Treating Bulimia Nervosa and Binge Eating

Myra Cooper is senior research tutor at the Oxford Doctoral Course in Clinical Psychology, University of Oxford.

Gillian Todd is based in the Department of Psychiatry at the University of Cambridge.

Adrian Wells is Professor of Clinical and Experimental Psychopathology at the University of Manchester.

Treating Bulimia Nervosa and Binge Eating explains how cognitive therapy can be used to treat those suffering from bulimia nervosa. The manual provides a step-by-step treatment guide, incorporating a number of case examples offering detailed explanations of the treatment process, questionnaires, worksheets and practical exercises for the client, which will provide a framework and focus for therapy. The authors use existing techniques, as well as new integrated cognitive and metacognitive methods developed from their recent research to take the therapist from initial assessment to the end of treatment and beyond, with chapters covering:

⊙ engagement and motivation
⊙ case formulation and socialisation
⊙ detached mindfulness strategies
⊙ positive and negative beliefs.

This practical guide will allow those treating patients with bulimia nervosa to take advantage of recent developments in the field and will be an essential tool for all therapists working with this eating disorder.

Treating Bulimia Nervosa and Binge Eating

An Integrated Metacognitive and Cognitive Therapy Manual

MYRA COOPER, GILLIAN TODD AND ADRIAN WELLS

Routledge
Taylor & Francis Group

LONDON AND NEW YORK

First published 2009 by Routledge
27 Church Road, Hove, East Sussex BN3 2FA

Simultaneously published in the USA and Canada
by Routledge
270 Madison Avenue, New York, NY 10016

Routledge is an imprint of the Taylor & Francis Group, an Informa business

Typeset in Stone Serif by Garfield Morgan, Swansea, West Glamorgan
Printed and bound in Great Britain by TJ International Ltd, Padstow, Cornwall
Paperback cover design by Andy Ward

This publication has been produced with paper manufactured to strict
environmental standards and with pulp derived from sustainable forests.

British Library Cataloguing in Publication Data
A catalogue record for this book is available from the British Library

Library of Congress Cataloging-in-Publication Data
Cooper, Myra, 1957-
   Treating bulimia nervosa and binge eating : an integrated
metacognitive and cognitive therapy manual / Myra J. Cooper, Gillian
Todd, and Adrian Wells.
       p. ; cm.
   Includes bibliographical references and index.
   ISBN 978-1-58391-944-6 (hardback) – ISBN 978-1-58391-945-3 (pbk.)
1. Bulimia–Treatment. 2. Compulsive eating–Treatment. 3. Cognitive
therapy. 4. Metacognition. I. Todd, Gillian, 1961- II. Wells, Adrian.
III. Title.
   [DNLM: 1. Bulimia Nervosa–therapy. 2. Bulimia Nervosa–psychology.
3. Cognitive Therapy–methods. WM 175 C777t 2008]
   RC552.B84C667 2008
   616.85'2630651–dc22
                                                    2008011597

ISBN: 978-1-58391-944-6 (hbk)
ISBN: 978-1-58391-945-3 (pbk)

Contents

Acknowledgements and an introductory note

We thank Professor Janet Treasure for kind permission to use the table 'A rough guide to a summary measure of risk', which appears in the Therapist Resources. We thank Professor Phil Cowen for help with medical and medication issues.

We are grateful to the adult eating disorder services at the Cambridgeshire and Peterborough Mental Health NHS Trust, and at the Oxfordshire and Buckinghamshire Mental Health Trust, for ongoing support, discussion and encouragement while preparing this book.

The case material in this book is based on our clinical and research work with patients with bulimia nervosa and binge eating problems. In order to preserve anonymity, any details that might enable patients to be identified have been changed.

The book is intended for those with a professional background in basic psychological treatment skills, thus it assumes that users have a relevant appropriate professional training and/or qualification, and will, in line with good practice, be receiving clinical supervision.

The appendix of this book contains worksheets that can be downloaded free of charge to purchasers of the print version. Please visit the website www.routledgementalhealth.com/treating-bulimia-nervosa-and-binge-eating to find out more about this facility.

Introduction to the book, a case example and an overview of treatment

This chapter begins with guidance on how to use the book, and discussion of who might benefit from the treatment. It introduces the reader to the symptoms and treatment of bulimia nervosa (BN) by presenting a case example of a patient (Jessica) with the disorder. It highlights the symptoms and problems that she experienced in relation to her illness, and then provides a detailed description of how her treatment with our version of cognitive therapy proceeded, as outlined in more detail in the remaining chapters of the book. It includes general information (for example, about the format of sessions) as well as a session-by-session summary of the course and content of the specific treatment received by Jessica. The treatment described here is a synthesis of our earlier work on the cognitive theory of BN (Cooper et al. 2004) with metacognitive therapy of psychological disorders (Wells 2000). We will continue to use the term cognitive therapy in this book for simplicity but we increasingly find ourselves moving towards a metacognitively focused approach.

INTRODUCTION TO THE BOOK

The book is designed to be used as a guide for therapists working with people with BN. It provides a structure, framework and focus for therapy. The book is written with individual therapy in mind, and provides a step-by-step guide from initial assessment to the end of treatment and beyond. The worksheets and patient information sheets are an important part of treatment, and therapists should aim to make maximum use of these, in addition to the advice and suggestions in the text.

Who can use the book?

All suitably trained therapists, from a range of professional backgrounds, should find this book useful. As with all psychological therapies, and problems treated, therapists must seek appropriate supervision and adhere to their professional code of ethics when using the programme.

Is the book just for bulimia nervosa?

The treatment is based on new developments in our understanding of eating disorders. These are not confined to BN, and our belief is that the book is also helpful for those who present with a range of binge eating problems, including sub-clinical BN, or variations of eating disorder not otherwise specified (ED-NOS), in which binge eating is a major problem. The experts do not agree on what the current diagnostic categories in eating disorders should be (e.g. Fairburn et al. 2003; Keel et al. 2004). In our work we have focused on conceptualising and explaining the symptoms of eating disorders, while at the same time juggling the complexities of the diagnostic categories used. Our experience is that the treatment will be useful to those with a range of binge eating disorders. We also have some experience of research into this group (e.g. Cooper et al. 2007a). Nevertheless, it is important to note that this group, and ED-NOS in general, has not been widely studied.

What about those with low weight?

Those with anorexia nervosa (AN) may experience binge eating, and some of these people will be on the border between AN and BN. We discuss low weight AN with binge eating further in Chapter 2. The treatment has not been developed on those with low weight who also binge eat, although there are many transferable strategies that can be used in this book, provided due attention is paid to the specific problems of low weight.

What about adolescents?

Bulimia nervosa is not confined to adults, and many adolescents are now seeking treatment. Some of our research has involved adolescents (e.g. Rose et al. 2006), and our view is that the model and treatment is applicable to this group. Our experience is that adolescents value the experience of individual treatment in this format, and much prefer it to the family focused treatments they have sometimes previously received. Nevertheless, there are inevitably systemic and developmental issues that arise and themes based on these topics may be an integral part of the problem. It is important to have some awareness of the normal developmental tasks of adolescence, and while this should be routine for those who have experience with adolescents, those who work mostly with adults with BN may need advice if seeking to treat adolescents, particularly those who are younger, with this programme.

In the remainder of the chapter we describe a case, Jessica, and her progress through the programme outlined in later chapters.

A CASE DESCRIPTION – JESSICA

Jessica was referred to Mental Health Services by her family physician for psychological treatment of her bulimia nervosa. She was aged 26, and had not had any previous psychiatric or psychological treatment. When seen for an initial assessment she said that her eating was 'out of control' and that she was obsessed with thinking about food and her figure. Every day she would plan to eat what she considered to be a healthy diet that had an upper limit of 1,000 calories, and would start off with good intentions. However, she would end up eating 'junk food' and then feel guilty and worried about gaining weight, having broken one of her dietary rules. This was followed by binge eating, which she felt was uncontrollable. She perceived herself as fat although her Body Mass Index (BMI = weight (in kilograms)/height (in metres)) fell within a normal range, and she reported feeling self-conscious about her weight and shape. In particular she felt disgusted by the shape of her stomach and thighs, which she saw as flabby and disproportionate to the rest of her body.

Jessica was constantly striving to lose weight because she believed that achieving her desired shape would make her feel happy, and confident to do things that she currently felt unable to do. Consequently she would set herself unrealistic targets for weight loss by trying 'lose weight quick diets' found in women's magazines, e.g. to lose 4kg in a week, or drop a dress size, even though she knew these diets were ineffective. Her rigid rules for dieting were unsustainable and she despaired of ever achieving significant weight loss because she frequently binged. She was miserable about her weight and eating habits, and often felt quite depressed. She said:

> I'm tired of getting so wound up about it all, I think about food and how I look all the time. Sometimes I think I'm going mad. I just want it all to go away. I can't carry on living like this – it's not a life. I want children, but I can't even cope with myself.

Her eating was erratic – she missed meals during the day to try and keep her calorie intake down, drank copious amounts of water to suppress her appetite and chewed gum obsessively so that she wouldn't be tempted to eat. She described binge eating at least once a day, and most of the time this was followed by self-induced vomiting in order to try to control the extreme distress she felt about her weight and shape, including great fear of gaining weight and getting fat, which always followed episodes of binge eating. She felt embarrassed and ashamed disclosing this information.

In a typical week Jessica would have eight to ten binges – usually when she returned home from work before her partner came home, and occasionally during her lunch break at work. Jessica had thought a great deal about why she binged, and recognised that at least some of her binges occurred as a way of coping with negative emotions such as worry, anxiety or sadness, rather than any overwhelming hunger. She felt frustrated by this, and described times when she repeatedly asked herself, 'Why am I doing this to myself?'

A typical binge consisted of several packets of crisps or savoury snacks (typically around five in total), four or five pastries, two or three packets of chocolate biscuits, several rounds of toast spread with butter, and two to three small chocolate bars or a tub of vanilla ice cream. Jessica also considered eating a 'forbidden' or 'bad' food, which could be a small amount, for example, one 25g chocolate bar, as bingeing. After bingeing Jessica would feel concerned about the impact of bingeing on gaining weight and would compensate for this by inducing vomiting as a means of getting rid of the calories and controlling her weight. On occasions, if she felt particularly fat, she would take 8–10 laxatives in addition to vomiting. She also followed a rigid exercise regime.

Jessica described having been worried about her weight and shape since her teenage years. She went through puberty before most of her peer group and recalled feeling self-conscious of her body shape and size in relation to others. She was concerned that other people perceived her as fat. She recalled a situation when a group of boys in the schoolyard said that they knew her name, F.A.T., and then burst into fits of laughter. She hated the way she looked and would try and conceal her body shape through wearing baggy clothes. Her mother, who also had issues with her own weight and was always following the latest diet fad, used to feed Jessica salads, and encourage her to eat less, while her siblings were offered family meals of normal size and more varied content. Her two older brothers referred to her as 'blubber' and would make 'fat' jokes, which everyone in the family found amusing. A friend told Jessica that vomiting was good for losing weight and she started to induce vomiting after normal eating. At first she would drink salt water or push a toothbrush to the back of her throat to stimulate the gag reflex and vomit. Later she could vomit spontaneously. Initially she lost weight, and everyone said how good she looked, which increased her sense of self worth. However, the belief that she could eat what she wanted if she induced vomiting and not gain weight encouraged her to use eating to reduce emotional distress, and bingeing and vomiting quickly became a way of life, that is, a way to manage and deal with emotional distress.

Jessica had a boyfriend with whom she had been living for about 8 months. Although he knew about her problem, Jessica said that he 'pretends it doesn't exist', and added that he was unaware of just how chaotic her eating was and, among other things, how much she typically ate in a binge. She expressed doubts about their future together, and also described feeling stressed in her job, which involved managing a small administrative team.

JESSICA'S TREATMENT

Jessica had 16 individual cognitive therapy (CT) treatment sessions, following the programme outlined here, over a period of five months. Each session followed a similar format, as detailed below.

A typical session format

At the beginning of each CT session Jessica completed the Eating Disorder Rating Scale (EDRS), a measure of key cognitions and behaviours relevant to BN and to the treatment model. (Questions included information on the frequency of behavioural symptoms, including bingeing, use of exercise to lose weight or prevent weight gain, and degree of belief in key cognitions relevant to the model, for example, related to negative and positive beliefs.) This provided an immediate indication of progress in changing important symptoms, and in changing the key thoughts relevant to the model on which treatment is based. The EDRS also provided a focus for the session; for example, it highlighted key thoughts and beliefs that were not changing or that might need to change for symptoms to decrease further. A copy of the EDRS can be seen in Appendix 1: Eating Disorder Rating Scale.

The format of the sessions followed a standard cognitive therapy protocol, similar to that described in detail elsewhere (Beck 1995). In brief, at the start of each session, the preceding week or time since the last session was reviewed, using the Weekly Evaluation Sheet, which she had completed prior to the session. This provided an opportunity for a personal review of the week. It indicated any progress she felt that she had made since last time, and highlighted any problems and difficulties she had experienced. There was also an opportunity for reflection on what she had learned. A copy of the Weekly Evaluation Sheet is displayed in Appendix 2. An example of a completed sheet can be seen in the box overleaf.

Homework assignments or tasks (a regular feature of treatment) were reviewed, and any further points for discussion were identified. An agenda for the session was set collaboratively, with both Jessica and her therapist contributing items. In the earlier sessions Jessica was unsure what to contribute to the agenda and the therapist took the lead in suggesting items. As sessions progressed Jessica became much more involved, and increasingly volunteered her own ideas. After setting the agenda the session moved on to tackle the specific items listed on it in some detail. Care was taken to ensure that a manageable number of items were identified for discussion, and that time was allocated in the most useful way. If necessary, items were prioritised, assigned as homework tasks and, also if necessary, deferred to the next session. Finally, further homework, based on the session's discussion, and including any findings from the previous week's homework, was decided upon by Jessica and her therapist together. The session concluded with the therapist eliciting any feedback and comments that Jessica had on the session. She was asked to comment, for example, on what had been helpful and what had not been so helpful or what had been difficult. Each session

WEEKLY EVALUATION SHEET

Date: 17 October

What have I achieved this week?

I managed to not binge and vomit for 2 days through using the binge postponement strategy. I told my family about my bulimia and they were cool about it. My Mum asked me to ask you if there is anything she should be doing to help.

What have I learned?

I felt really pleased with myself and thought that I can crack the bulimia. I was surprised Mum was so keen to help.

What has been difficult for me?

The other 5 days I binged and vomited between 2 and 5 times a day, which is rubbish. Working the late shift at the supermarket always gets to me. When everyone has left for work I binge my head off, because I can. I don't know why I do it, I just do it. It's so easy, like a bad habit that I've had for years. I just want to get rid of the bulimia and feel fed up with it ruining my life. I'm so worried that I'll get fat and have to think about what I'm eating to stop that from happening. It's exhausting.

What areas do I need to work on over the next week?

Stopping bingeing, I need more strategies. I also need to know why I keep on doing it. I'm a young woman and should be thinking about other things that are more important like going out and having fun.

What realistic, achievable goals can I set myself?

Try to cut down bingeing, especially in the mornings.

What problems am I likely to have?

It's hard to be on my own at home. There is so much food around.

How might I overcome these?

I need some other strategies, but I can't think of any right now.

What do I want to work on in therapy this week?

Cutting down my bingeing further.

Comments

The days I binged were awful and I felt a real failure, but it was a big achievement for me not to binge for two days, and I felt so much better about myself those days.

was audiotaped, and Jessica took an audiotape of the session away with her. Listening to the audiotape for homework was always recommended, sometimes with a specific aim identified in the session, but also to encourage learning, reflection and feedback to the therapist at the next meeting. At first Jessica commented that she hated the sound of her own voice and felt embarrassed hearing some of the things she had discussed. This made listening to the audiotape recording of the session difficult for her, although after persevering with the task she ultimately found it invaluable.

Treatment style

Treatment was based on an individual case formulation and the style was collaborative. Jessica was treated as an expert on her problem, and Jessica and her therapist worked in partnership to resolve it. Jessica was encouraged to contribute her own views and ideas right from the start, and to take an increasingly active role as treatment progressed, for example, in suggesting and designing exercises, such as behavioural experiments, and homework. The message conveyed by the therapist was that she was learning to be her own therapist, and that treatment would not stop when sessions stopped, but that she should continue to practise the strategies in the future, until she no longer needed them. Jessica was also encouraged to provide feedback to the therapist on all aspects of her treatment. The therapist actively and frequently sought this from her, and also frequently checked out Jessica's understanding of what was being discussed or done, both in the session and for homework.

The idea that therapy would help her to 'learn how to learn' was emphasised; that it would equip her with the tools to be her own therapist. The therapist enhanced the learning process by provision of frequent, capsule summaries. Regular summaries help to keep the session focused, keep the therapist and patient on track and promote self-reflection. The patient is encouraged to also make capsule summaries. Learning was enhanced by a distinctive questioning style. Termed Socratic questioning (e.g. Padesky 1993), the latter was embedded in a process of 'guided discovery' in which the therapist assisted Jessica to make her own discoveries about the problematic thoughts, and the model underlying her eating difficulty. Capsule summaries aimed to capture the essence of what Jessica had said, and give her an opportunity to correct any misunderstanding on the part of the therapist. As treatment progressed, Jessica was also encouraged to make her own mini summaries of what she had learned, and to apply Socratic questioning and guided discovery to her own thoughts by herself.

TYPICAL STAGES IN TREATMENT

A detailed outline of Jessica's treatment as it proceeded sequentially is presented below, but first, here is a summary of the main stages of treatment, including the topics covered at each stage.

STAGES IN JESSICA'S TREATMENT

Stage 1: Assessment

As a first step a detailed assessment of Jessica's problem was made using the Clinical Interview Proforma presented in Chapter 2 (see p. 31).

Using the Clinical Interview Proforma, an overview of the current situation and difficulties was obtained. This provided a general picture of the difficulties that Jessica had been experiencing in recent weeks. While Jessica was clear that her eating disorder was her main problem, she also mentioned relationship difficulties with her boyfriend, feelings of depression and problems at work. Most of these problems, including her eating disorder, had been going on for several years, although the problems with her boyfriend and stress at work had more recent origins.

A detailed picture of Jessica's eating over the last month was then gathered (see Part 1 of the Clinical Interview Proforma in Chapter 2), followed by some background information, including more detail on the history of the problem (see Part 2 of the Clinical Interview Proforma in

TYPICAL STAGES IN TREATMENT: A SUMMARY

Each session was preceded by completion of the Eating Disorder Rating Scale (Appendix 1). The Weekly Evaluation Sheet (Appendix 2) was also completed each week for homework, and discussed at the beginning of the session.

Stage 1: Assessment

Assess current problems. Use Clinical Interview Proforma (see Chapter 2, p. 31) to achieve this.

Complete self-report questionnaires – Eating Attitudes Test (EAT), Beck Depression Inventory (BDI), Beck Anxiety Inventory (BAI), Rosenberg Self Esteem Scale (RSE), Eating Disorder Belief Questionnaire (EDBQ), Eating Disorder Thoughts Questionnaire (EDTQ) and Eating Behaviour Questionnaire (EBQ). Copies of the EDBQ, EDTQ and EBQ can be found in Appendices 6, 7 and 5 respectively, and can often usefully be sent to the patient for completion prior to attending the first appointment.

Introduce the Weekly Evaluation Sheet (Appendix 2).

Read written information about cognitive therapy for BN (see Appendix 3: A Client's Guide to Cognitive Therapy for Bulimia Nervosa).

Stage 2: Motivation and fears about change

Identify advantages of BN and fears about change.

Employ strategies (e.g. other ways to cope with distress, there is an understandable cause, fears are part of BN and education) to manage typical fears, including cognitive restructuring and behavioural experiments (e.g. a cost-benefit analysis, using the specific questions presented in Chapter 5, and the PETS (Prepare, Expose, Test, Summarise) framework). See Appendix 9 for an outline of the PETS framework.

Tackle any specific fears.

Complete cost-benefit sheet (p. 232).

Discuss and tackle any realistic fears.

Read educational handouts (see Appendix 10: Myths about Bulimia Nervosa and Cognitive Therapy and Appendix 8: Consequences and Dangers of the Symptoms of Bulimia Nervosa).

Stage 3: Formulation

Formulate a recent episode of binge eating and any associated vulnerability factors. Use the worksheet Case Conceptualisation Interview Proforma to achieve this (see Chapter 6 p. 87).

Provide general education about the model and the basics of treatment. Revisit the handouts in Appendix 3 and Appendix 8.

Demonstrate the model: for example, that negative thinking causes distress, by contrasting negative and positive beliefs about eating and examining how believing only the positive would affect mood, thinking and behaviour.

Complete the worksheet Case Conceptualisation Proforma (see p. 87).

Stage 4: Detached mindfulness

Introduce and provide a rationale for detached mindfulness.

Give instructions on how to achieve detached mindfulness in relation to BN thoughts and symptoms.

Teach specific strategies.

Plan practice sessions and practical application in everyday life.

Stage 5: Uncontrollability of binge eating

Introduce behavioural experiments as a major treatment strategy and the PETS framework.

Identify key (negative) beliefs about uncontrollability of bingeing, including by reviewing the EBQ. Complete a modified dysfunctional thought record (DTR: see p. 237).

Use verbal reattribution strategies to challenge beliefs that eating is not controllable (e.g. verbal challenging of beliefs in sessions, use of the modified dysfunctional thought record).

Use written record sheet to record evidence for and against lack of control over eating beliefs.

Identify beliefs and evidence that eating can be controlled.

Make a record of evidence for beliefs that eating can be controlled.

Plan and conduct behavioural experiments to test beliefs about uncontrollability of eating (e.g. using the PETS framework).

Use behavioural experiment worksheet to record experiments.

Introduce the binge postponement strategy.

If necessary, introduce the idea of a graded hierarchy to build up the belief that eating can be controlled.

Plan to carry out follow-on experiments.

Stage 6: Negative consequences of eating behaviours

Identify key beliefs about negative consequences, including by reviewing the EBQ.

Complete modified DTR. Use verbal reattribution (as for Stage 5) to challenge these beliefs.

Identify and challenge cognitive distortions.

Plan and conduct behavioural experiments using the PETS framework (as for Stage 5).

Stage 7: Positive beliefs

Increase awareness of and identify key positive beliefs about eating, including by reviewing the EBQ.

Complete a modified DTR.

Use verbal reattribution strategies to challenge positive beliefs and to introduce flexibility (e.g. by verbal challenging of beliefs in sessions, use of the modified DTR, by introducing alternative strategies for self regulation).

Use written record sheet to record advantages and disadvantages of having particular positive beliefs.

Plan and conduct behavioural experiments to test positive beliefs about eating (e.g. using the PETS framework, by making use of follow-on experiments).

Use behavioural experiment worksheet to record experiments.

Stage 8: Negative self beliefs

Introduce core belief work with the prejudice model (Padesky 1990).

Complete the Positive Core Beliefs Questionnaire (see Appendix 14).

Create a positive or alternative core belief.

Weaken old and build new beliefs using one or more of the following: core belief worksheet, cognitive continua, historical test of beliefs and positive data logs.

Use behavioural experiments to test predictions from negative core beliefs (e.g. using the PETS framework, by making use of follow-on experiments).

Introduce the use of flashcards.

Introduce imagery modification and provide a rationale for tackling any remaining strongly held 'emotional' beliefs.

Employ proforma for imagery intervention in Chapter 10 (p. 170) to identify and modify these beliefs.

Stage 9: Planning for the future

Tackle residual cognitions and behaviours, and make plans for further work on these post-therapy.

Develop a blueprint.

Devise a plan to deal with signs of relapse.

Make follow-up appointment for one month's time.

Chapter 2). This revealed that Jessica was currently bingeing, and that binges took place mainly in the evenings. In the last six weeks, however, she had also begun to slip out of work at lunchtime to binge – this had happened three times in the preceding week. Jessica's lunchtime binges usually consisted of ready to eat sandwiches and desserts, bought at a local supermarket, bakery or convenience store, and large quantities of diet coke. On the way home from work Jessica would stop at garages or convenience stores to buy food (usually crisps, savoury snacks and pastries), going out of her way to make sure that she didn't visit the same shop too often, embarrassed that someone might recognise her and notice how much junk food she was buying. Typically, she would start eating the food while driving home, with an increasing sense of excitement and anticipation, knowing that when she got home bingeing would continue. At home she would eat any savoury snacks while simultaneously making and buttering toast. After eating several slices of toast, she would finish with as much sweet food (chocolate biscuits, chocolate bars or ice cream) as she could physically manage. She bought supplies of long-life bread and ice cream, as well as other 'binge foods', while doing the weekly shop, and hid these in difficult to find places in the kitchen, and in the bottom of the freezer. Jessica almost always made herself sick after bingeing. The only occasions when she didn't induce vomiting were if the binge was interrupted, or if the amount of food consumed in a binge was small, which made inducing vomiting difficult.

Vomiting was ritualistic – at the beginning of a binge she would line her stomach with a distinctive marker (e.g. beetroot, bran flakes or red cabbage) and would flush her stomach out with water and vomit until the food marker came back. If she had consumed large amounts of fat in a binge she would have several hot drinks (she had learned that this eased the process of inducing vomiting after such foods). She had taken moderately large amounts of laxatives in the past because she believed this would help her lose weight, and had found that she experienced diarrhoea, severe stomach pains and bloating as a result. She recognised that the laxatives were ineffective in controlling her weight and had decided not to persist with them other than at times when she felt fat after vomiting.

Jessica exercised compulsively with the sole purpose of burning off the calories eaten in a binge. She exercised hard at the gym every day and would do 90 minutes of aerobic exercise and 30 minutes of weights. Jessica would prioritise going to the gym above other activities and would feel guilty if she missed a day, even when she was physically unwell.

The impact of bulimia was that she felt low in mood and depressed at times, occasions which were characterised by self-critical thoughts. She felt ashamed of having bulimia and alone in so far as she did not feel able to disclose her problem to others. She felt deceitful that she hadn't told her boyfriend about the full extent of her eating disorder yet feared that he would leave her if he knew. This dilemma left her feeling unable to take the relationship further until she had sorted her bingeing out. She felt exhausted and tired, which made it difficult to function effectively at work. She was often late getting into the office and had taken several days off sick, which people had started to notice. She worried about losing her job and that increased her feelings of stress, which she would then cope with by binge eating, thus exacerbating her problems further.

Jessica completed self-report questionnaires that measured eating disorder symptoms, mood and self-esteem – all of which would be repeated at the end of treatment to assess overall progress. The Eating Disorder Rating Scale (see Appendix 1), which provides a weekly measure of key eating disorder behaviours and cognitions, was also completed for the first time. Further measures of the cognitions and behaviours that are important in the model were introduced and were to be completed for homework. Jessica also took away some written information about BN and cognitive therapy for BN, to read for homework and for discussion at the next session (see Appendix 3: A Client's Guide to Cognitive Therapy for Bulimia Nervosa).

Following the assessment the therapist wrote a letter to Jessica providing a summary of the assessment, and a preliminary formulation. Based on similar letters used by Schmidt and Treasure (1997) this aimed to enhance motivation and engagement in treatment. An example of an assessment letter that might be written to Jessica can be seen in Appendix 4.

Stage 2: Motivation and fears about change

Once the assessment had been completed, motivational issues for change were addressed and strategies to address these were identified and practised. The strategies included identifying the pros and cons of having bulimia nervosa and a discussion about the fears Jessica had about change. Both cognitive and behavioural strategies to deal with these fears were introduced. For example, psycho-education and challenging cognitive processes such as catastrophisation (see Chapter 2) were employed. Jessica expressed a particular fear that if she didn't binge she wouldn't have any way to deal with her distress. Part of the session was thus spent on helping her to identify the key cognition underlying her fear and planning a behavioural experiment to test this cognition. The positive thought 'bingeing is a helpful way to deal with distress' was identified and tested. The PETS (Prepare, Expose, Test, Summarise) framework (Wells 1997) for behavioural experiments was employed, and Jessica and her therapist made a plan for her to compare the effects of two conditions. One involved behaving as normal, that is, bingeing when distressed, while the other involved using cognitive distraction (focusing on and asking questions of herself about what was happening around her). In both conditions she agreed to monitor and rate several outcome variables, including how distressed she felt, and how long her distress lasted. She planned to complete this experiment for homework, compare the two outcomes in terms of her initial belief and return with her findings for discussion with her therapist at the following session. Jessica also planned to read some educational material about BN that discussed some of the common fears people with BN might have about changing (see Appendix 10: Myths about Bulimia Nervosa and Cognitive Therapy), and how these may not always be accurate. Based on the information obtained from the sessions and the self-report measures, including of relevant cognitions and behaviours, the therapist developed a preliminary formulation of Jessica's eating problem. Although not yet shared with Jessica this would help guide the development of a shared formulation in Stage 3.

Stage 3: Formulation

During Stage 3 a detailed case formulation was developed using the Case Conceptualisation Proforma (see p. 87). As noted above, the therapist had already started the process of developing a formulation, but this had not yet been fully shared with Jessica. The aim of developing a shared formulation was to allow Jessica to discover, for herself but with the therapist's help, the factors involved in the maintenance and development of her binge eating. In order to achieve this Jessica and her therapist explored two examples of a recent episode of bingeing, and completed a formulation for each of these. Jessica took a blank formulation worksheet away, so that she could practise eliciting and observing the thoughts and feelings involved in her personal binge eating episodes for homework.

Building on the information about cognitive therapy for BN that Jessica had read during Stage 1, the basic principles of CT were introduced. The model that was to form the basis for treatment, which was briefly outlined in the written material that Jessica had read on BN, was then discussed in more detail.

Jessica completed a socialisation exercise that aimed to help her understand two key features of the model (i.e. that there are conflicting positive and negative beliefs, and that negative thinking causes distress), as elicited in the formulation. The various stages and types of cognitions to be tackled in treatment were also discussed.

While the focus was initially on understanding Jessica's episodes of binge eating, the role of the model in understanding her other symptoms, particularly her compulsive exercising and obsessive thinking about food, and her weight and shape was also discussed. This part of treatment drew on metacognitive therapy examining beliefs about thinking (Wells 2000). For example, Jessica believed, 'Worrying about what and how much I'm eating stops me overeating and gaining weight'. With her therapist Jessica identified how this positive belief, in conjunction with the negative beliefs 'I can't stop worrying about food' and 'If I don't worry about food and calories I'll get fat and be rejected', maintained her obsession with food, and the distress associated with this.

Stage 4: Detached mindfulness

Before proceeding to tackle the specific cognitions in the model, strategies to encourage a state of detached mindfulness were taught, with the aim of enabling Jessica to become aware of but not respond to or engage with the thoughts and beliefs that triggered her BN, and to separate her sense of self from the products of cognition, that, is these thoughts and beliefs (Wells 2008). Detached mindfulness (DM) is a key part of metacognitive therapy (Wells 2000) on which our treatment model and practice are based. The state of detached mindfulness is designed to facilitate and enhance potential for therapeutic change, by providing a new way to relate to inner experience. Jessica practised the DM exercises used in session for homework, and learned how to apply them whenever she experienced triggers for bingeing (i.e. thoughts and feelings), so that she could interrupt the cycle of rumination/worry and behaviour in the course of her everyday life and replace them with DM. Jessica also reported finding detached mindfulness particularly helpful in dealing with triggers for repetitive worries she experienced when feeling indecisive (for example, when selecting what to eat in a normal meal) and when preoccupied with self blame (for example, when unable to exercise as normal).

Stage 5: Uncontrollability of binge eating

The main aim of this stage was to reduce or eliminate binge eating. Jessica worked on her beliefs that her eating was uncontrollable (all of which were examples of negative beliefs).

Jessica believed that she could not do a great deal to stop herself from bingeing. Initially, Jessica learned to identify these beliefs in the session and at home, using a written record sheet. She then learned to challenge them using both cognitive restructuring and behavioural experiments. One particularly important experiment involved building up a sense that she could control her eating. To achieve this Jessica worked to control her eating in increasingly difficult situations over the course of several days while also monitoring the effect on her weight and mood. Jessica also learned how to delay and demonstrated that she could control her binges using the strategy 'binge postponement'.

Stage 6: Negative consequences of eating behaviour

Jessica worked on the negative beliefs that reflected the negative consequences of binge eating. She learned how to identify and record them using a written record, and then how to challenge them using verbal restructuring and behavioural experiments. One exercise she found useful and which she undertook, first using a dysfunctional thought record and then as a behavioural experiment, involved testing the belief 'If I feel fat, it means I must have gained weight'. In preliminary verbal challenging of this belief she found that taking the perspective of a close friend and labelling the cognitive distortion in the belief (emotional reasoning) helped her to entertain the possibility that this belief might not be accurate. Follow-up behavioural experiments which involved recording 'feeling fat' in a range of situations and correlating these with an objective indicator (weight in kg) confirmed this interpretation.

Jessica had lots of negative beliefs about how others would react to her if she gained weight, and time was spent working on these. Jessica's thinking about this issue was very black and white. She had a tendency to catastrophise and typically assumed that a very negative outcome was most likely. In order to introduce some flexibility in her thinking, the therapist used guided discovery to explore her beliefs and her style of thinking further in the session. Jessica assumed that others would automatically judge her self worth by her weight. Using guided discovery, she explored with her therapist what other factors might be important in friendships and relationships. This exploration was continued for homework. To test out her belief, Jessica conducted a survey of her friends' opinions, and another involving asking her boyfriend for his views. She asked these people to identify five characteristics they valued about her, collated their replies and brought them along to the next session. This enabled her to discover that her friends listed a range of features that were not reflective of weight, and thus provided her with evidence that did not support her belief. At the same time, Jessica discussed the fact that, while probabilities can be estimated, some things can never be known with complete certainty.

Stage 7: Positive beliefs

Jessica first used written records to identify and record examples of positive beliefs in her everyday life. Important beliefs were 'eating helps me cope with distress' and 'eating is the only way I have to express my anger and frustration'. Once she was adept at spotting these, she learned how to challenge them, using a range of cognitive and behavioural strategies. Written exercises as well as behavioural experiments were used. A behavioural experiment she found particularly useful was experimenting with and learning new ways to express negative feelings. The latter proved to be particularly useful to Jessica, and she became very good at learning from each experiment that she conducted in order to plan and conduct further experiments. As part of learning to manage distress without bingeing, she also practised a range of behavioural techniques. These included alternative, less damaging activities, and tasks that captured attention, including word puzzles and exercises involving maintaining an external focus of attention. Part of her work involved improving communication with her boyfriend, who, contrary to Jessica's expectations, became a very helpful support.

Eating disorder problem behaviours in addition to binge eating were identified. Jessica completed the Eating Behaviour Questionnaire (EBQ: Cooper et al. 2006, displayed in Appendix 5), which helped to highlight which specific behaviours were problematic. These were then conceptualised using the model, just as binge eating had been, and links to cognitions were identified. Behavioural experiments then played an important role in modifying the relevant cognitions and thus the problem behaviours. Among other cognitions, Jessica's fears about relinquishing the behaviours were identified and behavioural experiments set up to test their accuracy. The EBQ indicated that Jessica had problem behaviours in three areas: dieting, checking of weight and shape, and food. Specific predictions were derived about what might happen if she stopped each of the behaviours and these were tested. One very successful experiment involved modifying frequent checking of her appearance, while another involved reducing dieting-related behaviour. In both cases her fears – that not checking and not dieting would cause large weight gain – failed to come true.

Stage 8: Negative self beliefs

Several sessions were spent on negative self beliefs. These sessions were spaced out over a longer period of time than the previous sessions, in recognition of the slower pace of change expected with core beliefs. Jessica learned to identify these, and when they were active, by honing in on situations when extreme emotion was present. The downward arrow technique was used to take important assumptions to a 'deeper' level of meaning, and beliefs were formulated by reviewing her treatment records. In session and for homework she practised and worked on a range of ways to challenge her negative self beliefs, including cognitive continua (for example, as described by Beck 1995; Padesky 1994) and a detailed historical test (also described by Beck 1995; Padesky 1994). She became aware of possible origins of her negative self beliefs. Particularly important in her case were the beliefs 'I'm unlovable' and 'I'm no good'. Historically, these seemed to be related to early, negative experiences with her family. Practice with cognitive continua was particularly crucial in helping her to re-evaluate these beliefs and recognise her propensity to dichotomous thinking. In line with suggestions made by Padesky (1994), alternative beliefs were identified before proceeding to challenge the negative self beliefs. Jessica developed two new, alternative beliefs: 'I'm lovable' and 'I'm capable'. She also began a positive data (or self-statement) log to record examples from her daily life of times when these beliefs were supported, using others' behaviour, and her own thoughts and feelings, as evidence.

Stage 9: Planning for the future

Time was spent with Jessica planning for the future. She had made considerable progress. She had not binged and vomited for several weeks, and her scores on most of the self-report questionnaires were now within normal limits. She still needed to work further on her negative self beliefs, and strategies to do this were identified. Jessica drew up a plan of how she would continue this work on her own, and she agreed to report back in one month's time at a follow-up appointment.

A blueprint (e.g. Butler et al. 1991) identifying the most helpful aspects of treatment was created. Jessica had found several things particularly helpful, including the idea that core beliefs were important, learning alternative ways to deal with distress, and the behavioural experiments – particularly those that she had conducted with her friends and boyfriend to improve her communication skills. Finally, a plan to deal with any signs of relapse was developed, drawing on what Jessica had found most useful in treatment.

CHAPTER SUMMARY AND KEY POINTS

In this chapter the nature of BN was described in a particular case. An outline of the cognitive therapy treatment presented in the book was provided, illustrated with a detailed summary of Jessica's own treatment with the new cognitive therapy for BN.

Key points to remember include the following:

⊙ Therapy is relatively brief – up to 16 sessions over five months
⊙ Each therapy session follows a similar, structured format
⊙ Regular features include completion of a self-report measure of cognitions and behaviours important in the new cognitive model for BN, review of progress, homework assignments, agenda setting, requests for feedback and summaries from the patient, and audiotaping of sessions (which are listened to by the patient as part of homework).
⊙ Treatment is based on an individualised case formulation
⊙ Therapy style is collaborative, and makes extensive use of guided discovery through the use of a Socratic questioning style of enquiry. It emphasises 'learning how to learn'.

Diagnosis and assessment

This chapter describes the main features and the diagnostic criteria for bulimia nervosa. It provides a brief summary of the epidemiology of BN, comorbidity and differential or additional diagnosis issues. The process of undertaking an assessment with the patient is then covered in some detail, including information on the usefulness of establishing a history of anorexia nervosa (AN), how to identify BN as the primary problem, suitability for the new treatment and advice on appropriate assessment measures. A detailed Clinical Interview Proforma is provided to help clinicians undertake the pre-treatment assessment. This covers the main areas in which information is required to undertake the new treatment.

THE KEY FEATURES OF BULIMIA NERVOSA

As the brief portrait of Jessica in Chapter 1 suggests, bulimia nervosa is a serious mental health problem with significant negative consequences for sufferers. Families and friends are often affected, and the burden in caring for sufferers can be high, particularly when the problem is long term.

Bulimia nervosa is characterised most dramatically by recurrent episodes of binge eating. A very large amount of food may be consumed. A review suggests that the number of calories consumed in a typical 'binge' for those with a diagnosis of bulimia nervosa (e.g. American Psychiatric Association 2000) ranges from 1,110 to 4,394 (Guertin 1999). The patient experiences a sense of loss of control over eating during a binge. The patient often describes feeling unable to stop eating once they have tasted a desired food and many believe their insatiable hunger or emptiness drives their bingeing.

Binge eating is followed by inappropriate compensatory behaviour, including self-induced vomiting, misuse of laxatives, diuretics, enemas, medications (such as diet pills), fasting or excessive exercise. A minority of patients may also use illicit drugs such as cocaine or ecstasy. Some buy drugs (e.g. thyroxin) over the internet that are normally available only with a medical prescription, in order to reduce their appetite and increase their metabolism. Some buy such drugs (e.g. ipecac) to aid vomiting or to function as a compensatory behaviour following bingeing, although this is not typical of the majority of those with BN. These more extreme, destructive behaviours are often associated with severe personality dysfunction, particularly Cluster B personality disorders (American Psychiatric Association 2000). Such patients may also engage in self harm, including overdosing, parasuicidal behaviour, cutting, burning or other extreme self-punishing behaviours. In patients where extreme behaviour functions as self punishment, the behaviour is usually best conceptualised and treated as self harm. Alternatively, treatment for borderline personality disorder may be most appropriate.

Occasionally, it may be unclear whether or not a patient with a more extreme form of compensatory behaviour is best treated using cognitive therapy for BN or not. In such cases the function of the behaviour (for example, repeated vomiting in the absence of binge eating) should be carefully explored. In BN such behaviour functions primarily to deal with or control distress associated in some way with weight, weight gain and shape. However, in self harm or severe personality disorder, the behaviour typically functions primarily as general emotional self regulation without this component. In the first case, then cognitive therapy for BN may well be appropriate; in the latter case, even if the patient also meets diagnostic criteria for BN, an alternative form of therapy is likely to be more appropriate. One possible alternative therapy might be dialectical behaviour therapy, as described by Linehan (1993).

BN is associated with certain typical cognitions and beliefs. For example, one belief often held by patients is that self worth is determined primarily by achieving a specific shape and weight. If an individual perceives herself as fat or overweight, this contributes to self-appraisals of worthlessness and unlovability. A typical negative belief might be 'If I'm fat, no one will like me', or 'If I'm thin people will approve of me'. However, the paradox is that individuals with BN are usually within the normal weight range (BMI range of 20–25), and their use of weight and shape to provide a measure of self worth and desirability is misplaced and ultimately self-defeating. Patients usually find, to their disappointment, that when they achieve their desired weight and/or dress size they continue to feel worthless or unlovable. They may then set themselves yet another weight and/or shape goal that is ultimately illusive. Alternatively, patients may acknowledge that they feel happy and more confident with their changed weight and shape but continue to appraise themselves extremely negatively.

DIAGNOSIS

The fourth version of the *Diagnostic and Statistical Manual* developed by the American Psychiatric Association (DSM-IV-TR: American Psychiatric Association 2000) is commonly used to establish a diagnosis of BN. The DSM-IV diagnostic criteria can be seen in the box opposite.

The criteria specify recurrent episodes of binge eating, and provide a clear definition of a binge. This includes criteria for the amount eaten, and for the accompanying sense of loss of control. Recurrent inappropriate compensatory behaviour is also necessary. Binge eating and its associated compensatory behaviour must have a minimum frequency (i.e. at least twice a week, on average, for three months). Undue self-evaluation in terms of weight and shape is also necessary. Two subtypes are sometimes identified, a purging and a non-purging subtype. The former is characterised by self-induced vomiting or laxative abuse and the latter by excessive exercise or periods of fasting. A diagnosis of anorexia nervosa cannot be given at the same time and in establishing a differential diagnosis anorexia nervosa 'trumps' bulimia nervosa (Garner and Fairburn 1988).

In Europe the International Classification of Diseases (ICD), Version 10 (World Health Organization 1992) is sometimes used to establish a diagnosis, although most research studies now report the DSM-IV status of their participants. ICD-10 criteria are somewhat broader, and are not specified in as much detail as those of DSM-IV. They also include more specific research criteria but, in practice, these are rarely used. A summary of the ICD-10 criteria can be seen in the box on page 24.

It is important to note that the diagnostic criteria are minimum criteria. In practice, the extent and severity of the symptoms can be very variable, and neither diagnosis per se nor extent or frequency of symptoms will necessarily match closely with risk, patient's concern or distress or with treatment priorities.

EPIDEMIOLOGY

Bulimia nervosa is a common problem in young women. It is one of the most common of the psychiatric problems affecting this group (Kendler et al. 1991). Prevalence in young adult women is thought to be between 1 and 2.5 per cent (see, for example, review by Cooper 2003). It is much less common in younger and older women (below age 14 and above age 35) and also relatively rare in men, although prevalence figures are difficult to

DSM-IV-TR DIAGNOSTIC CRITERIA FOR BN

A Recurrent episodes of binge eating

An episode of binge eating is characterised by both of the following:

1. Eating, in a discrete period of time (e.g. within any two-hour period), an amount of food that is definitely larger than most people would eat during a similar period of time and under similar circumstances.
2. A sense of lack of control over eating during the episode (e.g. a feeling that one cannot stop eating or control how much one is eating).

B Recurrent inappropriate compensatory behaviour in order to prevent weight gain

This includes self-induced vomiting, misuse of laxatives, diuretics, enemas or other medications; fasting or excessive exercise.

C The binge eating and inappropriate compensatory behaviour both occur on average at least twice a week for three months

D Self evaluation is unduly influenced by body shape and weight

E The disturbance does not occur exclusively during episodes of anorexia nervosa

Specify type

Purging type

During the episode of bulimia nervosa, the person has regularly engaged in self-induced vomiting or the misuse of laxatives, diuretics or enemas.

Non-purging type

During the current episode of bulimia nervosa, the person has used other inappropriate compensatory behaviours, such as fasting or excessive exercise, but has not regularly engaged in self-induced vomiting or the misuse of laxatives, diuretics or enemas.

Source: adapted from American Psychiatric Association (2000)

ICD-10 DIAGNOSTIC CRITERIA FOR BN

1. Overeating in which large amounts of food are consumed in short periods of time.
2. Attempts to control the fattening effects of food.
3. A morbid dread of fatness.

Source: adapted from World Health Organization (1992)

---

estimate. It is unclear how common BN is in ethnic minority groups in western countries, with some evidence in the UK that it may be more common than in the majority group (Mumford and Whitehouse 1988), although it seems less common in most non-western countries. It has been suggested that the incidence is rising (and this is widely believed to be the case), although the evidence for it is not clear cut (Fombonne 1995). A UK study found that the incidence over time may have decreased (Currin et al. 2005), while a study in the Netherlands found a non-significant decrease (van Son et al. 2006). There is also some suggestion that some people move between eating disorders, for example, from anorexia nervosa or eating disorder not otherwise specified to BN, and vice versa, although it also appears that over time the disorder may stabilise (Tozzi et al. 2005).

COMORBIDITY

Bulimia nervosa can co-occur with a variety of different disorders. These include both Axis I (current psychiatric disorders) and Axis II disorders (longstanding personality disorders), as described in the DSM-IV-TR (American Psychiatric Association 2000). A list of disorders that may co-occur with BN can be seen in the box opposite. They include mood disorders, anxiety-based disorders and at least one personality disorder. The main features of each disorder are noted below.

DIFFERENTIAL DIAGNOSIS

The precise nature of the boundaries between the different eating disorders continues to be debated, although there is good evidence for separating restricting from bingeing disorders, for example, from latent

KEY FEATURES OF DISORDERS THAT CAN CO-OCCUR WITH BULIMIA NERVOSA

Depression

Persistent low mood and/or loss of interest and/or pleasure in nearly all activities.

Dissociative identity disorder

The presence of two or more distinct identities or personality states.

Substance abuse disorder

A maladaptive pattern of substance use with recurrent and significant adverse consequences related to the repeated use of substances.

Obsessive compulsive disorder

Recurrent obsessions or compulsions that are severe enough to be time consuming or cause marked distress or repeated impairment.

Posttraumatic stress disorder

Development of characteristic symptoms following exposure to an extreme traumatic stressor that involves personal experience of an event that involves actual or threatened death etc., or witnessing such an event.

Social phobia

Marked and persistent fear of social or performance situations in which embarrassment may occur.

Borderline personality disorder

Pervasive pattern of instability of interpersonal relationships, self image and affect, and marked impulsivity beginning in early adulthood and present in a variety of contexts. Impulsive behaviours may include self harm, parasuicidal behaviours, risky sexual contacts, excessive anger and also binge eating.

class analysis (e.g. Keel et al. 2004). The treatment described here has been developed with BN in mind, thus it is important to distinguish BN from other eating disorders. These include AN, binge eating disorder (BED) and the DSM-IV category 'eating disorder not otherwise specified' (ED-NOS). It is also important to distinguish it from body dysmorphic disorder (BDD) and major depressive disorder (MDD).

Table 2.1 shows the main diagnostic features, behaviours and cognitive themes characteristic of each of these other psychological disorders (i.e. AN, BED, ED-NOS, BDD and depression) and of BN, and also organic illness.

Figure 2.1 shows a decision diagram which can be used to decide whether an individual patient has BN or one of these other diagnoses.

Table 2.1 Differential diagnosis: main diagnostic features, behaviours and cognitive themes characteristic of disorders related to BN

Disorder	Key diagnostic features	Key behavioural features	Key cognitive features
Bulimia nervosa	Binge eating Compensatory behaviour Weight and shape linked to self worth	Overeating (normally binge eating more than 1,000 calories in a discrete period of time, two hours) followed by self-induced vomiting or other compensatory behaviour	Negative thoughts about food, eating, weight and shape
Anorexia nervosa	Low body weight (less than 85% of expected body weight) Feeling fat when underweight Amenorrhoea	Avoidance of eating, marked weight loss	Negative thoughts about eating (negative thoughts about weight and shape may or may not be present) Perfectionism Beliefs about the importance of control Obsessional thoughts

continues

Table 2.1 (continued)

Disorder	Key diagnostic features	Key behavioural features	Key cognitive features
Binge eating disorder	Binge eating Can be normal weight, overweight or clinically obese	Binge eating that is similar to BN, but in the absence of any compensatory behaviour	Self worth linked to weight and shape Long history of overeating in response to emotional dysregulation (e.g. 'If I don't eat I feel deprived'), feelings of love and comfort linked to eating
Eating disorder not otherwise specified	Similar to BN and AN but fail to meet one key criterion for either diagnosis	Similar to BN, but less frequent	Similar cognitive presentation to BN and AN
Body dysmorphic disorder	Concern with imagined or exaggerated defect in physical appearance	Concealment or disguise of specific body part concerned	Negative thoughts about (specific) parts of physical appearance
Organic illness	Vomiting Binge eating (and others)	Vomiting Binge eating (and others)	Non-specific/ unremarkable
Depression	Persistent low mood and/or marked loss of interest and pleasure	Tearful, withdrawn, decreased interest and motivation, sleep and appetite disturbance etc.	Negative thoughts about the self, other people, the world and the future

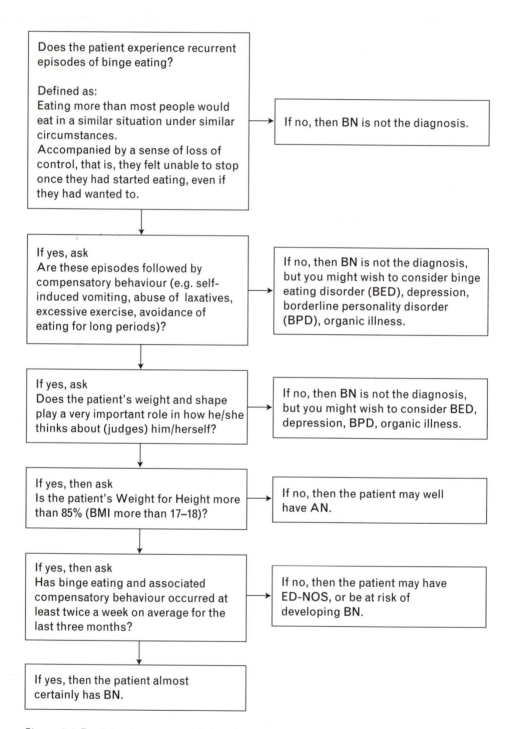

Figure 2.1 Decision tree to establish a BN diagnosis

ADDITIONAL DIAGNOSES

Even if the patient has a BN diagnosis it remains possible that another diagnosis is also appropriate, usually one of those listed above. Overleaf is a list of useful questions that can be used to indicate whether an additional diagnosis is warranted.

If the patient does have more than one problem, then we generally recommend that the clinician develops a formulation that takes this into account. Understanding the relationship between each of the presenting problems is helpful in understanding the precise nature of, and any interaction between, the factors maintaining the patient's problems (for example, any interrelationship between social phobia and BN). This can then help the therapist decide which is the primary problem, that is, which of the problems needs to be tackled first. This is important as improvement here is most likely to lead to overall improvement, including improvement in any secondary disorder.

ASSESSMENT

A general, psychological, problem-based assessment should be conducted. The aim is to get a reasonably detailed description of the patient's main problems as they have been experienced in recent weeks, together with some preliminary history. This includes any eating difficulties. It should include brief details on the general context in which the patient experiences his or her problems.

It is usually most useful to assess how the patient has experienced the eating problem over the last month first and then to follow this with questions about other potential problems. More detailed questions about the development of the eating (and, if relevant, any other problems) should then be asked. The Clinical Interview Proforma can be used to elicit this information.

Some tips on conducting the initial assessment and for using the Clinical Interview Proforma as a framework to obtain the necessary information are given below.

Introducing the assessment

The assessment can be introduced as follows:

Thank you for attending the clinic. Before we start shall I explain the plan for today? We will meet for one hour and during that time the aim is to find

QUESTIONS TO DETERMINE WHETHER AN ADDITIONAL DIAGNOSIS IS APPROPRIATE

Question to investigate body dysmorphic disorder

Is there any (specific) part of your body that you think is flawed or defective?

Question to ask if characteristic and/or general eating disorder concerns are mentioned

Do you think any other part of your body is flawed or defective (e.g. face, nose, hair, skin, teeth, breasts, genitalia, hands, head size)?

Questions to investigate depression

What has your mood been like over the last couple of weeks?

Have you been feeling down pretty much all the time, every day, over that period (even when you haven't been bingeing or worrying about your eating, weight and shape etc.)?

Have you lost interest in the things that you are normally interested in nearly every day over that period?

Questions to investigate borderline personality disorder

Have you ever done anything to hurt or harm yourself (apart from binge eating)?

Have you experienced episodes of uncontrollable emotions?

Have you experienced problems with close relationships?

Prompt for: reckless spending, substance abuse, self-mutilation, suicide attempts or threats.

CLINICAL INTERVIEW PROFORMA

Introduction to Part 1

I'm going to ask you about the problems you have been experiencing in the last month, so that we can get some more detail.

1. What brought you here today? What do you think is the main problem that you are wanting help with?

2. Thinking about the past month, what problems have you had with your eating?

3. I'd like you to take me through a typical day of eating. Starting with getting up in the morning I'd like you to take me through in detail everything that you had to eat and drink.

4. Binge eating
   In the last week how often have you binged?
   If every day, how many times a day?
   How often have you binged in the past month?
   Typically, what would you eat during a binge?
   What do you think is the reason for bingeing (identify triggers, function and beliefs about control)?
   How does that help?
   What do you think would happen if you didn't binge?

5. Compensatory behaviour
   After bingeing do you do anything to counteract the effects of bingeing (check for vomiting, use of laxatives, diuretics, excessive exercise and fasting)?
   How often do you induce vomiting (carry out other compensatory behaviour)?
   How do you feel after vomiting (or other compensatory behaviour)?
   What exercise do you do? How often?
   What is your goal when exercising?

6. Weight and shape
   What is your current weight? How tall are you (Use to calculate BMI.)
   What has been your highest weight, excluding pregnancy?
   When was that? How tall were you then? How old were you?
   Repeat for lowest weight.
   What has been your most stable weight?

What do you see as your ideal weight?
How often do you check your weight?
Do you avoid weighing yourself?
What's the reason for checking or avoiding weighing yourself?
How do you feel about your weight and shape?
Do you have any concerns about your body shape or figure?
What don't you like about your body shape or figure?
What effect does that have on you?
How much distress does that cause you?
What do you do to cope with that?
Do you check the particular body parts you are unhappy with? What do you do? How often do you do that?
What impact has your concerns about weight and/or shape had upon how you think of yourself? How do you think others perceive you?
Would you ever avoid situations because of concerns about your weight and shape?
If yes, how long has that been going on for?
Does anything make that worse? Or better? Was there anything in the past that made that worse or better?

7. Other problems
   Thinking about the past month, have you had any other problems?

Introduction to Part 2

Now I'd like to ask you some background information.

1. When did your problems with eating first start?
   What do you think the reason was for this problem developing? What's your theory?

2. Can you tell me a bit about your mood?
   What does that look like? How would you describe that?
   How often does that happen?
   What effect does that have on you? How bad is that for you? How distressing is that for you?
   How long has that been going on for?
   Does anything make that worse? Or better? Was there anything in the past that made it worse or better?
   What was happening in your life at the time that started?

3. Relationships (e.g. with partner, family, friends, colleagues at work)
   Can you tell me a bit about your family, friends, people at work etc.?
   Continue as above for mood.

4. Substance use
   Do you use any illegal or legal substances (e.g. drugs, cigarettes, alcohol)? Continue as above.

5. Employment or studying
   Are you working or studying? Can you tell me a bit about that? Continue as above.

6. Leisure activities
   What leisure activities do you enjoy or take part in? Continue as above.

7. Self harm
   Have you ever deliberately harmed yourself? Continue as above.

out more about some of the problems you are experiencing, and to establish if you have a treatable eating disorder. Initially it would be helpful to focus on the past month, then to discuss the background to the problem. I will need to ask you a lot of questions, is that all right?

It is usually useful to ask the patient to identify any problems before asking the more specific questions, for example, by asking:

What brought you here today? What do you think is the main problem that you are wanting help with?

Jessica's problems

Jessica identified a number of problems in response to the therapist's initial questioning. These included: 'I have bulimia and recently my eating feels more out of control. I'm bingeing at least once a day and feel unable to stop; I'm in a mess.' 'I'm fat and hate the fact that I've gained weight, I can't fit into any of my clothes which is depressing me. I don't want to have to buy a size 14 – that would be gross'. 'I feel ugly and revolted by my figure; my stomach and thighs are like a marshmallow covered in cellulite'. 'I'm so consumed with thoughts about my appearance and what to eat that I can't seem to concentrate on anything else. My work is affected, which stresses me out and I worry that I'll be fired'. 'Everything is going wrong for me; my relationship with my boyfriend is going pear shaped and I don't know what to do. I feel so low at times, and I keep thinking, what's the point? I hate feeling so miserable'.

Useful interview tips

The therapist should aim to make the patient feel safe, comfortable and able to disclose information that is likely to be very personal and sensitive. This will require good therapeutic skills, including reflective listening and demonstration of empathy, throughout the assessment. The therapist should make use of capsule summaries of what the patient has said before moving on to ask further questions. The therapist might choose to refer back to some of the information discussed at the start when eliciting more detail later on. This will help to demonstrate both active listening and empathy, which is likely to be validating for the patient and will help increase engagement.

Useful prompts to elicit more detail can include 'Can I pick up on . . .', 'Tell me more about that', 'What else?', 'I'd be really interested to hear more about . . .'. However, some patients find it difficult to adapt to the structure of cognitive therapy, and talk at great length, or include a huge amount of detail. It may be necessary, particularly early on and until they are accustomed to the format and style of therapy, to gently interrupt them, and encourage them to focus on the key issues.

Some useful questions to help with this include:

'Can I stop you/just pause you there for a moment?'
'Would it be OK with you if we were to come back to that later?'
'Can I just interrupt you there for a minute?'
'I'm sorry to interrupt but I was wondering if . . .'
'That's really interesting, perhaps we could pick up on that later?'
'I'm aware that we've got a lot to cover, and if time were no object we could continue, but perhaps we could come back to that later?'

Such questions should be interspersed with questions to check that the patient is still engaged. These might usefully include:

'Is that OK?'
'Can I just ask you if . . .'
'Is it all right if . . .'

Bulimia nervosa and identity

It is usually helpful to obtain a view of how the patient views her problem as a whole, in particular how much her identity is linked to its existence. The latter may need special attention (see below). Although commonly noted as a problem in AN, we have also observed it to be a problem for some patients with BN, especially those with a long history or past history of AN. Useful questions to explore this further include:

'If you didn't have BN, what do you think it would be like?'
'What function do you think BN serves for you?'
'What are the advantages of having BN?'
'What would it feel like if you no longer had BN?'
'What would it mean if you no longer had BN?'
'If you no longer had BN how would you think about yourself?'

Patients may express the way in which BN is linked to their identity in different ways. Comments from patients include, for example:

'It's my best friend, it's always there to fall back on if anything goes wrong in life'. 'It's the only thing I've got that is mine and no one can take it away from me'. 'It's the only thing I have control of in my life'. 'It's like a habit, a reflex action that I can't control'. 'My eating disorder and I are one – it's a part of me. Not having it would be like losing a limb, only worse'.

Establishing an AN diagnosis

It can be useful, but not essential, to establish whether the patient has ever had a DSM-IV-TR (American Psychiatric Association 2000) diagnosis of AN or EDNOS-anorexic subtype. The easiest way to do this is to use the decision tree in Figure 2.1. If AN appears a possibility then a diagnosis can be established using the Eating Disorder modules of the Structured Clinical Interview for DSM-IV (First et al. 1996). Although history of AN has not been found to be particularly relevant to treatment success in cognitive therapy for BN, history of low body weight does seem to affect outcome, and may alert the clinician to potential treatment difficulties, although this has not been the subject of systematic research. (It is important to note that binge eating followed by compensatory behaviour may also be characteristic of those with AN – the treatment outlined here has not yet been widely applied to this group, and its development is not based on this group.) Treatment difficulties may include a need to focus on desire to achieve a very low body weight once binge eating is under control, and difficulty in maintaining a normal weight. Severe dietary restriction or starvation, as well as other self-defeating behaviours, as a way to deal with core or negative self beliefs may also need to be addressed (Woolrich et al. 2006).

Bulimia nervosa as the primary problem

It is not usually appropriate to initiate treatment for bulimia nervosa, as the sole or main treatment, if BN is not the primary problem. For example, some patients with severe borderline personality disorder (BPD) may have periods of BN that serve as an emotion regulation strategy, and as self harm or punishment, but BN is not their primary problem. In this case BPD needs to be conceptualised as the primary problem, and might be treated using dialectical behaviour therapy (Linehan 1993) or schema focused CT (Young 1990), both of which have an evidence base (e.g. Giesen-Bloo et al. 2006; Safer et al. 2001).

We use two approaches to try to establish the primacy of BN in comorbid presentations: the timeline and the residual problems question.

Questions to help the therapist decide whether BN is likely to be the primary problem are listed in the box.

If major depression (or some other problem, for example, severe social phobia, generalised anxiety disorder or obsessional-compulsive disorder) is the primary problem then it is usually best to suggest that the patient discusses treatment options further with their family physician or psychiatrist. This is particularly important if there is evidence to suggest that medical interventions such as the prescribing of medication might be appropriate (see Appendix 11: Medical Aspects of Bulimia Nervosa for Family Physicians). Where another disorder is the primary problem then referral to a general psychological or primary care therapy service may be

---

QUESTIONS TO DETERMINE WHETHER BULIMIA NERVOSA IS THE PRIMARY PROBLEM

Which problem do you think came first, bulimia nervosa or (for example) depression/anxiety?

What do you see as your primary problem right now?

If you no longer had BN how much of a problem would your depression/anxiety etc. be?

In what way do you think your problem with depression/anxiety etc. is connected with your eating disorder?

If we were to work on your depression/anxiety etc. what impact do you think that would have on your eating disorder? What do you think would change?

advisable. Alternatively, if this is not possible, and the therapist has the necessary experience, then the primary problem can either be treated using a CT approach (see e.g. Wells 1997) before moving on to treat the BN, or a formulation that incorporates both problems can be developed and the different problems treated in parallel.

National Health Service (NHS) treatment in the United Kingdom (and also treatment in some other countries) usually involves a wait of some months between initial assessment and treatment, and so all patients should be reassessed when they reach the top of the waiting list, in case their symptoms or circumstances have changed markedly, and so that the appropriate decision can be reached about their treatment at that point. When someone is placed on a waiting list for CT it is useful to suggest self help or psycho-educational reading. Useful books include *Bulimia Nervosa: A Cognitive Therapy Programme for Clients* (Cooper et al. 2000), *Getting Better Bit(e) by Bit(e): A Survival Guide for Sufferers of Bulimia Nervosa and Binge Eating Disorders* (Schmidt and Treasure 1993), *Bulimia Nervosa and Binge Eating* (P.J. Cooper 1995), *Overcoming Binge Eating* (Fairburn 1995) and *Overcoming your Eating Disorder: A Cognitive-Behavioural Therapy Approach for Bulimia Nervosa and Binge-Eating Disorder* (Agras and Apple 2007). It might be helpful to provide information about relevant national charities that provide information and advice on eating disorders (for example, in the UK, BEAT, the working name of the Eating Disorders Association: www.b-eat.co.uk/Home), and any local eating disorder carer support groups. Some useful website addresses for similar organisations in other countries can be found in Appendix 13.

It is important to remember that great care in establishing the primary diagnosis may be needed in some cases. For example, where severe mood disorder or personality disorder is present, patients may not be clear about the exact relationship between them. In the case of personality disorder, patients may be unaware that they have what might be regarded by others as a significant personality dysfunction. Such cases need to be approached sensitively when discussing treatment options, and it may be useful to postpone such a discussion until the patient's case can be discussed with colleagues in supervision, and the possibility of alternative treatment options can be investigated.

Who should not have the treatment?

Provided that the patient's primary problem is BN, then there are no ubiquitous or definite indicators for exclusion from cognitive therapy treatment. It is always important, however, to assess the patient's motivation for change, as clinically this has been observed to be an important indicator of likely treatment success (e.g. Schmidt and Treasure 1997). This is particularly important when patients hold positive beliefs about the function of BN and when it is linked to their identity. The reason behind attendance at the clinic should also be ascertained as patients may attend for many different reasons, including pressure from parents, partner or their family physician, or as a result of a health scare such as chest pain, while still finding the idea of giving up BN inconceivable. Patients may also have unrealistic expectations of treatment, for example, clinging onto the idea that a magic wand will suddenly be waved and they will miraculously feel better, without making any effort or taking any responsibility for change.

At times, in consultation with a physician, CT may be best achieved in combination with psychotropic medication. Because BN carries a greater risk to an individual's physical health than is normal for the patient's peers, it is advisable that the family physician is involved in the medical monitoring of the patient.

The Eating Disorder Unit at the Institute of Psychiatry has information for physicians about assessing risk and medical monitoring of patients with eating disorders on its website (www.iop.kcl.ac.uk). These guidelines are reproduced with kind permission of Professor Janet Treasure at the end of Appendix 11. If the patient's family physician is not already familiar with these guidelines, it is useful to recommend them as helpful material to read. It is also helpful for the clinician to have knowledge of these issues, and we would recommend that therapists also read this information. More information relevant to medical issues in BN can be found in Appendix 11 (as noted above) and Appendix 12 (Medical Aspects of Bulimia Nervosa for Non-Medical Practitioners).

It is important that a physician is involved in the patient's care, and kept informed of treatment and progress, and that any medical problems or issues are raised and discussed with the physician. The most serious physical problems are usually associated with electrolyte imbalance, in particular with low potassium levels, and patients should have their electrolyte levels assessed at regular intervals if they continue to binge and compensate using vomiting, laxatives or other purging behaviour. This is important because there may be no obvious symptoms indicating that levels are abnormal, yet the consequences are potentially fatal. Regular monitoring is very important if the patient is pregnant and the eating disorder continues to remain active. More information on the physical health topics and assessments that should normally be conducted can be found in Appendices 11 and 12, particularly at the end of Appendix 11 in the section written by Professor Janet Treasure, and reproduced here with kind permission of the author.

ASSESSMENT MEASURES

Questionnaires and diaries are an important part of assessment, and will help to evaluate progress. The purpose and rationale for these should be explained to the patient. There are usually four main purposes:

⊙ to obtain information about symptoms, thoughts and behaviours necessary for understanding the problem
⊙ to quantify and observe patterns in behaviour, emotion and cognitions
⊙ to focus treatment on the key targets or maintaining factors involved
⊙ to measure change and to assess the effectiveness of the therapy.

We use the self-report questionnaire and interview-based measures detailed in the box overleaf, which may usefully be considered in the following two categories:

⊙ eating disorder related measures
⊙ general symptoms and psychopathology measures.

There are many other useful measures, and clinicians may develop a preference for certain ones. We have also found the Eating Disorder Examination (interview version) useful, particularly in establishing a diagnosis, and assessing frequency and intensity of binge eating. It assesses the same dimensions as the self-report questionnaire version, but does require training in its use. The interview version (Fairburn and Cooper 1993) is often considered the 'gold standard' measure in the field while the self-report questionnaire version (Beglin and Fairburn 1992) is more practical for everyday clinical use. The Eating Disorder Inventory 3 (Garner 2004) is also useful as a multidimensional measure of features associated with BN, while the Body Shape Questionnaire (P.J. Cooper et al. 1987) provides a useful measure of concern and distress about weight and shape.

Cut-off scores and categories used by researchers to indicate either eating disorder 'caseness' or severity of symptoms can be seen, where these are available (normally from those who have developed the relevant scales), in Table 2.2.

SELF-REPORT QUESTIONNAIRE AND INTERVIEW-BASED MEASURES

Eating disorder related measures

Eating Attitudes Test-26 (Garner et al. 1982)

This 26 item measure assesses some of the typical symptoms associated with eating disorders.

Eating Disorder Examination – Questionnaire (Fairburn and Beglin 1994)

This is a widely used measure that assesses the frequency and severity of eating disorder related behaviours including binge eating and compensatory behaviours, as well as restraint, and concerns about eating, weight and shape.

Eating Behaviour Questionnaire (Cooper et al. 2006)

This 47 item self-report questionnaire assesses six dimensions of eating disorder behaviours related to weight and shape, bingeing, dieting, food, eating and overeating.

Readiness and Motivation Interview for Eating Disorders (Geller and Drab 1999)

This is a semi-structured assessment tool that elicits information on individuals' experience of and attachment to their symptoms. It assesses readiness and motivation for change, as well as the extent to which change may depend on internal versus external factors.

Eating Disorder Thoughts Questionnaire (Cooper et al. 2006)

This 26 item self-report questionnaire assesses three dimensions of eating disorder thoughts relevant to the new cognitive model: positive thoughts about eating, negative thoughts about eating and permissive thoughts.

Eating Disorder Belief Questionnaire (Cooper et al. 1997)

This measures four cognitive constructs related to eating disorders: it includes negative self beliefs, and three types of underlying assumptions related to eating, weight and shape.

General symptoms and psychopathology measures

Beck Depression Inventory II (Beck et al. 1996)

This is a measure of the typical symptoms associated with depression.

Beck Anxiety Inventory (Beck and Steer 1990)

This is a measure of the typical symptoms associated with anxiety.

Rosenberg Self Esteem Scale (Rosenberg 1967)

This is a brief measure of how positive or negative the individual feels about herself.

Meta-Cognitions Questionnaire-30 (Wells and Cartwright-Hatton 2004)

This 30 item self-report questionnaire measures five dimensions relevant to metacognition, including three comprised of positive and negative beliefs about thinking and worry, one related to metacognitive monitoring and one to judgements of cognitive confidence.

Table 2.3 provides mean scores and standard deviations (SDs) obtained in samples of women without an eating disorder and women with BN for the Rosenberg Self Esteem Scale (RSE: Hunt and Cooper 2001), the Eating Disorder Belief Questionnaire (EDBQ: Cooper et al. 1997) and in these two groups for the Eating Disorder Thoughts Questionnaire (EDTQ) and Eating Behaviour Questionnaire (EBQ) (Cooper et al. 2006).

Table 2.2 Cut-off scores and symptom severity on self-report measures

Questionnaire	Cut-off for caseness or severity of symptoms
Eating Attitudes Test	26 item version, 20 (40 item version, 30)
Beck Depression Inventory II	0–13 minimal depression 14–19 mild depression 20–28 moderate depression 29–63 severe depression
Beck Anxiety Inventory	0–7 minimal anxiety 8–15 mild anxiety 16–25 moderate anxiety 26–63 severe anxiety

Note: Scores above 'cut-offs' indicate that the person is very likely to have an eating disorder diagnosis.

Table 2.3 Mean scores on self-report measures in women without an eating disorder and women with bulimia nervosa

Questionnaire	Non-eating-disordered women		Women with BN	
	Mean	SD	Mean	SD
Rosenberg Self Esteem Scale	31.5	5.0	20.1	3.3
Eating Disorder Belief Questionnaire				
Negative self beliefs	20.4	16.3	60.4	18.3
Acceptance by others	7.1	10.1	61.2	23.2
Self acceptance	40.9	25.7	86.5	15.0
Control over eating	10.0	13.9	81.5	17.7
Eating Disorder Thoughts Questionnaire				
Negative thoughts	7.2	11.0	90.9	9.7
Positive thoughts	2.0	3.0	39.8	28.6
Permissive thoughts	27.7	20.9	43.7	27.9
Eating Behaviour Questionnaire				
Weight and shape	9.7	9.7	67.0	18.3
Bingeing	2.2	2.7	52.7	21.4
Dieting	8.8	9.0	63.1	24.6
Food	21.5	14.3	26.6	24.0
Eating	10.5	18.4	39.0	29.4
Overeating	20.6	14.0	58.9	29.1

READING MATERIAL

Having made a decision to offer the patient cognitive therapy for BN, it is useful to provide some written information on the style and content of treatment. Appendix 3: A Client's Guide to Cognitive Therapy for Bulimia Nervosa can be used to achieve this, and might usefully be given to the patient to read as a homework task, with instructions to make notes of any questions or queries that are raised when reading it. The material, including any issues noted by the patient, and her reaction to it, should then be discussed at the next meeting.

OBSTACLES TO ASSESSMENT

Patients may have a variety of concerns when they arrive for assessment. Some of the more common ones that may need to be addressed can be seen in the box. Using general therapeutic skills such as reflective listening and being empathic and validating their experiences may be all that is required to deal with these at this early stage.

TYPICAL CONCERNS OF PATIENTS AT ASSESSMENT

1. I need help with this problem yet feel unsure if I want to change. When I went to my GP it seemed like a good idea; now I'm not sure.
2. I don't believe it is possible to overcome BN.
3. It will upset me, or I will feel ashamed talking about my problems.
4. If I'm truthful about my behaviour, the therapist will think I'm weird.
5. I'm worried that I will come across as a bit mad.
6. The therapist will want me to gain weight or get fat; the treatment will involve weight gain.
7. 'Normal eating' means I will gain weight.
8. I'll have to eat foods I don't like.

CHAPTER SUMMARY AND KEY POINTS

This chapter has outlined the key diagnostic features of BN and provided information relevant to its assessment, including detail on the information a therapist requires from an assessment before starting the new CT for BN.

Key points to remember include the following:

⊙ BN is a serious mental health problem.
⊙ It is particularly common in young women.
⊙ BN can co-occur with other disorders and an assessment of their presence and function needs to be made; the primary problem should always be identified.
⊙ In some circumstances CT for BN is best conducted together with additional treatment.
⊙ In all cases of BN the relevant physician should be involved and kept informed about the patient's progress.
⊙ The main focus of the assessment required should be psychological and problem based, and should include a detailed description of the eating problem.
⊙ Self-report questionnaires and diaries are an important part of the assessment.
⊙ Any concerns that patients may have about treatment at this stage should be identified and addressed.

Treatment of bulimia nervosa

This chapter briefly summarises existing cognitive behavioural treatment for bulimia nervosa and the evidence for its efficacy. Issues raised by existing treatment are identified, including the evidence that a significant number of people do not currently benefit a great deal from cognitive behaviour therapy (CBT) for BN. Possible reasons for this are explored. The case for a new cognitive model is then presented, together with some of the main influences and empirical evidence that has led us to its development. These include early writers on BN, more recent development of specific models of cognitive therapy for different disorders, work in the field of normal eating and the emergence and development of schema focused and, most recently, metacognitive theory and treatments.

CBT is widely recognised as the treatment of choice for bulimia nervosa (National Institute for Clinical Excellence (NICE) 2004). It currently has the strongest evidence base of all the different approaches to BN, including self help and pharmacotherapy, both of which are often used to treat the disorder.

EFFECTIVENESS STUDIES

Most studies of CBT draw on the manual based cognitive behavioural intervention developed by Fairburn et al. (1993). Indeed, it has formed the basis of the majority of treatment evaluation studies.

Cognitive behavioural therapy for BN developed by Fairburn et al (1993) has three overlapping phases. In the first phase the main aim is to educate the patient about BN and the processes that maintain the disorder. Educational material is presented including information on the negative consequences of bingeing, vomiting and dieting. Patients are asked to resume a normal eating pattern (three meals and three snacks a day) based on the premise that eliminating dietary restriction will reduce the urge and frequency of binge eating. They are also asked to resist urges to binge and purge. Daily records are kept of all food eaten, of binge eating, purging and any related events and thoughts. In the second phase normal food intake and elimination of dietary restraint continues. Regular meals and snacks made up of a wide range of foods, including any foods that have been avoided, are introduced. Cognitive procedures are employed to identify and challenge negative automatic thoughts and avoidance related to food, eating, weight and shape. Problem solving is taught, and the patient is encouraged to generate and implement alternatives when faced with a difficult situation (one, for example, that has led to binge eating in the past). In the third phase the focus is on maintaining change, and education about relapse prevention.

The evidence suggests that CBT including these phases and components is effective for some patients. Most of the relevant studies now use sophisticated, well-controlled designs with careful inclusion and exclusion criteria, and psychometrically robust assessment measures; thus the evidence is very credible. The most sophisticated and significant study is a large multi-centre study (Agras et al. 2000) which has provided very definite confirmation of the usefulness of CBT in patients with BN. The study involved two treatment sites, and recruited 220 patients with BN to take part. CBT was compared with interpersonal psychotherapy (IPT) immediately after treatment and at one year follow-up. CBT was more effective in reducing binge eating, purging, and dietary restraint at the end of treatment than IPT. These results constitute an important finding which extends the validity of the treatment beyond its original home (Oxford) and those who were initially involved in developing it (Fairburn's group). However, it is also important to note that interpersonal psychotherapy (which has no focus on food and eating, or weight and shape) was equally effective in reducing the core eating disorder symptoms at follow-up. At the end of treatment 45 per cent (29) of those who had CBT had recovered compared with only 8 per cent (5) recovered in the IPT group. At one year follow-up, however, there were no significant differences between the two treatments on any measure.

A detailed and comprehensive systematic review of a broad range of different CBT treatment studies for BN reaches the same conclusion (Hay and Bacaltchuk 2000). In other words, while cognitive therapy is clearly effective in the treatment of BN, it is by no means the only effective treatment, particularly in the longer term, where IPT can be just as efficacious. Interestingly, however, in Agras et al.'s (2000) study, cognitive therapy was more effective at the end of treatment than IPT, thus it appears to act more quickly. This could be important pragmatically when making decisions about type of treatment to offer. The National Institute of Clinical Excellence (2004) recommends that cognitive behaviour therapy be offered as a first-line treatment for BN, noting that IPT may be a useful alternative, but that it takes longer to work than CBT. There is some preliminary evidence that those with personality disorder features do less well with CBT (for more information see Cooper 2003). To date, however, what works for whom has not yet begun to be studied in detail; it may be that rapid gains are more important for some (yet to be identified) patients than others. Some may prefer and benefit most from a less structured approach or one that does not focus directly on eating. Personality as well as illness-related variables, individual experience and personal history may be related to this, although no consistent predictors of outcome have yet been established.

What is most important, however, is that overall many people do not benefit a great deal from either IPT or CBT. For example, 37 per cent of those treated with CBT had a DSM-IV eating diagnosis at long-term follow-up (Fairburn et al. 1995). Thus while it undoubtedly helps some people, it is not helpful for everyone, and alternatives will often need to be considered in practice.

An additional point is that the outcome for CBT for BN is generally much less good than CBT outcome in other psychological disorders, particularly when compared with that for the anxiety disorders. A meta-analysis of CBT confirms that less than half of those who complete CBT for BN can expect to recover (only one-fifth if intention to treat analysis is used), and that most patients have residual symptoms (Thompson-Brenner et al. 2003).

THE CASE FOR A NEW MODEL

One possible reason for less than ideal outcome with CBT for BN is that the treatment has not been delivered adequately and effectively. In relation to the treatment studies published this seems extremely unlikely. All therapists had experience, expertise and supervision in the treatments being used. Treatment adherence and treatment integrity has generally been taken very seriously by the investigators, and has been closely monitored. However, it is also important to remember that the criteria for inclusion in the trials conducted to date are very narrow, and thus participants may not be very representative of patients typically seen by many clinicians in the course of their everyday work, including services at secondary level. Such patients often have additional problems or comorbidity.

A more plausible reason for the limitations of current CBT for bulimia nervosa, and one suggested by some researchers (e.g. Jansen 2001), is that the cognitive models being used need further development. Several factors have led us to develop a new cognitive model of BN, while acknowledging that important advances have come from the original model.

First, as noted above, treatment based on earlier models might be improved – many people with BN are not helped very much by existing treatment.

Second, research data (and the general development of schema theory) suggests that the original model needs substantial revision. In particular, it needs to take account of evidence related to the presence of core or negative self beliefs in BN, and their role in the development of the disorder. It also needs to take account of some of the more detailed investigations of types of automatic thoughts related to the maintenance of specific behaviours, including binge eating, and how these interact with emotions and physiological processes. It also might benefit from attending to some of the newer cognitive constructs, including schema (or core beliefs) and metacognition, that have been explored in other disorders and that might also have a role in BN.

Third, there is a small but growing body of evidence that contradicts some of the assumptions of the original theory, including the importance of dietary restraint in the maintenance of binge eating. Several studies now suggest that dietary restraint may be rather less important than the original theory suggests (Byrne and McLean 2002; Steiger et al. 1999b; Stice 2005; Stice et al. 1996), although it does seem important in the development of the disorder. In contrast, affect may be rather more important, and perhaps more important than restraint or hunger (Waters et al. 2001). The latter finding has now been supported in a number of recent studies (e.g. Engelberg et al. 2007; Hilbert and Tuschen-Caffier 2007), while the former study also provides evidence for the role of altered self-awareness as a precursor to binge eating.

Much of the detail of this work and evidence is reviewed elsewhere (e.g. Cooper 1997a, 2005). Below we briefly summarise the main influences that have led us to the development of a new cognitive model of BN.

OUR MAIN INFLUENCES

Garner and Bemis (1982) first integrated Beck's theory of depression and psychological models of anorexia nervosa, while Fairburn et al. (1986) provided a specific model for bulimia nervosa – an innovative development in the understanding and treatment of what was then a relatively newly identified and little understood disorder. Both have been important influences on our model and work.

We have also been influenced by the work of several other researchers and theorists. These include Heatherton and Baumeister (1991), who proposed that binge eating operates as an escape from aversive self-awareness and emotional distress. The model we propose also has links with that of Grilo and Shiffman (1994), who described a model in which binge eating was predicted by cognitive state. Root et al. (1986) have also highlighted the development of individual identity and binge eating as serving a function, to deal with or dissociate from thoughts and feelings.

We have been influenced by the development of disorder specific models in cognitive therapy (for example, generalised anxiety disorder: Wells 1995). These have presented detailed accounts of the relationships between thoughts, feelings and behaviours in the maintenance of individual disorders. They have been accompanied by clear and precise descriptions of the cognitions and cognitive processes involved. This has not generally been the case in eating disorders. The model we describe clearly distinguishes levels of cognition, and different types of thought. Unlike previous models it provides a detailed account of the relationship between thoughts, feelings, behaviour and physiological processes. Importantly, it also introduces a metacognitive perspective, that is, it emphasises the role of the factors that control and regulate cognition, in addition to the emphasis on cognitive content that is typical of schema theory.

Work in the field of normal eating, both theoretical and empirical, has also been influential. The theory we describe is compatible with recent developments in these areas, notably the shift away from set point theory, and interest in cognitive determinants of normal eating, such as learned expectations (e.g. Hohlstein et al. 1998; Pinel 2000). One exciting consequence of this is that it becomes possible to use paradigms and techniques from the study of normal eating to understand (and help treat) disordered eating and eating disorders.

We have been influenced by the development and application of schema theory and treatment (e.g. Beck and Freeman 1990; Young 1990; Young et al. 2003). In particular we have taken note of its emphasis on core beliefs or schema, schema driven processes and the role of early experience in the formation of core beliefs.

It is noteworthy that others are moving in similar directions. Waller and colleagues, for example, have highlighted the importance of schemas in eating disorders, and have outlined a model in which bulimia nervosa, compared to anorexia nervosa, is characterised by secondary processing or a greater tendency towards an avoidant coping style (Luck et al. 2005; Waller et al. 2007). Fairburn et al. (2003) in their transdiagnostic model highlight the role of negative affect, core low self-esteem and mood intolerance. These concepts are similar to some of those that we have highlighted.

Despite these influences our most important influence stems from the growth and development of metacognitive theory, from its early beginnings as outlined by Wells and Matthews (1994) to its more sophisticated articulation in Wells (2000). Beliefs about cognition and emotion and the use of cognitive regulatory processes have a key role in our model. Control beliefs are a recurrent theme, and one that is evident at several levels of processing, from negative automatic thoughts, to core beliefs. For example, our model addresses beliefs about control (i.e. self-regulation) at several levels, including the way in which control of eating-related thoughts, control of emotions and control of behaviour contribute to the problematic symptoms of BN. The model shares similar features with the metacognitive model of generalised anxiety disorder (Wells 1995, 1997), although the cognitive content is very different. Overall, attentional and other processes involved in the maintenance of dysfunctional cognition patterns, as well as the content of the cognitions, play an important role in contributing to our understanding (and thus treatment) of BN.

CHAPTER SUMMARY AND KEY POINTS

This chapter has considered CBT for BN and evidence for its efficacy. Limitations of existing treatment have been identified. The case is made for a new model, and the main influences that have led us to its development have been summarised.

Key points to remember include the following:

⦿ CBT is widely recognised as an effective treatment for BN for some patients but a significant number do not benefit from it (or from IPT, which can also be effective).
⦿ One potential explanation for this is that the cognitive models of BN require further development.
⦿ Existing models of BN could be revised to take into account developments related to negative self beliefs (important in the development of BN), research on different types of automatic thoughts, specific behaviours and their interaction with emotion and physiological processes.

⊙ Metacognition and patterns of self-regulation of thoughts and feelings are likely to be of special significance in any revised model.
⊙ Research findings that are inconsistent with existing theory need to be integrated, as do developments in the field of normal eating, schema and metacognitive theory and treatment.

CHAPTER 4

A new cognitive model of bulimia nervosa

This chapter outlines a new cognitive model of bulimia nervosa. The model accounts for the development of the disorder as well as the maintenance of binge eating and other behaviours and concerns characteristic of BN. The empirical evidence that supports the new model and its key constructs and processes is presented. The model's implications for therapy are discussed.

THE NEW MODEL

How can we account for the repeated, and apparently uncontrollable, episodes of bingeing and vomiting in BN? How can we explain the other characteristic behaviours (overt and covert) associated with BN? In this section a new cognitive model of bulimia nervosa is described. An earlier version was previously described by Cooper et al. (2004) that incorporates precipitating, maintaining and vulnerability factors. The version presented here builds on that model by adding greater detail and being grounded more clearly in Wells' metacognitive theory of psychological disorder (Wells 2000). A diagram of the model can be seen in Figure 4.1.

The model differentiates between different types of beliefs that interact in the development and maintenance of BN. Negative self beliefs (e.g.'I'm unlovable', 'I'm a failure') constitute a vulnerability to the disorder. However, in line with metacognitive theory (Wells 2000; Wells and Matthews 1994) this leads to disorder when general negative self beliefs occur in conjunction with instrumental beliefs or metacognitions that interpret and control cognition and behaviour. In BN specifically, we propose that these instrumental beliefs or metacognitions include negative and positive beliefs about eating and eating-related cognitive processes (e.g. 'I cannot stop worrying about my weight', 'I must control my thoughts or I'll get fat', 'If I pay attention to my thighs I can remain thin').

Three types of negative belief exist in BN: that eating/food will lead to catastrophic weight gain, that bingeing is uncontrollable and that the thoughts and emotions associated with BN are dangerous (e.g. will never end). The last two types of belief represent metacognitive beliefs.

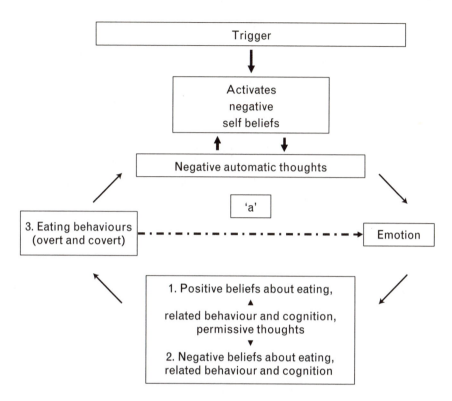

Note 'a' = Effects of distraction, direct effects on emotion/body state, interoception
1. Positive beliefs about eating, about worrying about food, about selective attention
2. Negative beliefs about uncontrollability of eating behaviour and thoughts, consequences of eating
3. Eating behaviour includes bingeing, purging, worrying, attention to calories/body parts, hoarding food etc.

Figure 4.1 A cognitive model of bulimia nervosa

Positive beliefs are of three types: that bingeing is a helpful behaviour, that it is necessary to focus attention on weight and shape-related information (e.g. waist size, feeling bloated) and that it is helpful to ruminate and worry about food, eating and one's body. The latter two types are also metacognitive beliefs. The preoccupations and attentional patterns they represent epitomise the construct that Wells and Matthews identified as the cognitive-attentional syndrome (CAS: Wells and Matthews 1994, 1996), a process involved in all psychological disorders. Examples of positive beliefs in BN include 'Bingeing will stop me feeling upset', 'Worrying about my weight and shape is useful', 'If I don't worry I'll lose control of my eating', 'If I dwell on food it stops me getting upset about other things', 'I must focus attention on how my waist feels and then I'll remain thin'.

The belief that bingeing is uncontrollable leads to failed or counterproductive attempts to control eating, thereby contributing to the persistence of binges. Preoccupation with and attention to food, weight and one's body increases negative thoughts, leading them to become more intrusive and harder to ignore. Changes in the body, for example, fluctuating (especially lowering) blood-glucose levels, also provide internal body state information that contributes to changes in the way cognition feels and operates, thus contributing to a sense of loss of control.

An important mechanism in maintaining binges is the conflict that exists between negative and positive beliefs about eating. In particular, the person believes that eating will lead to catastrophic weight gain but, at the same time, believes that they must binge in order to control negative emotions and thoughts. This conflict is resolved by permissive thoughts (for example, 'This will be the last time I binge'). However, these thoughts and the binge that results do not resolve the discrepancy between the two opposing types of belief; instead they provide only temporary relief from the original distress and concerns. The person goes on to have further episodes, reinforcing their (erroneous) sense of loss of control over eating, not least because occurrences of bingeing are subject to negative interpretation, not only as a sign of loss of control, but also as a sign of failure, defectiveness, and so on, which reinforces the negative self beliefs that render the person cognitively and emotionally vulnerable in the first place.

The act of engaging in eating-related behaviours such as bingeing has direct effects on emotion and feeling states and these are important in our model. Eating-related behaviours can distract from more upsetting thoughts and memories, thus improving mood and negatively reinforcing the activity. There are also direct physiological effects of eating that activate reward-mechanisms in the brain, as well as direct effects on cognition (for example, due to changes in blood glucose levels). These effects can make it harder to give up bingeing since it has direct payoffs.

The maintenance of binge eating

In the individual case an episode of bingeing and vomiting is typically activated in particular contexts or 'setting conditions'. Setting conditions for bingeing generally fall into three categories: those concerned with issues of weight, shape and eating, those concerned with different physiological states and those concerned with issues unrelated to these.

Common situations in the latter category are social situations or inter-personal issues.

A setting condition activates one or more of the patient's negative self beliefs (e.g. 'I'm worthless', 'I'm unlovable', 'I'm a failure'). These beliefs are expressed as negative automatic thoughts, and their activation typically creates considerable emotional distress.

Bingeing (or other problematic behaviours) then takes place to deal with, or to cope with, the distress that is experienced as a result of negative self belief activation. Bingeing is caused by positive beliefs about eating, such as 'Binging will take away my painful feelings', and further supported by permissive thoughts, such as 'This will be the last time I binge'. The eventual outcome of such thoughts is an episode of binge eating. As the episode of binge eating continues, negative beliefs about eating become more prominent. These are focused on the perceived (negative) consequences of overeating (e.g. 'I'll get fat'). These negative beliefs also become linked to the positive beliefs that offer a means of coping with them. Such beliefs include 'Worrying about my shape stops me from gaining weight'.

Compensatory behaviour, for example, the vomiting which typically follows an episode of binge eating, occurs when the relative balance of positive and negative beliefs shifts in favour of the negative, and the negative beliefs about eating predominate. Physiological pressures, for example, spontaneous regurgitation of food, may also play a role. Vomiting is one (extreme) example of a strategy to cope with negative beliefs.

Immediately after a binge, but before vomiting takes place, any high levels of arousal and any negative mood decrease. This process serves to reinforce the act of binge eating as an effective or helpful way to cope with distress. In the longer term however, once vomiting or other compensatory behaviour has been completed any initial sense of relief from having got rid of the food tends to disappear. Negative mood and arousal start to rise again, as the individual contemplates what she has done, and considers the potential negative consequences of yet another episode of bingeing and vomiting. Binge eating also leaves the initial negative self beliefs intact, as these have not been directly challenged or modified by bingeing. This means that the individual is vulnerable to episodes of binge eating in the future. (Clinically, we have observed that on occasion vomiting may occur in some patients after normal eating (or indeed excessive eating in a social context) as a means of weight control and when schemas are not activated. For example, individuals with BN might plan to eat a three-course dinner in a restaurant with friends with the intention of inducing vomiting and not proceeding on to bingeing.

However, the act of vomiting then typically activates schema, providing another route into bingeing. It is important to formulate such instances carefully in order to determine the precise cognitions involved.)

A clinical example of binge eating

Bethany had concerns about work and when she tried to explain these to a friend, she didn't think her friend understood her situation. This activated her schema or negative self beliefs that she was all alone, and that no one understood her, and she felt very disappointed and let down. On the way back to work she bought a muffin, and ate it, motivated by the thought that it would cheer her up. She then thought 'I'll get fat', and 'I've had one, why not have more, this will be the last time I'll binge'. She bought food to binge on and ate it rapidly, believing that she couldn't stop eating. While eating she felt detached, and unaware of what she was thinking. She described this as 'zoning out'. She stopped eating when she felt that she physically couldn't eat any more, and could feel the food rising up inside her throat. Her fear of gaining weight intensified. She then felt weak, hated herself and became increasingly self critical and blaming of herself. Figure 4.2 shows how the cognitive model was used to understand Bethany's experience in this situation.

The maintenance of other BN-related behaviours and concerns

The model provides an account of the maintenance of a range of BN related behaviours and concerns, and is not just a model of binge eating. These behaviours include frequent checking of weight and appearance, and various behaviours related to food and eating, for example, rigid counting of calories or fat grams, as well as dieting and extended periods of fasting. For example, a negative automatic thought might be dealt with by engaging in worry and rumination about being overweight. The person becomes preoccupied with thoughts of being fat, and an inability to stop thinking about being fat can be interpreted as evidence that the individual has lost control or is getting fat. Worry about and preoccupation with weight can distract attention from other negative automatic thoughts in the short term, but in the long term worry behaviour is negatively reinforced because it reduces more distressing affect associated with other more distressing thoughts.

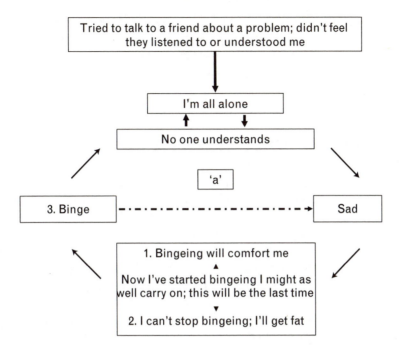

Note 'a' = Effects of distraction, direct effects on emotion/body state, interoception
1. Positive beliefs about eating, about worrying about food, about selective attention
2. Negative beliefs about uncontrollability of eating behaviour and thoughts, consequences of eating
3. Eating behaviour includes bingeing, purging, worrying, attention to calories/ body parts, hoarding food etc.

Figure 4.2 A cognitive model of bulimia nervosa: a case example

The development of BN

The maintenance of binge eating has been outlined above. The conjunction of negative self beliefs and positive and negative metacognitive beliefs together explain the development of BN, or the reasons why some people are vulnerable to BN. Both types of beliefs (self and metacognition related) are necessary for BN to develop; one without the other will not normally result in BN. We have seen how the metacognitive beliefs concern the uncontrollability or dangerous consequences of internal thoughts, actions and emotions, and positive beliefs about worry, attentional strategies and eating as a route to self-regulation.

There are also negative beliefs about eating, which fall into the 'catastrophic consequences of weight gain' category, and which typically reflect assumptions about the meaning of eating and body related behaviours and concerns. These assumptions can include beliefs such as 'If I gain weight, I'm not successful; if I get fat, no one will like me'. They can also include beliefs such as 'If I eat fat, it will turn into fat; if I eat normally, I'll gain weight'.

EMPIRICAL SUPPORT FOR THE NEW MODEL

Much of the empirical evidence which supports existing cognitive models of BN also supports our model. We have additional evidence, however, that supports some of the specific components of the model.

The basic ingredients of the new model were identified in a study described by Cooper et al. (1998, 2002). Additional evidence can be found in subsequent studies that we have published, including those noted below. We also note findings relevant to the model in studies conducted by other research groups. The review is meant to be illustrative, rather than exhaustive. A more detailed presentation of the relevant evidence can be found in Cooper (2003).

Positive beliefs

Positive beliefs are an important element of the new model. A study using the Eating Disorder Thoughts Questionnaire found that positive beliefs about eating predicted eating disorder symptoms, and that BN patients, compared with dieters and non-dieters, have high levels of these beliefs (Cooper et al. 2006).

A second study also suggests that positive beliefs are important in BN. Items endorsed by BN patients in dealing with negative events and emotions included 'Eating helped distract me', 'Eating helped me get rid of some angry feelings' (Sherwood et al. 2000).

Negative beliefs

These beliefs are also assessed on the Eating Disorder Thoughts Questionnaire (Cooper et al. 2006). Levels are higher in BN patients than in dieters and non-dieters. High levels were also associated with eating disorder symptoms in a cross-sectional study (Cooper et al. 2006).

Metacognitive beliefs

A metacognition questionnaire (MCQ-30: Wells and Cartwright-Hatton 2004) was found to be positively associated with EAT scores, a measure of eating disorder symptoms, both cross-sectionally and longitudinally in a population of 16–19-year-old schoolgirls (Todd 2006).

Vicious circle links

The model outlines a vicious circle of thoughts, feelings, behaviour and physiological responses. No test of the specific links outlined has been conducted, but the evidence is generally consistent with the links. There is ample evidence, for example, that binge eating in bulimia nervosa is preceded by considerable distress both emotionally and cognitively, including in recent studies using daily monitoring (e.g. Stein et al. 2007), and including evidence that one function of binge eating may be to decrease self-awareness (e.g. Engelberg et al. 2007). This 'distracting' function is discussed further below. The most commonly reported emotion immediately prior to bingeing is anxiety (Elmore and De Castro 1990) or tension (Abraham and Beumont 1982). Higher than average levels of depression have also been reported (Hsu 1990). There is evidence that the negative cognitions which precede or trigger bingeing include thoughts of loneliness (Abraham and Beumont 1982). A study using the Young Schema Questionnaire (Young 1998) found that core (including negative self) beliefs were linked to the two key symptoms of BN, bingeing and vomiting (Waller et al. 2000). A link exists between scores on the Weight and Shape Based Self-Esteem Inventory (Geller et al. 1997) and eating disorder symptoms, which is also consistent with the link we suggest. One study has found a strong correlation between self-esteem and body dissatisfaction in bulimia nervosa (Joiner et al. 1997).

Immediately after bingeing and before purging, negative emotions increase, particularly depression (Elmore and De Castro 1990; Hsu 1990). In one study negative cognitions focused on self-loathing, and guilt and disgust also intensified (J.L. Cooper et al. 1988).

Distraction from thoughts and emotions

There is evidence that episodes of binge eating provide a way of decreasing or distracting from distress, particularly emotional distress. Most commonly, bingeing appears to give relief from anxiety, which typically decreases during the course of a binge (Kaye et al. 1986). Depression also decreases as a binge proceeds (Hsu 1990), but before vomiting occurs.

Setting conditions

Other studies indicate that people with bulimia appear to be particularly sensitive to social interactions (e.g. Steiger et al. 1999a). The latter study in particular provides some support for the suggestion that negative events other than food and eating, weight and shape events can precede binge eating (see also Grilo and Shiffman 1994).

Negative self beliefs

Two studies (Cooper et al. 1997, 1998) demonstrated and confirmed the reliability and validity of a measure of negative self beliefs in BN. While core beliefs are usually of three types – beliefs about the self, other people and the world (Padesky and Greenberger 1995) – one of our studies (Cooper et al. 1996) indicated that negative self beliefs appear to be relatively more important in bulimia nervosa than beliefs about others and beliefs about the world.

Data from another research group are consistent with the importance of negative self beliefs in BN. Using the Young Schema Questionnaire (Young 1998), two studies have found that those with bulimic disorders had more dysfunctional core beliefs than controls (Leung et al. 1999; Waller et al. 2000).

Weight, shape and eating-related assumptions

Assumptions related to eating, weight and shape (included in our model as negative consequences, a type of negative belief) have now been quite extensively investigated using the EDBQ. Studies show that, like core beliefs, these are related to eating disorder symptoms (Cooper et al. 1997) and are at high levels in BN (Cooper et al. 1997; Cooper and Hunt 1998).

Early trauma

The many reports of early childhood trauma or early negative experiences in bulimia nervosa (Guidano and Liotti 1983) are consistent with our model. More specifically, childhood sexual abuse is common (though not specific to eating disorders) (Welch and Fairburn 1994), as is physical and emotional abuse (Rorty et al. 1994). Such experiences typically result in the development of the negative self beliefs commonly identified with a general vulnerability to psychological problems. Bulimic patients also report that parental relationships were unfriendly or hostile and disengaged, as well as autonomous (low control, low submission), and their self-concept ratings are correlated with their perceptions of their family (Rorty et al. 1994). Although one possibility is that poor parental relationships are the result of the eating disorder, an alternative possibility is that patients have internalised these negative relationships (Wonderlich et al. 1996).

Another study found that low perceived parental bonding behaviours (early negative experiences) were related to the development of core (including negative self) beliefs in bulimics (Leung et al. 2000).

Link between early experience, bingeing and negative self beliefs

One study (in a non-clinical group) found that core beliefs (defectiveness and shame) mediated the relationship between early childhood experience and bulimic symptoms (Meyer et al. 2001). This supports our suggestion that all three are linked in a meaningful way.

OTHER EVIDENCE CONSISTENT WITH OUR MODEL

A general review of evidence for cognitive models of eating disorders can be found elsewhere (Cooper 1997a, 2005). This considers the experimental psychology evidence for information processing biases – selective attention and memory, and interpretive bias – in bulimia nervosa. In brief, several studies find selective attention to eating, weight and shape related words in BN (e.g. Cooper et al. 1992; Cooper and Todd 1997). The bias seems to correlate with severity of eating disorder symptoms, and improves with treatment, including cognitive therapy (Cooper and

Fairburn 1994). However, a small number of studies have not found this bias (e.g. Carter et al. 2000). A review highlighting the methodological problems with this research suggests that these may explain the conflicting findings (Faunce 2002).

A small number of studies have investigated attentional bias using alternative methods. A study using a dichotic listening task, and including thin-related words, found selective processing of fat-related body words compared to thin in bulimics (Rieger et al. 1998). Such biases are consistent with the present model. In accordance with metacognitive theory (Wells and Matthews 1994, 1996) they are thought to be a product of attempts to control cognition (i.e. of positive beliefs about control strategies). In particular, such biases are considered to reflect a top-down strategy of focusing attention on threat-related information as a coping strategy.

One study provides some support for selective memory bias in bulimia nervosa that improves with treatment (Flynn and McNally 1999). Another study, however, by Hunt and Cooper (2001) provided only partial support for such a bias. Interpretive bias, assessed using ambiguous scenarios, also seems to characterise bulimia nervosa (Cooper 1997b). Two detailed reviews specifically of information processing biases relevant to eating disorders have been published, and provide additional relevant information (Lee and Shafran 2004; Williamson et al. 1999).

IMPLICATIONS FOR THERAPY

The model described suggests that the following cognitions should be a focus of treatment:

- negative beliefs about uncontrollability of bingeing and cognition
- negative beliefs about the consequences of eating and related behaviour
- positive beliefs about behaviours and cognition (worry, attention strategies) related to BN
- negative self beliefs.

Tackling negative beliefs about eating (including the uncontrollability of binge eating), as well as positive beliefs about eating, will interrupt the cycle of thoughts, feelings and behaviour that maintains binge eating. It will also decrease other BN-related behaviours. Tackling negative self beliefs addresses vulnerability (developmental) factors and makes emotional relapse less likely.

There is some evidence for the effectiveness of treatment based on the model described above. In both studies the primary focus was on achieving cognitive change. This includes work using a self-help version of the treatment (Pritchard et al. 2004), and a single case series, which employed individually tailored therapy for patients with BN (Cooper et al. 2007b). In both studies, emphasis on cognitive change also resulted in significant behavioural change.

Prioritising different aspects of the model during treatment

The treatment is presented sequentially here, in the order in which it is usually administered. Motivational strategies are followed by formulation, and by techniques to challenge negative automatic thoughts that focus initially on beliefs about uncontrollability of binge eating. This is followed by work on negative beliefs about the consequences of eating and other related behaviours. Positive beliefs about eating-related behaviours and cognitions are then modified and finally treatment tackles negative self beliefs.

Treatment may not necessarily proceed sequentially in the exact order in which it is presented here. At times, for example when setbacks in progress are encountered, it may be necessary to recap on previously learned skills. It may also be necessary to interweave work on concurrent problems with work on the eating problem, particularly if these are judged to be impeding progress with the latter. Occasionally, it may be necessary to move on to the next stage, even though less progress has been made than one might wish with a particular step. This is particularly true of progression to work on negative self beliefs. Clinically, some patients seem to reach a roadblock that is resolved only once significant progress has been made in negative self belief work. At this stage it may be necessary to interleave the core belief work with a focus on consolidating work done on eating, weight and shape topics and tasks. Work on two strategies simultaneously then seems to facilitate progress, with progress in one having a positive effect on progress in the other.

CHAPTER SUMMARY AND KEY POINTS

This chapter has outlined our cognitive model of BN. It has described its main constructs and the processes involved. It has also briefly summarised the empirical evidence consistent with it.

Key points to remember include the following:

- The model accounts for the development as well as the maintenance of the disorder's key features.
- Important constructs include negative self beliefs, positive and negative beliefs about eating and permissive thoughts.
- Beliefs about the uncontrollability of binge eating and metacognitive beliefs about eating, cognition and emotion are important considerations.
- A particularly important construct is that binge eating (and associated behaviours) reflects strategies of maladaptive cognitive and emotional regulation.

Important ideas include:

- Binge eating is a form of distraction from negative self beliefs and its associated affect.
- A vicious circle of thoughts, emotions, behaviours and physiological factors is involved in the maintenance of binge eating.
- The conjunction of different types of beliefs is important in the development of the disorder.
- Important targets for treatment are negative beliefs about lack of control, beliefs about the negative consequences of eating, positive beliefs about engaging in food or eating-related cognitions and behaviour, and negative self beliefs.

Engagement and motivation

This chapter provides ideas for enhancing patients' engagement in treatment, together with ideas for encouraging motivation for change. The chapter recognises that patients with bulimia nervosa often find it difficult to proceed with treatment, and that fears about change are common and will need to be tackled for treatment to be successful. Ideas for identifying fears about change, and suggestions for how to manage these, are presented. Six different strategies are described, together with a cost-benefit analysis examining the advantages and disadvantages of change. Finally, some specific fears and issues are briefly discussed.

ENGAGEMENT

Patients with BN can be difficult to engage in treatment. However, like all cognitive therapy, the treatment we outline can be applied effectively only if the patient is willing to make a commitment to treatment. Patient and therapist factors can both have an impact on this.

Patient factors

Patients with BN can behave in ways that make it difficult to engage them in therapy. Some of the behaviours that therapists may find difficult include missing appointments without notice, not completing homework assignments, leaving out crucial details in a story and difficulty in taking a psychological perspective on the problem. Unlike many other patients, those with BN may also not have a very positive view of therapy (Meyer 2001).

Dropout from therapy is a particular problem, and mean dropout rates of 15.3 per cent (Garner 1987) and 24.4 per cent (Blouin et al. 1995) have been found in controlled studies using CBT to treat BN. It is likely that the dropout rate is as high as 37 per cent in less rigorous effectiveness studies (Steel et al. 2000). This finding is consistent with that of a study of referrals to an NHS eating disorders clinic, where 36.4 per cent of those who were offered treatment, and who took this up, failed to complete a full course of therapy (Peake et al. 2005). This compares with a dropout rate of 8.2 per cent in a large sample of those who began treatment for a broader (but possibly overall less severe) range of mental health problems in one NHS Trust over a two-year period (Hostick and Newell 2004).

Therapist factors

Therapist behaviour and attitudes can also make therapy difficult. Indeed, negative attitudes by therapists are not unusual, and therapists may view patients with BN as manipulative, self absorbed, selfish, irrational and self destructive (Geller et al. 2001).

Implications

The therapist can help build a positive therapeutic alliance with BN patients by following several important principles. These include use of general therapy skills that are common to all psychological therapies where a good therapeutic alliance is important, such as genuine interest and curiosity; warmth and empathy; active listening, summarising and reflecting; and validating the patient's experience. Safran offers more detailed advice on developing a strong therapeutic alliance (e.g. Safran and Muran 2000), while Leahy (2001) outlines strategies for dealing with resistance in cognitive therapy. In those with BN particular attention needs to be paid to the following:

⊙ *Understand why the patient is behaving as she does.* Patients' behaviour makes sense given their beliefs; thus, it is important to try to understand the reasons behind specific behaviours that are affecting treatment progression. For example, many patients with BN are ashamed or embarrassed about their BN behaviours, and fear being judged negatively. This may prevent them from disclosing the full extent of their problem when first seen. Although it is frustrating for the therapist to learn certain important facts only later in treatment, the patient's behaviour makes sense given her beliefs.
⊙ *No blame.* It is not helpful to blame the patient (or anyone else), even if others do. Rather, the focus should not be on 'blame' but framed more positively as 'unconditional positive regard for the client', as outlined by Carl Rogers (e.g. Rogers 1951). This involves valuing patients as they are and conveying 'unpossessive warmth' for them, even when not approving of their behaviour.

⊙ *Use motivational strategies.* Many patients are, for very good reasons, ambivalent about treatment. If so, this needs to be acknowledged and openly discussed. The patient needs to be encouraged to take responsibility for change and take an active part in their treatment; the therapist should not assume that this will happen automatically. Miller and Rollnick (2002) outline five basic principles of motivational interviewing, all of which we have found useful when working with people with BN, and some of which have helped inform this chapter. They can be summarised as follows: express empathy, develop discrepancy or cognitive dissonance between present behaviour and broader goals, avoid getting into arguments, roll with resistance, and support self efficacy, or the patient's belief that she can change.

⊙ *Be proactive.* It is not usually helpful to make assumptions about a patient's likely motives or beliefs and not subsequently check whether these are accurate or not. For example, it is easy to assume that a patient who does not attend a session no longer wishes to have treatment. However, this may well not be the case for a patient with BN, and it is always worth attempting to follow-up patients who apparently drop out or 'do not attend' (DNA), and uncovering the reasoning behind the behaviour. The examples in the box illustrate this point.

REASONS FOR NOT ATTENDING SESSIONS: CLINICAL EXAMPLES

Lucy stopped attending cognitive therapy after eight sessions. The therapist had always considered her to be highly motivated and was very puzzled by this sudden change. The therapist wrote to Lucy and invited her to meet and discuss the situation. It transpired that Lucy didn't fully understand what she was supposed to do in the therapy and believed that to admit to this would be letting the therapist down. She had lost hope of ever overcoming BN and thought that she might as well give up now.

Melissa had received ten sessions of cognitive therapy. She had not binged and vomited for four weeks, and was feeling more optimistic about recovery. After a family argument she binged and vomited and thought, 'I've blown it, I've failed, I'm doomed to be bulimic for ever'. She lost all hope of recovery, discounted all the progress that she had made and decided that it wasn't worth attending her next session.

MOTIVATION

Motivational techniques are an important part of our treatment. This is not to say that BN patients are unmotivated. Indeed, many patients will already have tried other therapies, or used self-help literature. For many patients something will have happened in their life that has inspired them to change, for instance pregnancy and not wanting to be a bulimic mother, starting a new relationship or job. This all suggests a strong drive to do something about their problem, and an interest in change. However, BN serves a function and patients often have fears about changing. Consequently, it is often necessary to use specific strategies and exercises to fully engage and interest them. These also help to build the relationship before proceeding to the more specific (and 'difficult') therapeutic tasks.

One useful approach to understanding the different stages of motivation that can occur in those with mental health problems, including those with BN, is Prochaska and DiClemente's Transtheoretical Stages of Change Model (Prochaska and DiClemente 1982). Prochaska and DiClemente's model with the different stages of change identified can be seen in Table 5.1.

The Stages of Change Model has been widely used by others to understand the specific stages at which eating disorder patients might be in terms of motivation to change. Both Schmidt and Treasure (e.g. Schmidt and Treasure 1997) and Geller (e.g. Geller 2002) have been keen advocates of working with the stage of change the patient is at currently. Those with eating disorders, including BN, are often in the very early stages of change and, as outlined by Treasure (e.g. Treasure 2004), techniques from motivational interviewing (e.g. Miller and Rollnick 2002) can be particularly useful at such stages. Miller and Rollnick (2002) identify five important skills: use open-ended questions, listen reflectively, affirm, summarise and elicit self-motivational statements, all of which we have also found useful in work with people with BN, but particularly when working, as also described by Miller and Rollnick (2002), to tip the decisional balance in favour of change (see below). While motivational interviewing has been found clinically useful, it is important to note that the model, and its relationship to treatment, has been criticised as applied to eating disorders (Wilson and Schlam 2004). Nevertheless, although the link between the two may need clarification, as well as finding the treatment useful, we have also found that components of the model are useful in our research (e.g. Stockford et al. 2007).

Table 5.1 Transtheoretical Stages of Change Model

Stage of change	Characteristics	Techniques
Pre-contemplation	Not currently considering change: 'ignorance is bliss'	Validate lack of readiness Clarify: decision is theirs Encourage re-evaluation of current behaviour Encourage self-exploration, not action Explain and personalise the risk
Contemplation	Ambivalent about change: 'sitting on the fence' Not considering change within the next month	Validate lack of readiness Clarify: decision is theirs Encourage evaluation of pros and cons of behaviour change Identify and promote new, positive outcome expectations
Preparation	Some experience with change and are trying to change: 'testing the waters' Planning to act within one month	Identify and assist in problem solving re obstacles Help patient identify social support Verify that the patient has underlying skills for behaviour change Encourage small initial steps
Action	Practising new behaviour for 3–6 months	Focus on restructuring cues and social support Bolster self-efficacy for dealing with obstacles Combat feelings of loss and reiterate long-term benefits
Maintenance	Continued commitment to sustaining new behaviour Post 6 months to 5 years (after treatment has ended)	Plan for follow-up support Reinforce internal rewards Discuss coping with relapse
Relapse	Resumption of old behaviours: 'fall from grace'	Evaluate trigger for relapse Reassess motivation and barriers Plan stronger coping strategies

Techniques, including those based on motivational interviewing, that might be useful in enhancing engagement and motivation at each stage of change can also be seen in Table 5.1.

Initial motivation for change

Four stages are identified in the Prochaska and DiClemente model. Contemplation or preparation is the usual stage that patients present with in BN. If in contemplation they are ambivalent about changing and do not have any set plan to change within the near future. If patients are in the preparation stage they usually have some experience of change and are already trying to change. This contrasts with anorexia nervosa, where patients seem more likely to present at the pre-contemplation stage.

ENCOURAGING INITIAL MOTIVATION FOR CHANGE

If the patient is extremely reluctant, or has previously had a bad therapy experience, special care may be needed. A statement along the lines of the following may be useful:

You have taken a big step to come to the clinic today, which must have been very difficult for you, especially given your concerns about [reflect back a brief summary of the patient's concerns]. I appreciate that you have been honest with me about your reservations in embarking on a course of psychological treatment. Cognitive therapy is the treatment that is likely to be most useful in helping you overcome BN. For CT to be effective it has to be something that you really want to do. It is about making changes and requires commitment. Right now on a scale of 0–10 how motivated do you feel, if 10 represents highly motivated? How ready do you feel to make changes, again on a scale of 0–10, if 10 is extremely ready? In the last month have there been times when your motivation to change has been greater than this? What are the factors that lead to increases/decreases in your motivation? How able (e.g. confident, skilled) do you feel to change, on a scale of 0–10, if 10 represents extremely motivated?

Note: If the patient rates motivation at less than 5, this is an indication that CT might be unhelpful at this time. One option is to arrange a review appointment in three months' time for a reassessment; another is to suggest that the patient requests referral in the future when he or she feels more ready to undertake treatment. A third option is to agree on a limited number of sessions in order to examine motivational issues.

The therapist may usefully continue as follows:

There are several things we could do. The first option would be for you to go away and think over the things we have discussed today before making a decision. The second option would be to arrange a review appointment for three months' time, and we can reassess things then. The third option would be for us to plan four cognitive therapy sessions to discuss your uncertainty and fears about making changes. You mentioned [again, briefly summarise the patient's concerns], and these are some of the areas that we could focus on during these sessions. What ideas do you have or what would you like to do?

However, if the patient has been assessed and has expressed rather fewer reservations, then the initial stage of therapy can be introduced in the following way:

Last time we met we briefly discussed some of your reservations and fears about making changes to your eating disorder, and what a course of therapy would involve. I wonder if it might be useful for us to explore and understand a bit more about some of your fears in today's session, what do you think?

The therapist might then begin to address the topic by saying:

If I can reflect back to you what I understand you are saying. It's as if you are in two minds about changing. One side of you is determined to over-come bulimia because it is distressing and unbearable at times and is causing you a lot of problems with your health, work and relationships, and the other side of you needs bulimia in order to cope. Have I understood you? What do you fear would happen if you no longer had an eating disorder?

IDENTIFYING FEARS ABOUT CHANGE

The therapist will need to ensure that all the patient's initial fears about change have been identified. While some will have emerged in the assessment, it is usually useful to dedicate a specific portion of time at the start of treatment to making sure that all the significant ones have been picked up. When identifying fears, both immediate and longer term fears should be covered.

STRATEGIES TO MANAGE TYPICAL FEARS

Before introducing specific strategies to manage fears, it is useful to share with the patient the idea that therapy will provide him or her with an opportunity to try out and experiment with new ideas and making changes, while having the support of another person. It is also helpful to reiterative the collaborative nature of therapy, that is, the patient and therapist will have decided together what changes might be good. In other words, the patient is not alone; the patient and therapist are 'in this together' and new ways of managing the problem can be found and tried out in a safe setting.

An example of how a patient might be encouraged into a position of being willing to give the therapy a go and to live with the uncertainly and fears this may generate might begin as follows:

It must feel very frightening to believe that you will gain an enormous amount of weight and that people will reject you. If that were true, it makes sense to me why the thought of stopping bingeing and vomiting is worrying. We can choose to examine some of the possible evidence against your fear that this will happen. If you no longer believed this quite as much as now how might that change your fear?

In order to facilitate this process, guided discovery is best used first, followed by cognitive restructuring of fears, and relevant psycho-educational material (see, for example, Appendix 10: Myths about Bulimia Nervosa and Cognitive Therapy) can then be given for homework.

Below we present six strategies, each designed to deal with one or more of the more typical fears that patients may have about change.

Strategy 1: Energy in = energy out

One of the most common, and one of the most difficult to manage, is fear of weight gain. Many patients with BN are afraid that if they stop bingeing and vomiting they will gain weight.

This strategy generally has two parts, and aims to convey at least two messages: first, that weight gain in the majority of cases is due solely to eating more than the body requires while weight loss occurs when the amount of energy consumed exceeds the amount of food eaten, and second, that patients will need to learn to live with uncertainty; many factors contribute to weight gain and it is not an exact science; moreover attempts at overcontrol are likely to be a source of further distress.

Psycho-education

A useful place to begin to deal with this fear, especially if weight has been gained in the past, is through psycho-education. For example, explaining the 'energy in = energy out' equation can be useful. This can be achieved through guided discovery. Useful questions to achieve this might be:

What is it that makes you think that if you stop bingeing and vomiting you will gain weight? When you did gain weight in the past? What other explanation might there be?

A pie chart to determine and quantify all possible reasons might be useful here, such as described by Wells (1997):

Can you think of someone you know well who eats normally and whose weight is relatively stable? What have you noticed about their eating patterns?

This might lead to a behavioural experiment to collect information about how and what is eaten by most people who eat normally and don't gain weight.

If someone wanted to gain weight what would they have to do? What do film stars do when they need to gain weight to play a role? What's the mechanism? If you give one person 2,000 calories of vegetables a day and one person 2,000 calories of chocolate, which person is most likely to gain weight?

(Patients invariably say the person who ate the chocolate). The therapist can then ask: 'How can that be, they've both had the same amount of energy?' This can help to create a dialogue around the importance of energy as opposed to content of foods – the message being that it does not matter what you eat if you stay within a regular, daily allowance of food that takes into account levels of activity. In such cases weight will remain stable. It is also useful to discuss normal fluctuations in weight and explore reasons why weight might change, apart from excessive energy intake or energy deficit. For example, factors that underlie weight fluctuation may include dehydration, hormonal changes and bowel habits. Finally, it is useful to encourage patients to adopt a wait and see attitude, bearing in mind that whatever happens to their weight they have some degree of control over it, so that if they do show a trend to gain weight over time then they can adjust their energy input and output accordingly.

Living with uncertainty

Implicit in any discussion involving psycho-education, particularly when considering possible reasons for weight gain in the individual case, is that it is impossible to predict with any accuracy in everyday life the precise circumstances under which an individual will gain weight. This can be particularly hard for patients with BN to accept, as they often have a more general black and white approach. They are also often uncomfortable with not always knowing for certain, and as reflected in the metacognitive beliefs in the model presented here they tend to have a strong need to be in control of a range of behaviours, as well as of their emotions and cognitions, all of which are likely to be associated with distress. As well as addressing this explicitly, and assessing, for example, the pros and cons of a black and white thinking style in relation to weight gain (and perhaps more generally), some specific techniques can be useful to make patients aware that complete certainty is impossible. One adaptive alternative coping strategy (instead of demanding a 100 per cent guarantee) might be to de-catastrophise the feared consequences, while another might be to consider explicitly the advantages and disadvantages of complete control.

Strategy 2: Other ways to cope with distress

In the model, bingeing is a solution to manage unbearable distress, and some patients may be afraid that they will be unable to cope with their distress if they no longer allow themselves to binge. It can be useful to ask: 'Has there been a time when you have felt distressed and haven't binged? What happened? How did you cope?' It is usually useful to elicit the worst case scenario from the patient, for example 'What's the worst that could happen if you don't allow yourself to binge when you are really upset or anxious?', and to obtain a picture or detailed description of what that would look like. Alternative strategies to cope with distress should then be introduced that build upon the patient's existing and more positive coping strategies. Plans should be made to implement these when the patient is distressed in the future. Strategies that aim to distance the patient from their distress may also be useful and include distraction, such as counting backwards from 100 in 7s, describing an object out loud, reciting a verse or poem, taking gentle exercise, relaxation, absorbing activities and seeking social support. Once the patient feels less distressed, she might employ problem-solving strategies and, when more skilled, cognitive restructuring. The patient and the therapist can subsequently determine whether or not the patient's worst fears were realised when she did not binge, how successful the alternative coping strategy was and how its effectiveness might be enhanced next time.

One important strategy is to introduce tolerance of emotions. Patients often catastrophise emotional experience and erroneously assume that a negative feeling will last indefinitely. Here the therapist can question if the patient has ever experienced a permanent emotion, and challenge the idea that emotions work this way, that is, they last indefinitely.

Strategy 3: There is an understandable cause

Sometimes patients find their behaviour puzzling. One patient noted that coping with problems through binge eating was like a reflex action – that there seemed no logical reason for it. It can be useful to explain this as a familiar template of thinking and behaving that has developed over a long time, that longstanding patterns of behaviour often become automatic and that while it will take time to develop an awareness of the cognitive and emotional triggers, as well as of the setting conditions in which these occur, it is possible to do so and is half of the battle.

Strategy 4: Challenging the process of catastrophisation

Some patients' fears of changing are so catastrophic and so widespread that they create an enormous barrier to change. In such cases challenging individual fears can start to seem like an endless task. If this is the case then it can be useful to modify the cognitive distortion of catastrophisation. Useful questions to ask in such cases can be seen in the box overleaf.

Strategy 5: Fears are part of BN

It can be useful to remind the patient that the fears are part of BN and if they no longer had the fears they would be unlikely to have BN (i.e. they are an integral part of the disorder and can be understood to arise from the model). This is particularly useful if the patient is finding it difficult to accept and deal with ambivalence about treatment and recovery, and finding work on barriers to change and motivation difficult.

USEFUL QUESTIONS TO CHALLENGE CATASTROPHISATION

How do you know for sure what will happen (e.g. to your weight)?

How can you predict with certainty what will happen in the future?

When were you last convinced that something bad was going to happen, and it didn't turn out to be true?

How often when you have feared the worse has it actually come true?

What bad things have happened to you in the past? How did you cope with them?

What do you say to your friends when they are feeling anxious and thinking the worst about a situation?

What do your friends say to you when you are catastrophising?

What are the disadvantages or consequences of making negative predictions about the future?

In what way do you think that thinking this way impacts on your ability to make changes in your eating disorder?

How will you know what will actually happen in the future unless you put it to the test?

When you are catastrophising how might you challenge this way of thinking?

What might you say to yourself as an alternative?

Relationship fears

Patients may fear that getting better will lead to a relationship break-up, either because they will get fat and their partner will abandon them, or perhaps because having the illness displays vulnerability or dependence, and this is what holds the relationship together in some way. Similarly, younger patients, living at home with their parents, may fear that the family is staying together only because they are ill. Once they get better, then parents may separate and the family will split up. In all these cases, negative self beliefs are typically activated, and via this mechanism patients can fall into bingeing and vomiting in order to cope. They may also worsen their situation by putting pressure on themselves to recover, or through worry about hurting others by being unwell. Again, this is

Strategy 6: Education

Patients may benefit from education about the effects of giving up binge eating, and from information about the aims and format of the treatment. This can usefully be approached using written materials, which can then be discussed in a session using guided discovery. Some of the important messages this should convey include:

- Giving up binge eating and vomiting will not usually lead to any significant or lasting weight gain.
- Weight gain may need to be on the agenda if vomiting is helping to maintain a very low BMI.
- Apparent weight reducing strategies such as use of laxatives and diuretics are more or less completely ineffective. Vomiting is also relatively ineffective.
- The therapist does not have a hidden agenda – the aim of treatment is not to get the patient to gain weight.

This information is summarised in Appendix 3: A Client's Guide to Cognitive Therapy for Bulimia Nervosa, Appendix 8: Consequences and Dangers of the Symptoms of Bulimia Nervosa, and Appendix 10: Myths about Bulimia Nervosa and Cognitive Therapy.

COST-BENEFIT ANALYSIS

It can be very useful to ask the patient to examine the advantages and disadvantages of change, both in the short term and in the long term. This can be achieved using a worksheet and writing any conclusions down can be helpful here. In the process of doing this the therapist should also help the patient, through guided discovery, to explore other possibilities, and elicit a full picture of these, for example by asking, 'How would you imagine life will be like in five years' time if you continue to have these problems?', 'If you could wave a magic wand, what would be different?', or 'What would you be able to do if you no longer had these problems?'

Most patients are well aware of the disadvantages of having BN and can feel criticised and embarrassed if asked to state them without a context. It is always best to start with the advantages of having BN and approach this with interest and curiosity. Patients are then likely to feel that the function of their bulimia is validated. After this stage, patients can then be invited to consider the disadvantages.

Useful initial questions include the following:

'What are the advantages of having BN?'
'What are the advantages of continuing to have BN?'
'What would be the disadvantages of not having BN?'
'What would be the advantages of not having BN?'
'What do you imagine your life will be like in three or five years from now if you still have an eating disorder?'
'What would you like your life to be like three years from now?'
'What would be different?'

A sample cost-benefit sheet (also reproduced in Appendix 15) and a completed example can be seen in the boxes.

A COST-BENEFIT SHEET	
Advantages of change	**Disadvantages of change**
Conclusion	

A COMPLETED COST-BENEFIT SHEET

Advantages of change	Disadvantages of change
I won't be so focused on food and eating I'll have more time for friends I'll be healthier – have a better diet, fewer health worries I'll have more money to spend on going out, clothes and presents If I control my eating and control my spending I'll be less anxious when I have to eat with other people I won't argue so much with my parents I won't be ruining my teeth any longer I'll have more time and energy for other things My self-esteem will improve, I'll feel better about myself	I'll gain lots of weight People won't like me I'll try and fail and it might be worse than having BN I will have no means of rewarding myself I might not be able to cope with my emotions I'll no longer have guilt-free eating I'll have to monitor what I eat

Conclusion

There are more potential advantages than I had realised, and some of them are really important things – like my health and my relationships with other people. The disadvantages seem very real and frightening but the truth is that I don't actually know what will happen unless I decide to give it a go. I could end up stuck like this forever.

In the course of conducting cognitive exercises and behavioural experiments, the therapist should be attempting to highlight any discrepancies, and ultimately to tip the balance in favour of advantages, so that these are seen to outweigh the disadvantages of change. When discussing the advantages it is important to cover all the key areas of a patient's life that may benefit from stopping binge eating. These will probably include health, weight, social life, friendships, career, family relationships and relationships with partners. Patients do not always spontaneously mention all these aspects, and some may need to be raised by the therapist for discussion. The importance of the advantages of having BN should not be underestimated, and it is unlikely that the patient's belief in the advantages of having BN will diminish completely.

Cognitive strategies

Although behavioural experiments are important in changing fears, cognitive strategies can also be very useful. These may be particularly useful as a prelude or introduction to the planning of an experiment. Some useful questions to help patients challenge their fears are listed below.

USEFUL QUESTIONS TO HELP CHALLENGE FEARS ABOUT CHANGE

What is the basis for your fear? What evidence are you basing this fear on?

In the past when your fear was founded, what other explanation might there be other than stopping bulimic behaviours?

How do you know for certain that if you changed X that would happen?

What are the consequences of thinking this way?

When you are feeling fearful, how might you manage this?

A summary of how a patient used some of these questions to challenge her fear of becoming obese can be seen in Sam's case example.

COGNITIVE STRATEGIES TO CHALLENGE FEARS: A CASE EXAMPLE

Sam feared that if she gave up bingeing and vomiting she would have an enormous out-of-control appetite for food and without vomiting would become obese (as she had been as a child). Her mother and father were both clinically obese.

Through guided discovery Sam's rational response was, 'There is some truth in this fear, I was fat as a child and there is a family predisposition to obesity which makes me think it's in my physical make-up. However, when I felt unhappy I used to eat all day and night, anything that was in the cupboard. Even now I don't really know what drives me to eating in all circumstances. The truth is that I don't know if my appetite is normal because I can't remember a time when I've had proper meals and for as long as I remember I've binged and vomited. Just because I overate as a child doesn't mean that I have to do it now. I can choose to binge or not, it's in my control'.

SPECIFIC FEARS

Some patients have a particularly strong illness identity, that is, their whole life and sense of who they are is determined primarily by being bulimic. Giving up their eating disorder may threaten their whole sense of self. Four case examples of such fears can be seen in the box overleaf.

A long history

Some patients, particularly those with a long history of BN, or eating-related disorders, may have little idea what it is like to live without the disorder. Thinking about the issue may be quite abstract as they have little relevant life experience to draw on. This can be particularly problematic as there is some evidence that a longer history predicts poor outcome (e.g. Reas et al. 2000).

Some useful questions to elicit and begin to challenge fears in those with a long history or strong illness identity can be seen below.

'What would my life be like without bulimia?'
'If I don't have bulimia then [patient completes the sentence stem]?'
'What are my fears about letting go of bulimia?'

SENSE OF SELF BEING TIED TO HAVING BN: FOUR CASE EXAMPLES

Sarah had a 20-year history of BN and believed that it was an illness that controlled her. She felt that the impact of having BN had ruined her life, which had been dominated by endless dieting and constant rumination about her shape. If she came to believe that she actually did have control over bingeing and vomiting it would mean that she had wasted her life, which would be unbearable.

Rebecca believed that having bulimia was a way of occupying time and without it life would feel empty.

Anna feared that without bulimia she would be more unhappy, lonely and isolated than she currently was with bulimia and that giving it up would mean that she would no longer have the resource she currently turned to for support.

Angela believed that she was incapable of leading a normal life happy life without bulimia. If she no longer had bulimia she would discover a deeper more serious problem which she was unaware of at the moment, and which would mean that she would never have a normal life. She believed, 'It's better to have BN and be miserable than to live with the fear of discovering something worse about yourself and be even more unhappy and sad'.

'What is a more realistic response to my fears?'
'What concrete things could I do to overcome my fears?'

If there are chronic identity and self-related problems, then the following tips are useful:

1. Start with guided discovery, for example, 'In what way do you think your eating disorder is part of who you are?', 'If your eating disorder was taken away what do you think that would be like?', 'If you were to ask those who know you well what they valued about you what would they say about you?', 'How do you know what you would be like if you did not have an eating disorder?', 'What would it mean to not have an eating disorder?', 'How do other people of your age group define their personality?', 'What steps would you need to take to reinvent yourself without an eating disorder?'
2. Behavioural steps can then be examined, such as taking up new interests, increasing social contact.

3. Keeping a positive data log can be helpful to confirm new or developing positive self schema (see Chapter 10).
4. Identify long-term goals and ambitions. One patient, for example, wanted to become a nurse. 'What would you like to do in the future if you no longer had an eating disorder?' 'How might your life be different?'

Motivation over time

Motivational strategies are often emphasised at the beginning of treatment, and can be vital in encouraging the patient to embark on a course of treatment. However, it is also important to remember that motivation for change is likely to fluctuate during treatment. Such shifts need to be recognised and acknowledged. If necessary, motivational strategies may need to be reintroduced or revisited, even on occasions when the patient has already completed a number of sessions and therapy tasks. In general the therapeutic approach needs to be motivational throughout the therapy.

CHAPTER SUMMARY AND KEY POINTS

This chapter has discussed how patients' engagement in CT for BN might be enhanced. It has discussed motivation for change, drawing on the Stages of Change Model, and has highlighted the importance of identifying any fears that patients may have about changing, and how these might be addressed, using a range of specific verbal strategies as well as behavioural experiments.

Key points to remember include the following:

⊙ Patients with BN can be difficult to engage in treatment, and building a positive therapeutic alliance may need to be given specific attention.
⊙ Motivational techniques are an important part of CT for BN. The Stages of Change Model can be useful here.
⊙ Fears about change should be identified, and strategies to manage these should be introduced. Six specific strategies, as well as a cost-benefit analysis, can be useful.
⊙ Behavioural experiments have an important role in dealing with fears about change; verbal strategies may also be useful.
⊙ A number of very specific fears may need to be addressed.
⊙ Motivational strategies are likely to be useful throughout treatment.

CHAPTER 6

Case formulation and socialisation

This chapter outlines how the individual case is conceptualised using the framework of the Cooper et al. (2004) model of BN combined with a more recent shift to metacognitive emphasis, and how socialisation into the model can be achieved. It presents a detailed case conceptualisation interview as a proforma that can be used to formulate an individual case, together with sample worksheets for recording this information. It also introduces useful specific assessment measures that can assist with formulation, and the process of treatment. The section on socialisation introduces important points to be conveyed to the patient about therapy, and some suggestions for demonstrating the model.

THE FORMULATION INTERVIEW

A formulation interview provides the basic framework for conceptualising the individual case. Idiosyncratic cognitions and behaviours are identified by asking detailed questions about the last time the patient had an episode of bingeing and vomiting or other compensatory behaviour. The last time is chosen because this is likely to be fresh in the patient's memory, thus relevant thoughts and feelings are more likely to be identified. For most patients the occasion will be within the last day or two; it may be within the last few hours. We have provided our case conceptualisation interview as a proforma in the box opposite. It proceeds in a series of steps.

Identifying initial triggers for bingeing

A range of triggers exist for binge eating, including thoughts and feelings. Triggers for binge eating are not always immediate; they can be related to situations or events that occurred the previous day (or earlier, but which the patient has been ruminating on or reliving in some way). In such cases it is important to ask about memories.

CASE CONCEPTUALISATION INTERVIEW PROFORMA

I'd like you to focus on the last time you had an episode of binge eating and vomiting (or other compensatory behaviour). I'm going to ask you a series of questions so that we can find out what happened.

1. What thought, image, feeling, sensation or memory triggered your binge eating?
2. When you had that thought (etc.) how did that make you feel emotionally?
3. How did that feeling affect your thoughts about bingeing etc.?
4. Did you see any advantages to bingeing etc?
   (Probe: is this helpful in some way?)
5. Did you see any disadvantages to bingeing etc.?
   (Probe: what's the worst that can happen?)
6. How controllable did you think your bingeing was?
7. What thoughts made it easier to binge etc.?
8. What did you do next?
9. How did the thought (etc.) that triggered your binge eating make you think about yourself?
   (Probe: what did that say about you, what did that mean, suppose that were true, what would be so bad about that?)

Interoceptive cues can also act as triggers for bingeing, and may not be picked up unless specifically explored, so it can also be helpful to ask about these. Common examples include physiological symptoms of anxiety, feeling the tightness of clothes against the body, feelings of fatness and feelings of fullness.

Some case examples of initial triggers for bingeing are presented in the box overleaf.

Negative self beliefs

Identification of negative self beliefs at this stage is optional. The decision about whether to identify them or not may depend on several factors, including complexity of the case formulation, anticipated distress if they are identified at this stage or general level of distress associated with the discussion of a recent episode of bingeing and vomiting.

INITIAL TRIGGERS FOR BINGE EATING: SOME CASE EXAMPLES

Trigger related to eating

Amanda was invited to a dinner party. She had starved herself all day so that she would feel able to eat normally that evening. The host served a three-course dinner that included some of her binge foods, and which felt unsafe. Amanda didn't want to draw attention to herself by leaving any food. She also considered it rude to leave any food. She continued eating when she felt full, and became very conscious of how full she felt.

Trigger unrelated to eating, weight and shape

Hayley was asked if she would be willing to cancel her holiday because there wasn't enough cover at work. She was unable to say no, and believed that to do so would make her unpopular. She agreed to work because no one else had offered but felt used and taken for granted.

Trigger related to perceived failure

Samantha, a 19-year-old university student, finished her essay and thought, 'I haven't worked hard enough. It's not going to be good enough. It's really bad and won't make the grade'. She felt like a failure.

Trigger related to food cravings

Sonia, a 28-year-old secretary, was sitting at her desk thinking about how she would spend that evening when her husband went out to the rugby club. She started thinking, 'I'll treat myself to a box of chocolates on the way home'.

Trigger related to interoceptive cues

Lucy woke up and felt fat. She focused on the feeling of her stomach and buttocks pressing against the bed sheets and felt obsessed with rolls of fat, which she visualised as grotesque. She felt distressed and thought, 'I'm ugly'.

Connie usually avoided eating during the day. On this occasion she had eaten lunch and had then reluctantly agreed to an impromptu invitation to go clubbing with friends. She felt fat, and monitored feelings of fullness. She thought, 'I'm disgusting'.

Trigger around boredom

Thea was alone watching TV, eating lunch and thinking of ways of avoiding eating more. She felt bored, isolated, lonely, worried and guilty. She thought 'I'm not strong-willed enough and give in too easily. It's my fault that I've cut myself off from my friends'.

Trigger related to weight and shape

Sarah tried on her favourite skirt and found that it was tight on the waist. She thought, 'I've gained weight. I'm fat now. I'll never fit into my clothes again. It's all down hill from now on. I'm ballooning. I'm 22 years old and passed it'. She felt upset and anxious.

Positive beliefs about eating

Examples of positive beliefs about bingeing can be seen in the box below. Positive thoughts about bingeing focus on the perceived benefits or helpfulness of bingeing.

EXAMPLES OF POSITIVE BELIEFS ABOUT BINGEING

Bingeing will make me feel better.

Bingeing will help me to stop thinking about food.

Unless I binge I'll go mad with thoughts about food.

Bingeing is time for me, my treat.

I won't have to think when I'm bingeing.

Bingeing releases the buildup of pressure, it calms me and helps put things into perspective.

Bingeing is my source of pleasure and enjoyment.

Bingeing provides a focus.

Bingeing helps to control my feelings.

Negative beliefs about eating

Negative beliefs concern the undesirable consequences of engaging in bingeing. Examples of these can be seen in the box below. They include beliefs about the uncontrollability of bingeing.

EXAMPLES OF NEGATIVE BELIEFS ABOUT BINGEING

I'll get fat.

I can't help bingeing.

I'll gain weight and will therefore be more unlovable.

I'll keep on gaining weight and won't be able to stop.

I'm destined to be a fat person.

I'll be dirty and contaminated with food.

I'll get huge and disgusting.

My binge eating is out of control.

Permissive beliefs

Examples of permissive beliefs are shown in the box below. Permissive beliefs facilitate eating or bingeing, that is, they make it easier to start and/or to carry on eating once binge eating has begun.

EXAMPLES OF PERMISSIVE BELIEFS ABOUT BINGE EATING

Now I've started bingeing I might as well carry on.

There's no reason to stop bingeing.

I deserve to stuff myself and feel bad.

I don't have anything but bingeing to do or in my life.

A little bit more won't hurt.

I've earned a treat.

Example dialogue

An extended dialogue with a patient employing the case conceptualisation interview proforma structure and questions (see p. 87) is reproduced below:

Therapist: If you cast your mind back to the moment in time before you binged, what were you doing?

Patient: I was in my room trying to write my dissertation and struggling to string a sentence together.

Therapist: What was running through your mind at that time?

Patient: I was thinking, 'My dissertation is rubbish, it's not good enough, I'm bound to fail'.

Therapist: When you thought that, how did you feel?

Patient: I felt tense and angry with myself.

Therapist: It sounds like you were quite distressed, is that right?

Patient: Yes, I felt horrible and couldn't imagine ever getting a degree.

Therapist: How did that feeling affect you? Did it affect how you thought about bingeing?

Patient: I was so fed up and anxious, I just wanted something really nice to take my mind off things.

Therapist: At that moment in time did you see any advantages to bingeing?

Patient: I know it doesn't help, but yes I needed the comfort of food. I felt that I deserved a treat, something yummy like chocolate.

Therapist: At the time did you see any disadvantages to bingeing?

Patient: I knew I'd hate myself, I'd feel disgusted and repulsed with doing it because it's a disgusting thing to do. Who in their right mind does something like that? There's also the problem with gaining weight.

Therapist: It sounds like you were really cross with yourself. How controllable did you think your bingeing was?

Patient: I didn't think I was going to be able to stop myself.

Therapist: What were you saying to yourself that made it easier to binge?

Patient: I was thinking to myself, if I'm going to think about food all the time I might as well eat it and get it over with. I know I'll binge anyway. And then I thought well, I'm justified because I'm hungry, I can always throw up afterwards.

Therapist: What happened next?

Patient: I ate three Jaffa cakes, they're my favourite, and that started me off.

It is useful to draw the formulation out in the form of a diagram in collaboration with the patient (ideally, ask the patient to draw it out, and use a duplicate book so both therapist and patient can have a copy for future reference), either on paper or on a whiteboard.

Figure 6.1 illustrates a formulation for a patient. The different types of thought are labelled for ease of reference (see also Appendix 15 for the original diagram).

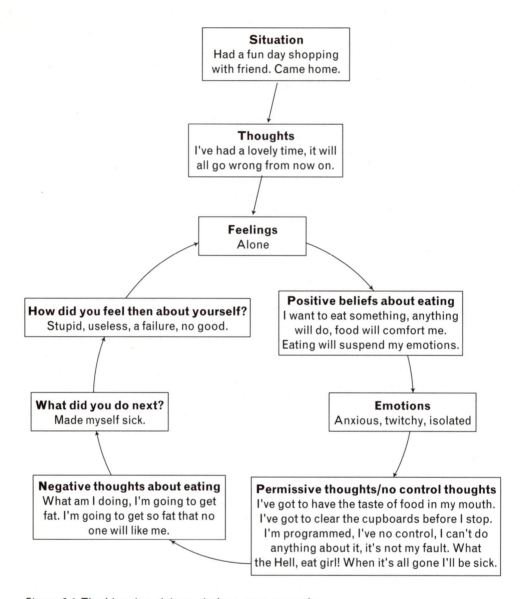

Figure 6.1 The bingeing vicious circle: a case example

Worksheet to elicit the bingeing formulation

Patients can work on eliciting their own formulations of binge eating using a worksheet, with some key questions as prompts. A sample blank worksheet (also reproduced in Appendix 15) and a completed example can be seen in the following two boxes.

WORKSHEET TO ELICIT FORMULATION

What thoughts were running through your mind? What were you thinking to yourself?

What did that mean or say about you?

Did you start eating?

How did you think that would help?

What did you think would happen if you didn't eat?

What thoughts made it easy to keep eating?

How did you feel about your sense of control?

What did you do next?

How did you feel then about yourself?

It is usually helpful for the patient to repeat this exercise with a number of problem situations in order to detect patterns in the key thoughts and processes associated with binge eating.

Schema

Useful questions to elicit negative self beliefs, if these are identified here, can also be seen in the box above.

A series of 'downward arrow' questions (see Burns 1980) can be used to achieve this. In the context of feeling anxious or worried about eating, food, weight and shape, these questions are repeated and varied, as appropriate, to elicit general rules or 'if then' statements, usually focused on weight and shape, but also on food and eating. Once a rule or assumption has been uncovered, then the downward arrow questioning is continued until an absolute, 'bottom line' belief about the self is reached. To qualify as a 'core' belief this should be one that the patient believes is generally

WORKSHEET TO ELICIT FORMULATION: A CASE EXAMPLE

What thoughts were running through your mind? What were you thinking to yourself?

I shouldn't have left that job for Charlotte to do – it's my fault it went wrong.

What did that mean or say about you?

I'm not trustworthy, I'm useless and stupid.

Did you start eating?

Yes – ate a piece of apple pie, then all the party leftovers.

How did you think that would help?

It would stop me feeling stupid and so unhappy.

What did you think would happen if you didn't eat?

I'll get really upset, and won't be able to stand it. I'll scream and cry.

What thoughts made it easy to keep eating?

I can always be sick afterwards, I can't help myself.

How did you feel about your sense of control?

I can't stop eating.

What did you do next?

Made myself sick.

How did you feel then about yourself?

Stupid, useless, a failure, no good.

true, and which applies in a range of situations and circumstances. Such beliefs are also absolute and unconditional.

Formulating other eating behaviours

Problem eating behaviours that do not involve binge eating (for example, purging, worry, checking, selective attention) can be formulated using the same sequence of questioning and strategies outlined above, substituting reference to bingeing for the relevant behaviour being formulated.

EATING DISORDER RATING SCALE

The Eating Disorder Rating Scale provides a useful weekly measure of the key behaviours and cognitions that are important in BN. It tracks changes in bingeing and vomiting (and other compensatory behaviours), associated distress and beliefs from week to week. The beliefs assessed include examples of the cognitive dimensions that the model indicates are important in bulimia nervosa. As well as providing an indication of progress, it is useful in identifying cognitive targets to focus on in sessions. It is most useful therefore to ask patients to complete it immediately prior to the start of each session. A copy of this measure can be found in Appendix 1.

SPECIFIC MEASURES

Eating Disorder Thoughts Questionnaire

The Eating Disorder Thoughts Questionnaire (EDTQ: Cooper et al. 2006) can be useful in identifying any positive, permissive and negative beliefs about eating and bingeing that the patient may have. It can be used to help develop the initial formulation, and will give information on the presence and relevance of positive (and other) beliefs about eating. A copy of this measure can be found in Appendix 7.

Eating Behaviour Questionnaire

Characteristic behaviours are observed in BN, many of which are assessed on the Eating Behaviour Questionnaire (EBQ: Cooper et al. 2006). These behaviours play a role in maintaining the beliefs that are important in BN. Treatment involves work on decreasing these behaviours, and completing the EBQ identifies these behaviours, which can also be included in the formulation. A copy of this measure can be found in Appendix 5.

Weekly Evaluation Sheet

This sheet helps the patient reflect on what they have learned and achieved since the last session, and helps her to think about goals for the following week. It is best completed by the patient at home, immediately before attending the session. A copy of this sheet can be found in Appendix 2.

SOCIALISATION

Socialisation involves 'selling' the model and providing a basic mental set for understanding the nature of treatment (Wells 1997). This involves educating the patient about cognitive therapy, discussing the patient's role in treatment and presenting the formulation. Educational material is provided to assist this process (see Appendices 3, 8 and 10). Demonstrations in session are used to illustrate the links in the model between thoughts, feelings and problem behaviour, including binge eating.

The principles of cognitive therapy and information about the structure of a typical session can be most efficiently covered in written educational material (see Appendix 3).

Prior to the assessment it is useful to send out the self-report measures (see Chapter 2) and ask for these to be returned before the appointment. As well as providing useful information for the formulation this can help with engagement. Feedback should also be sought from the patient on completing the questionnaires at the first appointment. Comments made by patients who have completed some of these measures include 'At last someone understands me', 'It's as though they were written for me', 'It was such a relief to know that others think and do similar things to me'.

Patients' reactions to reading any written information for homework should be discussed at the next appointment.

Topics to be covered in treatment

The patient should be introduced to the basic topics that treatment will cover, so that she will know roughly what to expect, and in what order and timescale: a brief summary of the material in Chapter 1 (pp. 9–12) can be useful here.

Basic features of treatment

The patient should also be introduced to some important treatment basics.

- *Audiotaping of sessions*, with the patient listening to the tape for homework and providing feedback at the following session.
- *Agenda setting*, designed to make the best use of the limited time available (an hour per session), and to make sure that items important to both patient and therapist are allocated enough time, and covered in sufficient detail.
- *Collaboration*, with both patient and therapist jointly designing therapy.
- *Likely time and effort needed*, since treatment is likely to be hard work, and will require time, effort and commitment.

Unlike standard cognitive behaviour therapy for BN, patients are not routinely asked to keep a detailed diary of binges, compensatory behaviour, problematic thoughts and food intake (e.g. Fairburn et al. 1993). There are several reasons for this. First, the primary focus is on changing cognition – since in the model this maintains behaviour, and behavioural change is expected to follow cognitive change, for example, through the use of behavioural experiments that aim to test negative predictions. Second, anecdotally we have observed that doing so increases some patients' problems with eating, particularly preoccupation with weight and shape, food and eating. This is perhaps not surprising given that food-related behaviour is a maintaining mechanism in the model. However, it is important to keep track of the frequency of bingeing and vomiting in order to monitor behavioural as well as cognitive change. This can be done easily and quickly using the weekly Eating Disorder Rating Scale (see Appendix 1).

However, food diaries can form an important component of treatment in several specific situations. First, they can be useful for gathering data or general information to help understand the problem in more detail. Second, they can form an integral part of testing specific hypotheses derived from the formulation (and should be explicitly framed or set up as such). Third, where patients have extremely chaotic eating patterns or are attempting to adhere to a severely restricted diet, they can form an important part of treatment by helping to identify binges that are likely to be significantly related to hunger. Fourth, keeping a written record can help to reduce shame and avoidance. Finally, monitoring binge eating can help patients to make the link between bingeing, triggers and setting conditions. In all cases, however, as for testing other specific hypotheses about eating, their use should always be explicitly formulated and framed to test one or more specific predictions.

Demonstrating the model (socialisation)

It is very useful to demonstrate key aspects of the model to the patient early on using behavioural experiments. It is particularly helpful to demonstrate the link between positive, permissive and negative (including control) beliefs about eating and binge eating. Behavioural experiments can be a very useful way for patients to gain insight into the link. In this case, the behavioural experiment is used to help the patient understand how specific thoughts and behaviours may be connected, rather than to test the validity of any thoughts and/or negative predictions.

Two central features of the formulation should be illustrated: that there are conflicting positive and negative beliefs about eating, and that negative thinking causes distress.

One useful exercise involves patients in guided discovery and discussion, contrasting their positive and negative beliefs about eating and assessing how each might make them feel if they believed them completely. This is particularly helpful when the formulation has not clearly illustrated the existence of the two types of conflicting or opposing beliefs. As well as highlighting the conflicting pressure of positive and negative beliefs, it can also usefully help to demonstrate how negative beliefs create distress. Using guided discovery can also begin to help emphasise the dissonance between these two types of belief, and thus help to enhance motivation for change.

Guided discovery

Some typical guided discovery questions that are useful in verbal identification of the key links in the formulation can be seen in the worksheet to elicit formulation (p. 93).

CHAPTER SUMMARY AND KEY POINTS

This chapter has presented a framework within which the individual case can be conceptualised, and a case conceptualisation interview which can be used to achieve this. It has also provided details on how socialisation into the cognitive model for BN can be achieved, with examples of strategies that can be used to reach that goal.

Key points to remember include the following:

⊙ The case conceptualisation interview should be grounded in the most recent example of bingeing and vomiting or other compensatory behaviour.
⊙ Triggers for bingeing can include interoceptive, as well as other cues.
⊙ The key thoughts in the vicious circle maintaining binge eating (and other problem behaviours) are positive beliefs and negative beliefs.
⊙ Detailed treatment of negative self beliefs at this stage is optional.
⊙ The downward arrow technique is useful in identifying underlying assumptions or compensatory rules and core beliefs.
⊙ Specific self-report measures can be a useful aid in identifying relevant vicious circle behaviours and cognitions.
⊙ Socialisation is important in selling the model to the patient. It can be achieved through education, including written material, which covers the basic elements of treatment, and through behavioural experiments, which allow the model to be demonstrated in action.

Detached mindfulness strategies

Our model proposes that bulimia nervosa is in effect a strategy for dealing with the activation of negative beliefs, thoughts and feelings. In this perspective the metacognitive appraisal and regulation of inner experiences is a central feature of the problem. It follows from this that metacognitive therapy principles (Wells 2000) could be applied in the treatment of BN. We have found that enabling patients to develop alternative strategies for relating to inner events is useful in increasing flexibility and subjective sense of control. One specific strategy is the use of detached mindfulness (DM) techniques. This chapter outlines the nature of detached mindfulness (Wells 2000, 2006), its role in the treatment of BN and example strategies for presenting its rationale to patients. A range of DM strategies, including metacognitive guidance, free association and the tiger task, that can be applied in practice are described, and their specific practical application is discussed.

WHAT IS DETACHED MINDFULNESS?

Detached mindfulness is derived from Wells and Matthews' S-REF theory of psychological disorder (Wells and Matthews 1994, 1996). Its theoretical underpinnings have been outlined in Wells (2006) and it has been incorporated as a key strategy in metacognitive therapy of disorders including posttraumatic stress disorder (Wells and Sembi 2004) and obsessive compulsive disorder (Fisher and Wells 2007).

The state of detached mindfulness has been described as 'a state of awareness of internal events, without responding to them with sustained evaluation, attempts to control or suppress them, or respond to them behaviourally' (Wells 2006: 340). Furthermore it consists of a separation of a sense of self from the products of cognition, that is, thoughts or beliefs (Wells 2008). Detached mindfulness facilitates and enhances the potential for therapeutic change, because it introduces options for relating to inner experience and it gives rise to the experiential knowledge required to control cognition and develop a flexible relationship with it.

DETACHED MINDFULNESS AND BN

The emphasis in our theory of BN on metacognitive beliefs about use of eating, and about weight cognitions, in particular, that binge eating (and associated behaviours) reflects strategies of maladaptive cognitive and emotional regulation, makes DM a useful strategy in our treatment. As in other disorders, training in detached mindfulness in BN aims to increase metacognitive awareness, for example, of unhelpful thinking styles, and provides a means of interrupting these processes, which improves the patient's ability to respond to their thoughts in a flexible way.

INTRODUCTION OF DM

Detached mindfulness training is normally introduced to the patient in the early stages of treatment, after engagement and motivational issues have been addressed and after the formulation has been developed, but before strategies to modify negative and positive beliefs are introduced. The idea of DM and the rationale for using it should be explained to the patient. Specific strategies designed to help the patient achieve this state are then introduced.

THE RATIONALE

In presenting the rationale for DM it is helpful to reflect on the formulation developed with the patient, and discuss how their problem has a number of layers. The first layer to focus on concerns recognising the triggers for bingeing (i.e. thoughts and feelings), and interrupting the cycle of rumination/worry and behaviour. These responses should be replaced by DM. The importance of metacognitive beliefs should be re-emphasised, and how, in relation to metacognitive beliefs, it is easy to become locked into a perseverative style of thinking in the form of worry and rumination, which not only helps to maintain problems but also is distressing in itself. Guided discovery should be used to explore how the process of worry and rumination maintains symptoms. The aim of DM should be introduced, for example, as a way to suspend worry and rumination, and change the way the person relates to inner experience.

The introduction and explanation of the rationale should emphasise the following important points:

- BN involves counterproductive ways of dealing with concerns about eating, food, shape and weight and other symptoms, including worry or rumination, overcontrol, attentional monitoring for threat and negative appraisals (as discussed when deriving the formulation with the patient).
- These strategies help to maintain the patient's symptoms and decreasing the use of these strategies will help to decrease symptoms, and also enable the patient to derive maximum benefit from the strategies that will be learned later in therapy.
- The goal of detached mindfulness is to enable the patient to take a new perspective on their thoughts and symptoms, in which instead of 'engaging with' these worries and problems, they are able to observe them in a detached way, without attempting to interpret, analyse, control or react to them in any way.

EXPERIMENTS

One or more experiments should be conducted in the session to demonstrate that there is typically a different outcome when engaging with (for example, avoiding or suppressing) compared to simply observing a thought and/or image. Furthermore these experiments build awareness of the concept of DM. The experiments described below are based on the approaches described by Wells (2006) in metacognitive therapy.

The blue rabbit

This experiment has two conditions. In condition 1 the patient is asked to try not to think of a thought (e.g. a blue rabbit), and after a short while is asked what he notices. In condition 2 the patient is asked to let his mind roam freely and if he has any thoughts of blue rabbits to watch them in a passive way as part of an overall landscape of thoughts. Again, after a short while the patient is asked what he notices. Patients typically discover that in condition 1 either the thought recurs or they manage to suppress it but they remain aware that it is there in the background. In condition 2 they usually find it difficult to hold on to the thought. This can then generate a conclusion and discussion about how, when no attempt is made to try to control thoughts, they are difficult to sustain, that is, avoidance or attempts to control thoughts are not helpful. The discussion can be extended to the unhelpful role of responding to thoughts with bingeing and rumination. These behaviours imbue inner experience with overimportance when the aim should be to detach from them.

There are usually three different responses to the blue rabbit exercises:

- Some people immediately understand the principles and readily recognise ways in which they can apply DM to their own thoughts and images.
- Others describe not having been able to hold on to the image but find they are distracted with other (typically examples of their own) worrying thoughts or images. In this situation it is useful to ask: 'What do you think might happen if you were able to view your own worrying thoughts or images in the same way without trying to control them?'
- Others, despite clear instructions not to try to control the blue rabbit thought do try to control it. In such cases it can be useful to ask: 'What do you think happens when you try and control your own thinking in this way. What do they think would have happened if you had just observed the blue rabbit?'

It is useful to follow these exercises by asking the patient to think of a current or recent thought that triggers bingeing and apply the process of DM:

I want you to allow that thought to occur and take a step back from it. Just watch the thought but do nothing with it. It might change but don't make it change, it may do nothing. Just watch the thought in a detached way.

ACHIEVING DM

Patients are given specific instructions on how to achieve a state of detached mindfulness in relation to their BN thoughts and symptoms, as follows:

When you start to worry, ruminate or become preoccupied with food, or eating, try to be aware of the triggering thought or feeling. Acknowledge to yourself that these thoughts or feelings are occurring, and remind yourself that engaging with them is unhelpful. Some people find it useful to say: 'This is just a thought and thoughts do not necessarily represent facts. I don't need to do anything about this thought. I am going to leave it alone. I'm not going to try and avoid or control this thought. I'm not going to worry about it or dwell on it. I don't need to react in any way'. Remember that engagement includes bingeing, worrying or dwelling on yourself. This includes asking questions involving 'why' and 'what if'. It includes worrying about symptoms as well as trying to control, avoid or even attend in detail to things. Try to let your thoughts and symptoms occupy their own space and time without engaging with them.

SELF-AWARENESS AND COPING

Detached mindfulness is not just a state of self-awareness or self-focused attention (both of which are particularly associated with psychopathology). Unlike these states, it has the goal of assuming an objective or decentred (i.e. detached) perspective in relation to thoughts and symptoms. The distinction is important given the potential of enhanced self-awareness and self-focused attention to increase distress – neither is the aim of DM. Detached mindfulness is also not just another coping strategy. The goal of DM is different from that of common coping strategies including many that the patient has probably already tried in order to deal with her symptoms. Detached mindfulness is not aimed at feeling better or comforting oneself, it is aimed at interrupting unhelpful thinking patterns and developing experiential knowledge for interpreting and dealing adaptively with thoughts and feelings.

ANALOGIES

Use of analogies can help to demonstrate the way in which thoughts and symptoms should be treated. The 'recalcitrant child' and 'pushing clouds' analogies may be useful (Wells and Sembi 2004). In the pushing clouds analogy the patient is asked to consider problematic thoughts and symptoms as if they were clouds in the sky. That is, they are treated as something that is passing by and something we can do nothing about. They are part of a self-regulating system and attempting to stop or push them away is not necessary or possible. Even if we could, this would disturb the balance of nature. They have to be left to occupy their own space and we can watch them only passively, as they change and move independently of us and our actions.

AVOIDANCE

Many patients with BN will have previously tried to avoid problematic thoughts and symptoms. It is important that they understand that avoidance, for example, trying to exclude or block thoughts, is a form of engagement, and is not the goal of DM.

OTHER DM TECHNIQUES

A range of techniques to facilitate a state of DM have been devised by Wells (2006), who describes ten particular strategies for use in meta-cognitive therapy. These include attentional control training, for which a detailed protocol can be found in Wells (2000). Three examples are metacognitive guidance, the free association task and the tiger task.

Metacognitive guidance

In this technique the therapist uses a series of questions with the aim of promoting meta-awareness, decentring and freeing of attention. It is taught in relation to a neutral situation and once mastered can be applied in anxiety provoking situations.

The questions used are as follows:

Do you ever assume your thoughts are just facts indistinct from what you see in the outside world? Have you ever paused for a moment to become aware of the inner stream of thoughts that are constantly with you? I would like us to walk together and as we do so for you to use your attention in a new way.

During the walk:

Can you become aware of your thoughts and images? Can you see your thoughts and the outside world at the same time? Try to hold onto a thought while focusing on what is happening in the street around you. Ask yourself: do I live by my thoughts or by what my eyes reveal in the moment?

(Wells 2006: 346)

Free association task

This aims to facilitate passive observation of the ebb and flow of internal events that are cued by verbal stimuli. It facilitates meta-awareness, decentring, attentional detachment and low conceptual processing.

The task is introduced as follows:

In order to become familiar with using DM it is useful to practise it in response to spontaneous events in your mind and body. By doing this you can learn how to relate to these events in a new way. In a moment I will say a series of words to you. I would like you to allow your mind to roam freely in response to the words. Do not control or analyse what you think, merely watch how your mind responds. You may find nothing much happens, but you may find that pictures or sensations come into your mind. It doesn't matter what happens, your task is just to passively watch what happens without trying to influence anything. Try this with your eyes open to begin with. I'm going to say some words now: apple, birthday, seaside, tree, bicycle, summertime, and roses.

What did you notice when you watched your mind?

The idea is that you should apply this strategy to your negative thoughts and feelings, just watch what your mind does without getting actively caught up in any thinking process.

(Wells 2006: 346–347)

The task is presented with neutral and/or positive stimuli first, and then words related to the patient's concerns and worries can be gradually introduced.

Tiger task

In this task the patient is guided in observing non-volitional aspects of imagery as a means to experiencing DM. The task is practised initially with a neutral image (we use a tiger). Later on it can usefully be applied to spontaneous intrusive and repetitive images.

The task is presented as follows:

To enable you to practise DM I'd like you to conjure up in your mind an image of a tiger. Don't try to influence or change the tiger's behaviour; just watch it. It may move, but don't make it move, it may blink, but don't make it blink, it may change, but don't make it change. Just watch how the image develops over time but do nothing to influence it, just watch the tiger in a passive way.

(Wells 2006: 348)

The therapist should check what happened to the image, and also if the patient made it move.

The following experience was reported by a patient, who described what was happening as follows:

The tiger is prowling around, quite slowly and rather leisurely, sniffing the ground a bit. Now he's stretching out and yawning. Now he's off again, looking around.

Asked if she had made the tiger move and what the experience was like, she said:

It feels as if he's out there, at a bit of a distance from me, and doing his own thing – it's a bit like watching a movie on a screen. I don't know what he's going to do next, but it's quite interesting just watching and waiting to see. I'm not trying to make him do anything or influence his behaviour. It feels as if he has a separate existence from me, which isn't how I normally feel about what I'm thinking. It's quite restful just watching him.

APPLICATION

As suggested above, DM should usually be practised first on neutral thoughts and images. Once the patient is able to demonstrate proficiency with this, the strategy should be applied to any thoughts or feelings that trigger eating behaviour. The patient is asked to apply DM in response to any such thoughts or images that occur in his or her daily life, and this is set as a homework task.

It is important to ensure that the patient is applying DM consistently to the full range of problematic thoughts and images identified in the formulation. The patient's use of DM should be carefully monitored and, if necessary, further practice in session undertaken. The latter may be useful in assisting generalisation to all relevant cognitions.

Frequency and consistency

The therapist should ensure that the patient is using DM consistently and frequently. It is useful to check use with the patient by asking her to estimate the percentage of time she has been able to apply DM to her problematic thoughts. Any change in use over time should be assessed and, if use decreases, the reasons for this should be determined. Patients may decrease their use of DM if their distress decreases. It is important to emphasise that they should continue to employ the strategy whenever they experience an inner trigger for worry, rumination or bingeing.

MINDFULNESS MEDITATION TRAINING

An alternative mindfulness approach, which has been employed clinically in patients with BN, is mindfulness based cognitive therapy (MBCT) (Segal

Table 7.1 Key differences between detached mindfulness and mindfulness based cognitive therapy

Detached mindfulness	Mindfulness based cognitive therapy
Designed for a wide range of emotional disorders	Designed for depression
Forms one part of a comprehensive treatment package	Is a treatment in itself
Can be taught and learned relatively quickly	Requires several sessions to teach and learn
Focuses explicitly on reducing self-focused attention, and increasing the flexible control of attention	Does not necessarily focus on reducing self-focused attention or enhancing attentional control
Employs exercises designed to teach metacognitive skills of gaining distance and detachment from thoughts	Employs Buddhist meditational strategies to increase here and now awareness (for example, focusing attention on breathing)

et al. 2002). A detailed account of the key similarities and differences in the theoretical bases of DM and MBCT can be found in Wells (2000). While MBCT has some overlap in aims and techniques with DM, it also has some key differences. The key differences are summarised in Table 7.1. One aspect of DM that we have found important clinically in working with people with BN is the explicit focus on responding to inner thoughts that trigger dwelling and bingeing. While MBCT may also achieve this specific type of awareness, and improve attentional control, this is not a necessary aim. Patients with BN are often excessively focused on and distressed by, for example, their bodies and internal experiences, and it can be particularly helpful for them to learn strategies that involve letting go of sustained self-processing, rather than to engage in strategies that focus on internal body sensations and processes. Indeed, some of our patients have found the latter a source of increased distress.

CHAPTER SUMMARY AND KEY POINTS

This chapter has outlined the role of detached mindfulness in BN. It has explained how its rationale can be presented, and described how a range of strategies can be employed to achieve its goal. The practicalities of its application have also been addressed.

Key points to remember include the following:

⊙ Detached mindfulness is a component of metacognitive theory based on the S-REF model, a general model of psychological dysfunction.
⊙ The aim is to be aware of internal events (particularly thoughts) but not to respond to them in any way.
⊙ Experiments to demonstrate the rationale should be conducted.
⊙ Specific instructions to achieve DM are given.
⊙ DM is not a coping strategy or avoidance.
⊙ Three techniques that may be used to teach DM are metacognitive guidance, the free association task and the tiger task.
⊙ Regular practice is needed, graduating from less to more emotionally distressing thoughts.
⊙ DM differs in key ways from meditation and mindfulness based cognitive therapy.

CHAPTER 8

Negative beliefs about eating: uncontrollability and consequences

In our model instrumental beliefs or metacognitions have a key role, in combination with general negative self beliefs, in the development and maintenance of bulimia nervosa. These beliefs or metacognitions include both negative and positive beliefs about eating and eating-related control processes. This chapter introduces negative beliefs about eating, including beliefs about the uncontrollability of eating and the negative consequences of eating behaviour. It describes strategies to identify key negative beliefs, and outlines ways to deal with them, including strategies involving verbal reattribution using a modified dysfunctional thought record (DTR). Behavioural experiments, including behavioural experiments to test lack of control thoughts, ideas for building up a sense of control over eating and tips on helping patients devise their own experiments, including follow-on experiments, are presented. The idea of realistic and unrealistic beliefs is introduced, and the chapter ends with some tips for troubleshooting, and a discussion of the time scale over which experiments may be planned.

THE ROLE OF BEHAVIOURAL EXPERIMENTS

Before discussing negative beliefs in detail first we examine the approach we use in designing and implementing behavioural experiments, as these now become crucial techniques.

Behavioural experiments are a powerful means of effecting change in beliefs and behaviour in cognitive therapy (Beck et al. 1979; Bennett-Levy et al. 2004; Wells 1997). They are often more powerful than verbal reattribution strategies, and they may have additional benefits, for example, effecting change in strongly held emotional beliefs that are typically hard to shift with verbal strategies. This advantage can be particularly important in BN where beliefs may not always be strongly believed at a rational level, but nonetheless remain strongly held at an emotional level. Such beliefs can be very hard to shift with standard thought challenging strategies, but may respond well to behavioural experiments.

The sequence or steps involved in planning and conducting behavioural experiments can be usefully expressed as a four-step protocol called PETS (Wells 1997). PETS stands for: Prepare, Expose, (putting it to the) Test and Summarise (the results). Behavioural experiments should be set up using the PETS framework (Wells 1997) and, in the first instance, carried out during the session. An outline of the PETS model can be found in Appendix 9. More detailed treatment of this topic, including both planning and working with behavioural experiments, can be found in Wells (1997) and Rouf et al. (2004).

In brief, the thought to be tested out is identified and the relationship between the thought and relevant stimuli and behaviours is formulated. An experiment to test out the thought is planned and conducted, and the results are summarised and a conclusion drawn.

BEHAVIOURAL EXPERIMENTS

Behavioural experiments can be introduced using a metaphor. One of the authors (AW) tells the following story. The bricklayer was teaching his apprentice to build a wall. When the wall was 6 feet high the builder told his apprentice that he would need to hold the wall while the cement dried in order to prevent it falling down. The apprentice stood there patiently holding on to the wall. How do you think the apprentice can find out if it will fall over or not? A typical response is to suggest that the apprentice take his hands off the wall. This is followed by the question: 'How can he be sure it won't fall over?' Typically, the patient will respond by suggesting that the apprentice give it a push. This provides a nice illustration of the ideas of testing out predictions, as well as the notion of a 'disconfirmatory manoeuvre'.

A relevant way of linking these ideas to the patient's eating disorder can be presented as follows:

Although you feel convinced that if you no longer had bulimia that X would happen, how can you be sure that would actually come true? How do you know what will happen? What is the impact of having this fear on your thoughts and behaviour? How might we test this?

Below is a sample experiment, presented in the PETS framework. It includes the preparatory verbal challenging and the setting up of a behavioural experiment. It also highlights the role and importance of linking these interventions to the formulation.

The experiment planned was designed to test the positive belief (see Chapter 9) 'Bingeing and vomiting helps me cope with stress; if I didn't binge and vomit I'd fall apart'.

Prepare (P)

(Use a modified DTR to focus on the patient's key fear, negative thought or negative prediction.)

Identify target thought(s): 'Bingeing and vomiting helps me cope with stress; if I didn't binge and vomit I'd fall apart'.

(Use modified DTR to identify the evidence for and against the thought, and use verbal challenging of the evidence that supports the thought.)

Explore evidence (against the thought, 'Bingeing and vomiting helps me cope with stress'): 'I feel exhausted and have difficulty concentrating after bingeing and vomiting. I feel more stressed. I struggle to get through the day at work. The evening is always ruined'.

(Use modified DTR, and verbal strategies, to develop an alternative perspective.)

Alternative perspective: 'In the short term I feel relief when bingeing because I'm not thinking about anything other than the next mouthful of food, but that's short lived and I feel more stressed in the end'.

Explore evidence (against the thought, if I didn't binge and vomit I'd fall apart): 'When I haven't binged and vomited I feel more confident, and my mood and emotions aren't nearly so likely to be all over the place'.

Alternative perspective: 'Bingeing and vomiting actually make me feel tearful and upset, and more vulnerable. I'm stronger and more confident when I haven't been bingeing and vomiting.'

Identify stimuli and behaviours: 'Weekly sales meeting at work. I always binge and vomit before the scheduled meeting.'

Make a specific prediction: A useful prediction in the current situation, where 'falling apart' meant bursting into tears, might be 'If I go to a sales meeting without bingeing and vomiting beforehand, I'll burst into tears'. The patient should then be asked to rate her belief in this thought. A scale from 0 ('I do not believe this at all') to 100 ('I am completely convinced that this is true') is useful here.

Rationale for experiment

This could be discussed as follows, with the therapist saying:

If I understand you correctly, you always binge and vomit before the sales meeting at work because this is the way you've learned to reduce anxiety and feel calm. Is that right? How can you be sure that without bingeing you would fall apart (e.g. burst into tears, have to leave the room, colleagues would make nasty comments etc.)? What we could do is design an experiment to find out what actually happens if you go to the sales meeting without bingeing and vomiting beforehand. It's a bit like setting up an experiment similar to the ones you probably did in science class at school. It's gathering new information or data that may help you revise your negative thoughts and then making a decision about changing based on what you find. Shall we give it a go?

Expose (E)

The therapist agrees a suitable situation for testing the prediction. Typically this involves reversing avoidance behaviour and/or actually engaging in the behaviours believed to lead to a negative outcome. It involves exposure to the feared stimuli.

In the current situation this might involve asking the patient to enter a situation that is normally associated with triggering the problem, for example, to go to a sales meeting.

Test (T)

Agree with the patient a disconfirmatory strategy, that is, something the patient will do or not do that provides a rigorous and unambiguous test of the prediction. For example, here the patient should ban bingeing and vomiting prior to the meeting. Furthermore, she might decide to take a more active role in the meeting than usual, perhaps by asking at least three questions during the course of the meeting, and see if that leads to 'bursting into tears'. The patient then completes the experiment, exposing herself to the feared situation and also completing the disconfirmatory manoeuvre previously agreed upon.

Summarise (S)

The patient and therapist then discuss the results of the experiment in terms of the original prediction (belief) made and re-rate the current level of belief in the negative thoughts. Here, in doing the experiment, the patient concluded that 'Bingeing and vomiting as a way of coping para-doxically made it more difficult to cope with stress'. She noticed that without bingeing and vomiting prior to the sales meeting she was able to concentrate and contribute significantly to the discussions and had a greater sense of satisfaction.

Together, therapist and patient should then plan further experiments. If necessary, the original experiment can be refined, and repeated in a revised form, drawing on what has been learned from carrying it out. As before, the aim is to challenge the negative prediction and discover any disconfirmatory evidence. Further experiments should be targeted at achieving this, and with the aim of decreasing belief in the negative thought to zero or as near zero as possible. If the original experiment has been conducted in the session, or with the help of the therapist, then further experiments will often involve repeating the same experiment alone, outside the session, for homework.

As well as discussing the outcome, it is also important to make time to reflect on the process of planning and developing the behavioural experi-ments with the patient and use guided discovery to help them develop the skill of setting up their own experiments for themselves in the future. It is also very important to prepare the patient for the fact that when con-ducting an experiment the outcome is unknown and that sometimes the unexpected happens, or experiments backfire in other ways. These experi-ences should be framed as opportunities to learn important things about the patient's problem, that is, as opportunities, not failure.

NEGATIVE BELIEFS ABOUT EATING

Beliefs are of central importance in the new cognitive model of BN. Negative beliefs reflect fears about weight gain and about eating or bingeing (e.g. 'If I eat a biscuit, I'll get fat'), and contribute to ambi-valence about change. Negative beliefs include a range of beliefs about the uncontrollability of eating (e.g. 'I can't stop myself from eating sweet things'), as well as the negative consequences of eating behaviour (e.g. 'I'll gain weight and get fat; if I get fat people will reject me; if I eat fat it will turn into fat on my body'). Together with positive beliefs about eating (see Chapter 9), negative beliefs play an important role in main-taining episodes of binge eating and vomiting. For complete recovery it is, therefore, essential to challenge and change these ways of thinking. If the beliefs are no longer present or credible then the problematic behaviour is not likely to occur. Among the range of negative beliefs that may be present, beliefs reflecting lack of control over eating are usually best tackled first.

The first step in challenging negative beliefs about eating, including uncontrollability beliefs, is to become aware of them. These beliefs can be very idiosyncratic and personal, as shown in the following example.

Miranda had the following worrying thoughts before a party she had planned that involved providing a buffet supper: 'I'll eat the desserts, I won't be able to stop, I've no willpower, I'll end up fat and unlovable' and 'I'll pile on weight and it won't stop – image of self obese'. These thoughts led to rumination. Miranda believed that she had no control over the situation and feared losing control. This negative belief about uncontroll-ability of eating was important in maintaining Miranda's problem, including her worrying thoughts about weight gain.

Identifying uncontrollability thoughts

A modified dysfunctional thought record (DTR) can be used to record lack of control beliefs (see Table 8.1; also in Appendix 15) and then becomes a useful tool and record for challenging these beliefs. The relevant subscale of the Eating Disorder Thoughts Questionnaire (see Appendix 7) can also be used to identify examples of these thoughts.

To identify lack of control beliefs, it can be useful to ask 'What do I say to myself in the middle of a binge?', 'How much do you believe you can control your eating once you've started?' Some questions that can be used to identify these beliefs can be seen in the box on page 117. The beliefs uncovered can then be recorded in the left-hand column of the modified DTR.

Challenging uncontrollability

In most cases it is usually helpful to begin with some initial work using verbal reattribution strategies, for example using modified DTRs to test key thoughts, and then to follow these (fairly quickly) with behavioural experiments designed to reinforce and extend what has been learned from verbal thought challenging. The advantage of preceding behavioural experiments with verbal thought challenging is that it often allows an initial loosening of beliefs, which then provides a lever or stage from which to develop and build a behavioural experiment. In other words, it acts as a way in, to help the patient see that alternatives might be possible

Table 8.1 A modified dysfunctional thought record form to record uncontrollability beliefs about eating

Situation	Feelings (0–100)	Beliefs (0–100)	Behaviour
Where was I? What was I doing? What was I thinking? What was I worrying about?	How did I feel?	What was running through my mind while I was bingeing/ contemplating bingeing? How much did I believe I could control my bingeing?	What evidence do I have against my belief? What evidence do I have that I can control my bingeing?

USEFUL QUESTIONS TO ELICIT NEGATIVE BELIEFS ABOUT UNCONTROLLABILITY OF EATING

General

What was running through your mind when you felt anxious, worried etc.?

What anxious thoughts did you have?

What were you saying to yourself?

Did you have any images or pictures in your mind?

Could you describe these?

Specific

What thoughts did you have about your sense of control?

and that an experiment might be a useful strategy. One function of the experiment is then to confirm and reinforce any initial shift that has already begun to take place.

Verbal reattribution strategies

Lack of control beliefs can be challenged using verbal reattribution strategies. Responses to questioning should be recorded on the modified DTR (see Table 8.2 for an example of a patient's completed record).

Useful general and more specific questions that can be employed to challenge these beliefs are listed in the box on page 119.

Planning behavioural experiments

After one or two examples of reinterpreting the evidence using verbal reattribution strategies have been completed in the session, and perhaps also for homework, it is usually useful to begin to plan some behavioural experiments. This is likely to be where most of the change in lack of control beliefs about eating will take place. The reasons and rationale for

Table 8.2 A modified dysfunctional thought record form completed for uncontrollability beliefs about eating

Situation	Feelings (0–100)	Beliefs (0–100)	Behaviour
Out with friends, worrying about having eaten too much food at dinnertime, drinking cocktails, feeling very fearful of bingeing, avoiding going home to flat	Scared 90% Tired 80% Excited 70% Vulnerable 65%	I've eaten too much 100% I'm out of control 95% (bought chocolate to take home to binge on) I can't control my eating 100% I might as well carry on and binge 100%	I ate more than I would usually which felt uncomfortable, but I wasn't out of control. I ate the same as everyone else. I was able to stop eating. I do have some control, and I can choose whether or not to proceed with bingeing 50%
Where was I? What was I doing? What was I thinking? What was I worrying about?	How did I feel?	What was running through my mind while I was bingeing/ contemplating bingeing? How much did I believe I could control my bingeing?	What evidence do I have against my belief? What evidence do I have that I can control my bingeing?

USEFUL QUESTIONS TO CHALLENGE UNCONTROLLABILITY BELIEFS

General questions

What would someone else suggest or say? What would my best friend say if they knew I felt like this? How would they try to help? How can I try to put that into practice myself?

What would I say to someone else in my position? How would I help them? What would I do or suggest? How could I put that into practice for myself?

Lack of control questions

Is it really true that I have no ability to control how much or what I eat? Does eating a small amount mean that I have 'lost control'? What would loss of control mean or look like to someone else? How does that compare to what I've just done or have planned?

---

conducting behavioural experiments at this stage should be carefully explained to the patient.

A behavioural experiment to test a lack of control thought

Below is a sample experiment, presented in the PETS framework, designed to test a lack of control thought. The example includes the preparatory verbal challenging and the setting up of a behavioural experiment. It also highlights the role and importance of linking these interventions to the formulation.

Prepare

(Use a revised DTR to focus on the patient's key negative belief about eating.) Key cognition: 'If I have chocolate I'll lose control and binge'. Identify evidence for and against the thought. Use verbal challenging of the evidence that supports the thought.

A useful prediction given the above thought might be: 'If I eat a whole Mars bar I will binge eat (1500 cal +) within 10 minutes of eating it'. The patient should then be asked to rate her belief in this thought. As before, a scale from 0 ('I do not believe this at all') to 100 ('I am completely convinced that this is true') is useful here. The therapist agrees on a suitable 'test' strategy with the patient, that is, a strategy that involves behaving in a way that enables the patient to discover that negative predicted outcomes do not occur, or a 'disconfirmatory strategy'.

Expose

The experiment is then carried out. In the session the patient is asked to eat a chocolate bar (the therapist might need to model this behaviour, which helps to enhance compliance with the experiment). The patient is then given a half-hour break and asked to return to the session.

Test

The patient is asked to implement the disconfirmatory manoeuvre, such as leaving the session for 15 minutes while carrying another three chocolate bars in her pocket.

Summarise

The patient and therapist discuss the results of the experiment in terms of the predictions made and re-rate the belief in the negative thoughts.

Further experiments

Together, therapist and patient plan further experiments for homework. As before, the aim is to challenge the negative prediction and discover any disconfirmatory evidence. Thus further experiments should be targeted at achieving this with the aim of decreasing belief in the negative thought to zero or as near zero as possible. Further experiments in the current situation might involve repeating the same experiment outside the session for homework.

A behavioural experiments worksheet

It is useful to have a specially designed worksheet when planning and recording the outcome of behavioural experiments (see worksheet).

A BEHAVIOURAL EXPERIMENTS WORKSHEET

Thought I want to test (Belief 0–100)	Situation in which I'll test it	Test strategy (what I will do)	Outcome (Belief 0–100)

Binge postponement

One very useful strategy to modify lack of control beliefs is binge post-ponement, a manoeuvre similar to that of 'worry postponement', described by Wells (1997). The patient, when experiencing a desire to binge, agrees to delay bingeing for increasingly longer periods of time. For example, she might begin by saying, 'I won't do it now, I'll do it later'. It can be useful to engage in a distracting activity for the following 15–20 minutes, and patients may find it helpful to have a list of activities that will occupy their attention to choose from. Paradoxically, many patients find that after introducing a delay the urge to binge either decreases or disappears. Deciding to postpone binges has been used in other treatments for BN (see, for example, P.J. Cooper 1993). However, it differs here from use elsewhere in the rationale; the explicit aim is to provide evidence to help support the belief that eating and bingeing can be controlled, rather than (as in P.J. Cooper 1993) to allow the urge to binge to decay.

Using a hierarchy

Sometimes it is often useful to plan a series of graded behavioural experi-ments designed to build up the patient's evidence base that she can control her eating. This involves developing a hierarchy of situations, starting with those in which it would be relatively easy to demonstrate a sense of control, through to those that are very difficult, and in which binge eating is most likely to occur. The patient then works through the hierarchy, starting with the easiest situation, and completes the designated task. Ratings of 'I can control my eating' (0 = not at all to 100 = com-pletely) are taken before and after each task. Once a task is mastered successfully, the patient proceeds to the next most difficult task. To help the patient it can be useful to refer to the hierarchy as a 'ladder' of situations with rungs at different levels, and draw it out on paper as a vertical line, with the top labelled 100 per cent and the bottom 0 per cent. Patients often find it easiest to identify the top and bottom rungs before proceeding to fill in the situations that come between these. A list of activities and strategies that might make each task easier can be generated, and put into practice, while completing the task.

Sophie was concerned that some foods were particularly 'risky' and that she would be unable to control the amount of them that she would eat. She was unwilling to test herself on highly risky foods that she associated with binge eating. A hierarchy was drawn up of safe foods through mildly to highly risky foods, and in each session she was asked to eat a specific amount of food at the appropriate stage on the hierarchy (for example, five crisps from a small packet).

Identifying beliefs about negative consequences

The patient will nearly always need some help to identify beliefs about the negative consequences of eating behaviour. As with lack of control beliefs, they can usefully be recorded on a modified DTR (see Table 8.1). Once the patient is familiar with the technique she can then be asked to identify and record examples of these beliefs on the DTR for homework.

Patients may have a number of beliefs when asked to self-monitor them. Not all of these will be important in maintaining the eating problem. In the individual case it will be important to identify those that are most important in maintaining the problem. Typically, those associated with most distress will be those that it is important to modify, as these beliefs will be most closely associated with any problem behaviour. Patients will generally be able to identify these in response to the question, 'Which of those beliefs do you find most upsetting', or, in response to a question designed to discover how the belief fits with the formulation (for example, it might be useful to ask 'Which of these beliefs is most likely to lead you to binge or worry excessively about your appearance etc.'). Some tips on identifying key thoughts and some useful questions to achieve this can be found in the following boxes.

How to identify key beliefs in practice

The therapist should identify a typical problem situation (e.g. a situation in which the patient feels worried or anxious about her eating) and work through this, completing the form with the patient in a session as a first step. Specific questions that can be asked one after the other, to identify beliefs about negative consequences, can be seen in the box overleaf.

It is important for the patient to demonstrate an ability to complete a DTR in the session before setting this as a homework task. It is also helpful to get the patient to think about any specific problems that she may have with identifying and recording her thoughts before going away, for example, with a record sheet on which to record key cognitions for homework. Useful questions to elicit potential problems might be:

TIPS ON IDENTIFYING KEY THOUGHTS

A thought is likely to be significant if

It is emotionally charged, that is, linked to affect and activation of negative self beliefs.

Ask the patient

'Out of all of your thoughts [therapist repeats back or patient and therapist look at the DTR], which ones hurt the most, were the most distressing or overwhelming. Which could you feel in the pit of your stomach?' 'Which thought was the most emotionally intense?' 'How much did you believe the thought to be true out of 0–100% [key or significant thoughts are mostly believed more than 70%]?' 'How did it make you feel [emotional language for key thoughts is typically strong, using words such as angry, furious, distraught, utterly gob smacked etc.]?'

Remember

Validate the patient's experience and be empathic. Discussing the thoughts can reactivate the underlying schema and lead to rumination, which is often a golden opportunity to work with the patient's distress in the session and help them experience both how the different parts of the cognitive model fit together in action, and how (for example) to employ detached mindfulness to deal with the triggering thoughts.

As a therapist, ask

'How does the thought fit with the formulation? Does it map on to a core belief or assumption?' Ask, for example, 'Has the patient expressed this type of thought on previous occasions – does it reflect a recurrent theme in their thoughts?' 'What does this thought mean to the patient?' Frequent thoughts with greater or more extensive meaning attached are more likely to be key thoughts.

Ask the patient

It can also be helpful to ask the patient for her view. For example, ask the patient which thought is the most salient thought, or which thought they would like to consider further.

Remember

Reflect on the process of discovering any links with the patient.

USEFUL QUESTIONS TO ASK TO IDENTIFY KEY THOUGHTS

Of those thoughts you have identified, which is the most significant?

Which thought makes you feel most anxious, upset etc.?

Which thought is most likely to lead to the problem behaviour, such as binge eating?

SPECIFIC QUESTIONS TO IDENTIFY BELIEFS ABOUT NEGATIVE CONSEQUENCES

What might happen then?

If that's true/likely/if I do that, then what might happen next?

What's the worst thing that could happen?

What would that mean?

'What might get in the way of you completing this?'
'What difficulties or problems do you see with doing this?'

Any potential problems should be discussed and possible solutions decided upon before the patient leaves.

It is not uncommon for patients to find that they dislike completing the DTR and prefer to record this information in a notebook, and there is no reason why they should not do this.

Challenging negative consequence beliefs

As with uncontrollability beliefs, it is helpful to challenge negative consequence beliefs using verbal strategies before proceeding to design and carry out behavioural experiments. Some specific questions to help challenge negative beliefs about consequences can be seen in the box overleaf. An example of a completed DTR, including the patient's response, can be seen in Table 8.3.

SPECIFIC QUESTIONS TO CHALLENGE NEGATIVE BELIEFS ABOUT CONSEQUENCES

How likely is that?

What evidence am I using?

Is there any evidence that contradicts that?

What alternative views are there?

How useful is it to think that way?

What tells me that this might not happen?

Table 8.3 Modified dysfunctional thought record completed for identifying negative beliefs about consequences

Situation	Feelings (0–100)	Beliefs (0–100)	Response to beliefs (0–100)
Karen asked me to lunch on Friday. I didn't really want to go but I couldn't say no as I'd already let her down twice before.	Anxious 75% Worried 90% Panicky 65%	I'll eat too much 95% I'll have to eat something fattening 85% There won't be anything I can eat 80% I'll end up feeling fat and bloated afterwards 90%	I don't have any evidence for this – the café has a big choice of food, and I won't have to eat anything I don't want to – if I am given something I'd rather not eat, I can always leave it 70%

Note: The key thought is circled.

Cognitive distortions

One way to challenge negative beliefs about consequences is to identify and then challenge the cognitive distortions that they contain.

Four common distortions in BN are:

- *catastrophising*: making negative predictions without considering other possible outcomes
- *selective attention*: focusing on one aspect of the problem while discounting or ignoring others

- *emotional reasoning*: interpreting feelings as facts
- *double standards*: having one rule for oneself and another for everyone else.

Some typical examples of each type of cognitive distortion in BN can be seen in the box.

EXAMPLES OF TYPICAL COGNITIVE DISTORTIONS

Catastrophisation

I'll gain a kilo if I eat chips with my lunch today.

If I eat a biscuit I'll lose control and eat everything in the cupboard.

If I get fat no one will ever speak to me again.

Selective attention

One critical comment (for example, in the context of many positive comments) means the person thinks I'm useless and a failure.

I'm fat and ugly (the result of focusing on one part of the body).

Noticing only articles on dieting and food in a magazine or paper.

Noticing that only the people who are skinny are in a relationship.

Emotional reasoning

If I feel fat it means I am fat.

If I feel other people don't like me then it must be true.

If I feel a failure then I must have failed.

Double standards

I can't allow myself to make any mistakes.

I must control my eating at all times.

If I don't exercise every day I'm worthless.

(Further information on cognitive distortions can be found in Beck et al. 1979; Burns 1980.)

Many people with BN have typical distortions that they use over and over again. Spotting distortions and any patterns in them can help patients to gain some distance or perspective on the way in which they think and to avoid distortions in the future. Most distortions will also need to be challenged directly, for example, by examining the evidence the patient is using to support them. Some questions that may be useful for challenging each type of cognitive distortion can be seen in the box.

QUESTIONS TO CHALLENGE TYPICAL COGNITIVE DISTORTIONS

Catastrophisation

Are you thinking the worst? Are you getting things out of all proportion? How often have you thought the worst and it's not turned out to be true? What's more likely to be true? What's the impact of thinking the worst?

Selective attention

Are you paying attention to one detail while excluding other important details? Do you have any evidence that this is not always true, or that it is not true all the time? How does focusing your attention in this way affect how I feel and think? What's the disadvantage of thinking this way?

Emotional reasoning

Are you focusing on how you are feeling without considering other factors?

Double standards

What would you say to someone else in this situation?

Ideas for experiments to test negative beliefs

We have found two types of behavioural experiment particularly useful when challenging negative beliefs about uncontrollability and consequences. These are:

- *Paradoxical experiments*, for example, designing an experiment with the aim of trying to lose control over eating.
- *Reversing avoidance behaviours*, for example, asking patients to predict what will happen if they do not avoid a forbidden food.

In the box are some examples of experiments designed to test negative (specifically, loss of control) beliefs, using each of these strategies.

EXAMPLES OF BEHAVIOURAL EXPERIMENTS DESIGNED TO CHALLENGE NEGATIVE BELIEFS

Paradoxical experiment

Angela believed that if she did not check food labels for calories and fat content she would lose control of how much she was eating, and binge. Her therapist asked, 'How does this stop you from bingeing?' Angela believed that it achieved this by stopping her from getting too upset by other people. She predicted that if she focused on other people, for example, what they were saying when she talked to them, then she would lose control. In a paradoxical experiment, Angela tried to see if she could make herself 'lose control' and binge by concentrating hard on other people and their conversations and concerns, and, in a disconfirmatory manoeuvre, actively seeking out people and talking to them about personal and sensitive topics.

Reversing avoidance

Bethany had severe BN, and was too frightened to keep any food in her flat. She predicted, 'If I keep food in the flat I'll lose control and eat everything there is'. In a behavioural experiment she reversed her avoidance behaviour, and went shopping for two days' groceries, which she put in her kitchen. In a disconfirmatory manoeuvre she planned to make and eat a meal using some of the shopping she had bought.

Planning an experiment

Below is an extract illustrating a dialogue in which the therapist and patient work together to plan a behavioural experiment to test a lack of control belief.

Therapist: How much do you believe the thought 'Once I start eating, I won't be able to stop' to be true if, on a scale of 0 to 100, 100 per cent is that you are totally convinced that it is true, and 0 per cent is that you don't believe the thought at all?

Patient: 85 per cent.

Therapist: What makes you think that this thought is true?

Patient: If food is there I have to eat it, I've no willpower, it feels as if I'm programmed to do it.

Therapist: What reasons have you got to believe that the thought isn't entirely true?

Patient: When I'm eating with my family or friends I can stop eating, in fact I usually eat less than them because it makes me feel better.

Therapist: What situations do you feel unable to stop eating in?

Patient: When I've had a hard day at work, when I'm feeling lonely, fed up and bored. I'm always bored on a Sunday afternoon and always binge eat then.

Therapist: Is there any other evidence that goes against the thought 'Once I start eating I can't stop'?

Patient: Yes, there have been times when I've stopped myself from bingeing and have had some control.

Therapist: What would be an alternative way of looking at this thought in light of the evidence?

Patient: I can control my eating at times, that's a fact, however when I'm at a low ebb it's more difficult to stop.

Therapist: You've mentioned that Sunday is a day when you are at a low ebb and which often ends in you binge eating. What experiment could you do to test out this (your prediction)?

Patient: I could plan to not have second helpings at lunchtime and find things to do to take my mind away from thoughts of eating more.

Therapist: What could you do?

Patient: I could practise my piano, then read a book, maybe phone a friend.

Therapist: Those are all good ideas, let's make a note of them. What problems are you likely to encounter?

Patient: I'll stay in the kitchen and start picking at food after lunch.

Therapist: How could you deal with this?

Patient: I could put my plate straight into the dishwasher, then leave the kitchen until the urge to nibble has gone.

Reflecting on experiments

Reflecting on the process of having completed an experiment is important and can help the patient to understand the process and skills acquired more thoroughly. An example of a dialogue in which this is achieved can be seen below:

Therapist: Let's reflect on the experiment we have just done. If we were to break it down into steps what do you think they are?

Patient: We started by questioning the thoughts from my thought record in the usual way and looking at what effect the thoughts were having on what I do.

Therapist: What did we do next?

Patient: I realised that avoiding having food in the house for fear of losing control was making me miserable and making me think that I was a freak. It reminded me of all those years when I wouldn't fly because I was convinced that the plane would crash, then after my friend died of cancer I thought that you could sit at home wrapped in cotton wool and still die. So I started flying and haven't looked back since. The fear of the unknown is illusory and not a fact. Coming back to the eating problem, the next step is changing the behaviour to see what happens. Then discussing what I've learned. Oh, then doing another experiment.

Therapist: How about if we plan an experiment together that you can have a go at over the next week?

Patient: Yes, I'd like to have a go, but feel a bit apprehensive.

Therapist: How about if we work on your thought 'Once I start eating I can't stop'.

Patient: Yes, definitely.

Notes about evidence for negative beliefs

The patient and therapist need to be able to distinguish between realistic and unrealistic negative beliefs concerning the consequences of eating, and this can cause some confusion at first if they are not adequately separated. The belief 'I'll get fat or gain weight' (or a variant of it) generally causes most problems. Many patients will, realistically, gain weight if they repeatedly binge. This may be a disadvantage of continuing and may be the evidence that the patient is using to support her belief. However, it is important to distinguish this from an unrealistic prediction of weight gain based, for example, on eating one 25 gram bar of chocolate. In summary, it is very important to elucidate the precise nature of the patient's evidence. When this is done, many fears of weight gain will turn out to be unrealistic given the patient's evidence.

Troubleshooting

Tackling negative beliefs using verbal restructuring and behavioural experiments is not always straightforward. Some potential problems and suggestions for ways to deal with them are given below.

'Yes but' statements

Sometimes patients respond to verbal restructuring with 'yes but' statements whenever an alternative response has been identified. There are two different reasons for this. The first is that challenging the belief has reinforced any negative predictions by encouraging rumination. This needs to be dealt with by helping the patient disengage from this process. It can be helpful to proceed as follows:

'Can I just pause you there for a moment? Thinking about your own thinking, what are you doing now?'

This can open up discussion of rumination, and help the patient develop a metacognitive perspective. It can be useful to then ask:

'What was the trigger for the rumination? If you spot yourself doing this in the future, what could you do?'

This can lead to a discussion of DM.
   The second is when challenging the belief has altered 'intellectual' but not 'emotional' belief. The patient may say, for example, 'I know it's ridiculous but I feel it's true'. One way to deal with this is to ask, 'Are there times when you can accept the evidence against the thought?', in order to highlight the discrepancy between these two ways of looking at it, and to conduct some behavioural experiments organised around the question, 'What would it take to convince you?'.

Negative outcomes to experiments

Sometimes behavioural experiments do not go to plan. It is important to set them up correctly, as a 'no lose' experiment, so that whatever happens they will tell us something helpful. But patients may still be disappointed at the result and lack of 'success'. It is important to consider possible reasons for this. For example, the steps taken may have been too big, the task was too ambitious, there were not enough alternative strategies available, there was no back-up plan, the experiment simply had not been thought through enough and a risk assessment (i.e. what could go wrong) had not been considered.

Guilt and choosing to binge

Most binges are planned, but the difficulty is that the patient believes her bingeing is beyond her control. However, some patients are clear very early on that they do make a planned decision to binge, that is, they choose to initiate it, despite being aware of many of the pros and cons. These patients often feel blamed, or that it is (or the therapist is saying that it is) their own fault, when the topic of control is raised. It is important to give the message that choosing to do something doesn't mean they are to blame – rather, there are likely to be some very good reasons why they make this choice – and that what is needed is to start to understand this process. It is also important to remember that although these patients recognise that they have choice over starting a binge, they invariably feel a sense of lack of control *while* eating, thus lack of control beliefs are invariably still present, even if confined to actual bingeing behaviour.

Short-term experiments versus longer term negative belief predictions

Several of the strategies demonstrated in this chapter involve experiments or tasks that take place over a relatively short period of time. Many patients will have negative beliefs about what will happen if they persist with new behaviours over time, and it is important that these are also addressed. Such beliefs are usually examples of negative beliefs that go beyond the ability to control eating in the here and now. For example, a patient may express the fear that she will gain weight over time if she substitutes normal food for low calorie or diet foods, that is, the effect will not show up immediately but only after several days. Education and appropriate verbal challenging may be used to tackle fears such as these. For example, it can be helpful to say that we cannot predict what will happen several days from now and explain that a stable weight lies within a range and is not static, and that weight will invariably fluctuate for lots of different reasons – 'What might those be?' Verbal challenging can also be used to normalise weight gain by asking, for example, 'If the worst happened and you did gain 10 kilos, how might you deal with that; what do other people do to lose weight?' Most patients will recognise that resuming bulimic behaviours or extreme dieting is not the answer and will refer to healthy eating and moderate exercise as the option of choice in such circumstances. Challenging of such beliefs may need to continue in parallel with the challenging of positive beliefs (see Chapter 9).

CHAPTER SUMMARY AND KEY POINTS

This chapter has outlined strategies to identify and challenge negative beliefs concerning uncontrollability and consequences of eating, using both verbal reattribution and behavioural experiments.

Key points to remember include the following:

⊙ Negative beliefs reflect beliefs about the uncontrollability of eating, and other effects or consequences of eating.
⊙ Negative beliefs play an important role in maintaining episodes of binge eating and vomiting.
⊙ Lack of control beliefs are best tackled first – they can usefully be recorded on a modified dysfunctional thought record, and challenged initially using verbal reattribution followed by behavioural experiments.
⊙ A behavioural experiments worksheet can be useful for recording experiments and their outcome.
⊙ It is important to help patients learn how to plan their own experiments, including follow-on experiments.
⊙ It can be important to distinguish realistic and unrealistic beliefs.
⊙ Troubleshooting for specific problems may be necessary.

Positive beliefs about eating

In our model positive beliefs about eating and eating-related cognitive processes occur in conjunction with negative beliefs (discussed in Chapter 8) and general negative self beliefs. Together they interact in the development and maintenance of bulimia nervosa. In Chapter 8 negative beliefs were considered, and strategies to modify them were identified. This chapter introduces positive beliefs about eating. It describes strategies to identify key positive beliefs, and outlines ways to deal with them. These include strategies involving verbal reattribution, such as an advantages versus disadvantages analysis, reviewing the counter-evidence, taking a longer term perspective and introducing flexibility into thinking. Behavioural experiments are also discussed, as are specific ideas for troubleshooting, and assessing the risk of potentially dangerous behaviours. Two types of positive belief are considered:

- ◉ positive beliefs about bingeing
- ◉ positive beliefs about eating-related behaviours such as worry, checking, selective attention to food, eating, weight and shape and compensatory behaviours such as purging and dieting.

POSITIVE BELIEFS ABOUT EATING

Bingeing, and a range of other behaviours, provide a means of regulating negative thoughts and feelings. Positive beliefs drive bingeing and eating-related behaviours as part of a self-regulation strategy. Examples of positive beliefs in BN are: 'Focusing on how tight my jeans feel is the only way I know I'm fat', 'Worrying about how much I eat keeps me in control', 'Imagining how bad I look if I were to gain weight helps me keep thin' and 'Purging stops me gaining weight'. Positive beliefs need to be weakened in order to increase the patient's flexibility of responding to negative internal experiences. The plan and strategies presented here are modelled closely on those outlined for modifying positive beliefs about worry in generalised anxiety disorder and in metacognitive therapy (see Wells 2000).

Identifying positive beliefs

Positive beliefs may not be readily apparent in the patient's stream of consciousness. However, these beliefs can be elicited through careful questioning about the advantages of observed behaviours or the costs of not engaging in, for example, bingeing and other behaviours (e.g. calorie counting, worrying about being fat, purging).

The positive beliefs subscale of the Eating Disorder Thoughts Questionnaire (see Appendix 7) can also be useful in identifying positive beliefs about binge eating.

Behaviours and positive beliefs

Behaviours play an important role in maintaining positive beliefs, and thus in maintaining BN. Behaviours prevent patients from reality testing their beliefs and erroneous assumptions and also from reality testing other people's reactions. Many of the behaviours involved are perceived as having a safety function for the patient in preventing something bad from happening and these can be particularly difficult to relinquish. Bingeing, for example, may function as a means to avoid the perceived danger of excessive distress.

MODELLING BEHAVIOURS

Behaviours that help maintain positive beliefs include extreme dieting, checking, avoidance and seeking reassurance about weight and shape concerns, as well as binge eating. Identifying key maintaining behaviours can be a useful first step in identifying the cognitive processes such as self-focused attention, worry and rumination that are characteristic of positive beliefs. Unlike many of the problematic behaviours we have discussed in previous chapters, the behaviours involved here can be subtle, secretive and covert, making them difficult to detect and modify.

Examples of the different behaviours that may be associated with positive beliefs in BN can be seen in Table 9.1.

Engagement in these behaviours reinforces and typically increases the strength of positive (as well as negative) beliefs. In a vicious cycle, the positive beliefs then maintain the problematic behaviours.

It is important to note that the same behaviour may function to maintain or increase strength of negative or positive beliefs at different

Table 9.1 Examples of behaviours that may be linked to positive beliefs and potential associated positive beliefs

Behaviour	Positive belief
Dieting	It keeps me slim. It gives me control. I need to think about food or control my eating to stay slim.
Checking	I need to make sure people see me as slim. Checking my weight will prevent me from gaining weight.
Hoarding food, buying excessive amounts of food	I must have food available – it's my security. If I don't have food to binge on I won't be able to cope with distress.
Counting calories, fat grams	I'll stay safe – thin and slim. Knowing exactly how much I've eaten stops me getting fat.

times, and differentially in different patients. Checking weight by frequent weighing can increase or maintain belief in the positive thought (for example, 'Checking keeps me safe; as long as I keep a close eye on how much I weigh, I won't gain weight') but it can also increase or maintain belief in the negative thought 'I'm getting fat'. Rumination can function in a similar way. For example, excessive thinking about how much one has eaten, and its calorie content, may increase preoccupation and belief in the positive belief, 'It's OK I haven't exceeded my limit for the day, I should lose some weight'. Equally, it may function to increase belief in a negative belief (for example, 'I'm overeating, I'll gain weight'). This means that it is important to uncover the function of specific behaviours related to BN, so that an accurate formulation can be derived, and the appropriate belief targeted.

INCREASING AWARENESS

One way to identify more subtle problematic behaviours is to ask the patient to complete the Eating Behaviour Questionnaire (EBQ: Cooper et al. 2006). This may help to highlight behaviours that are not spontaneously reported by patients.

Eating Behaviour Questionnaire

The Eating Behaviour Questionnaire can be found in Appendix 5. The scoring key for the EBQ is also shown in this Appendix.

The EBQ has six subscales. These are weight and shape; bingeing; dieting; food; eating; and overeating. Table 2.3 (p. 42) includes the mean scores for samples of BN patients, dieters and non-dieters on each subscale. Note, however, that this scale does not capture strategies of worry, preoccupation and attention which the therapist should ask about directly.

Guided discovery

Guided discovery can be used to help the patient identify positive beliefs. Below is an example of a dialogue between a patient and therapist illustrating how guided discovery, and a modified DTR form, can be used in this way.

Therapist: I'd like to introduce you to a worksheet that you might find useful. It's a thought record that has been modified specifically for recording the positive beliefs that are important in binge eating. For today I'd like us to concentrate on the first three columns of the worksheet. We'll think about the other columns in future sessions. How about if we both record this recent situation that we have just discussed?

Patient: OK.

Therapist: What were you doing?

Patient: I was sat at my desk responding to emails.

Therapist: Fine, so we put where you were in the 'situation column'. The situation can be an actual event that happened or it can be to do with a stream of thoughts or images that you are having at the time. Is that clear?

Patient: I think so. It's what I'm doing or thinking before I binge.

Therapist: What was the first thing you noticed before you binged – was it a thought or a feeling?

Patient: I was feeling bored.

Therapist: When you were feeling bored, what were you thinking?

Patient: That I'm fat and ugly.

Therapist: How did that make you feel?

Patient: I felt depressed, anxious, I was thinking about the food I was going to eat.

Therapist: What did you do then, how did you behave?

Patient: I bought a muffin from the vending machine.

Therapist: After you bought a muffin, what happened next?

Patient: I ate the muffin and thought, 'I've blown it now' and started to plan to buy more food.

Therapist: At the time, what did you think were the advantages of continuing to eat?

Patient: Well, I knew that bingeing was inevitable. I did feel it might help cheer me up, make me feel better.

Therapist: What went through your mind just before you started to binge?

Patient: A binge will make the day easier, it will cheer me up.

Therapist: Then what happened?

Patient: I went to the shop and bought chocolate and lo and behold a binge followed.

Therapist: OK, so how about if we record those thoughts on the worksheet in the 'Positive beliefs column'?

Patient: OK (therapist and patient record the positive beliefs on the dysfunctional thought record).

Some questions are more useful than others in eliciting positive beliefs. With practice and experience therapists often find ones that seem to work for them. However, there are some questions that are particularly useful. A selection of questions that we have found useful here can be seen in the box.

USEFUL QUESTIONS TO IDENTIFY POSITIVE BELIEFS ABOUT BINGEING

At the time of binge eating did you think eating would help?

How did you think it might help?

What did you think might happen if you didn't eat then (elicit the consequences of not eating, e.g. fear of not been able to cope with or control emotions)?

What are the advantages of eating when faced with a trigger?

Ideas for discovery-related behavioural experiments

Some ideas for experiments that can be conducted to help patients become aware of their positive beliefs can be seen in the box overleaf.

Fears associated with changing different types of behaviour

Some typical examples of the fears which may be associated with relinquishing different problematic behaviours can be seen in Table 9.2. As

IDEAS FOR EXPERIMENTS TO DEMONSTRATE THE ROLE OF BEHAVIOURS IN MAINTAINING POSITIVE BELIEFS

Example experiment 1

Ask patient to identify key belief experienced when she looks at herself in a full-length mirror.

Rate degree of belief currently (0–100).

Rate distress associated with this belief currently (0–100).

Stage 1

Ask patient to spend five minutes gazing at herself – body shape, appearance, parts she feels are overweight or ugly – in a full-length mirror.

Repeat ratings of belief and distress.

Stage 2

Ask patient to engage in a distracting task, such as a computer game or word puzzle, for five minutes.

Repeat ratings.

Example experiment 2

NB: This needs to be carried out over several consecutive days.

Ask patient to identify key negative belief when she searches for and buys only diet or very low calorie food.

Rate degree of belief currently (0–100).

Rate distress associated with this belief currently (0–100).

Stage 1

Behave as usual – searching for and reading about diet and very low calorie food – for three days.

Repeat ratings once a day at the same time.

Stage 2

Change behaviour – stop searching for and reading about diet and very low calorie food – for three days.

Repeat ratings.

Table 9.3 Fears and negative predictions associated with relinquishing problem behaviours

Problem behaviour	Predictions if the behaviour were to cease
Buying unnecessary stocks of food	It will be unbearable if I want to binge and there's no food in the house.
Wearing baggy clothes	People will see how fat and ugly my arms and legs are.
Avoiding high calorie and non-diet foods	I'll overeat, and get fat.
Reading ingredients on food items in supermarkets	I'll balloon if I eat any high calorie foods.

can be seen in Table 9.2, many of the fears involve catastrophising and black and white thinking.

Guidance in how to complete the modified DTR form for positive beliefs is often necessary, even after the patient is proficient in using it to identify negative beliefs. This may be necessary because, for some patients, positive beliefs can be more difficult to identify at first than any negative beliefs.

A DTR form completed by a patient with BN for a positive belief can be seen in the box overleaf (see also Appendix 15, p. 238).

The patient has provided a brief description of the situation in which the thought occurred, the emotions and body sensations experienced and the associated thoughts. The key positive belief in the example has been identified and circled.

As for negative beliefs, it is important for the patient to demonstrate an ability to complete a DTR in the session before setting this as a homework task. It is also helpful to get the patient to think about any specific problems that she may have with identifying and recording her thoughts before going away, for example, with a record sheet on which to record key cognitions for homework.

CHALLENGING POSITIVE BELIEFS

Two verbal reattribution strategies are particularly useful when dealing with positive beliefs: examining the advantages and disadvantages of continuing to hold the belief, and reviewing the counter-evidence for the belief.

A COMPLETED DYSFUNCTIONAL THOUGHT RECORD SHEET FOR A POSITIVE BELIEF ABOUT EATING

Situation	Feelings / sensations	Beliefs	Behaviour
Meeting at work to review progress on the new project. Given some tasks and deadlines for the next stage that I don't think I can manage. I felt inefficient and inadequate. I can't bear to feel like this. I want to leave it all behind. I walked past the vending machine on the way back to my office and started to crave chocolate.	Depressed 80% Angry (with self) 70%	Chocolate will make me feel better – it will wipe out the bad feelings; I need a break, eating's an escape.	Went back to the vending machine and bought three cream eggs. I ate the eggs in the toilet because I didn't want anyone to see me. Then I took an early lunch and went to buy more food. Binged.

Advantages versus disadvantages analysis

This can be a useful first verbal strategy, in which the patient is asked to reflect on the advantages and disadvantages of having a particular positive belief, or categories of belief. The patient is initially asked to list all the advantages or reasons why she should or feels obliged to continue with the belief, even if these seem trivial or superficial. Next, she is asked to list all the disadvantages. The data should be used to highlight the discrepancy between the advantages and disadvantages, with an emphasis on the emotional and behavioural consequences of any disadvantages. Finally, the advantages should be questioned, and reconstructed, if possible, as additional disadvantages, when considered more rationally.

A useful form for recording advantages and disadvantages for a positive belief can be seen in the box, containing an example completed by a patient (see also Appendix 15, p. 239).

AN ADVANTAGES AND DISADVANTAGES ANALYSIS FOR A POSITIVE BELIEF

Positive belief

Eating will take my mind off my worries

Advantages	Disadvantages	Evaluation of advantages
It will provide me with relief, a break from feeling so anxious; I'll forget about my worries for a while; I'll be able to fall asleep for a bit.	It won't sort anything out – the problems will still be there when I wake up; in the past I've just started worrying all over again, and then I end up bingeing again, and again . . . it's a never-ending cycle; it makes me feel worse about myself in the longer term, and less inclined to try not to binge again next time.	I'm not sure how else I can deal with my worries. I'm not sure what else I can do. It feels like I have no other options.

Conclusion

Bingeing is only useful in the short term. Long term I need to think about dealing with my worries, and learn how to manage them better. I need to look at alternatives to bingeing.

Reviewing the counter-evidence

An alternative verbal strategy involves reviewing the evidence and counter-evidence for the positive belief. This can be accomplished with the help of a modified dysfunctional thought record form, a completed example of which can be seen in the box (see also Appendix 15, p. 240).

KEY POSITIVE BELIEF ABOUT EATING, AND THE EVIDENCE FOR IT

Situation	Feelings (0–100)	Beliefs (0–100)	Counter-evidence
Younger sister borrowed make-up without asking, and left it all in a mess. Had a big argument and said some hurtful things. She'll hate me now, I'm a bad person.	Angry 75% Upset 85% Guilty 90%	Eating will take away my worries 95% If I don't binge I'll go out of my mind with worry and guilt 90% Eating is a solution 100%	Eating does relieve my worry in the short term, but in the long term I feel worse and the problem is still there.

Conclusion
I need to find other ways to cope – worry and bingeing and vomiting doesn't get me anywhere – I need to talk to her and apologise.

Some useful questions to help reinterpreting positive beliefs about binge eating are suggested in the box.

USEFUL QUESTIONS TO REINTERPRET POSITIVE BELIEFS ABOUT BINGE EATING

In the past when I've believed that eating is a solution to coping with a problem, what have I learned from doing this? What's the worst that could happen if I don't binge? Realistically, what is most likely to happen? Would that be really so terrible? Would it be worse than bingeing?

How can I find out next time I feel like this?

If it does feel bad, how can I cope without bingeing? What could I do instead? What could I say to myself that would help? What would help me to put that into practice next time this happens?

What would someone else suggest or say? What would my best friend say if they knew I felt like this? How would they try to help? How can I try to put that into practice myself?

What would I say to someone else in my position? How would I help them not to binge? What would I do or suggest? How could I put that into practice for myself?

Two strategies that are particularly valuable in dealing with positive beliefs are considering the long-term perspective and introducing flexibility into thinking.

Examining the long-term perspective

Many of the advantages or benefits that patients derive from their positive beliefs are very short term. Thus, it can be very useful to encourage patients to consider what the longer term impact of, for example, continuing to hold a particular belief might be. This might entail patients drawing on both current and past evidence and contemplating how they are likely to feel in say half an hour's time, or over a much longer time frame, say one or two years' time. Useful questions might include: 'What's happened in the past?', 'If you continue as you are, how will things change?' Often, as the time period is extended, the patient is able to see increasingly significant disadvantages to their positive belief. An example of asking such a question of one patient is presented below.

Rebecca believed 'Eating/bingeing takes away painful feelings'. She believed this to be 90 per cent true.

Therapist: When you got a grade C in your exam and considered yourself to be a failure, at that time how did you think eating would help?

Patient: It's just that when I eat I don't have to feel so bad – it sort of deadens the pain somehow.

Therapist: So, eating seems helpful in stopping you from feeling bad, is that right?

Patient: Yes, that's how it works. I feel that I deserve something nice and find food and eating a great comfort.

Therapist: At what point during bingeing does eating no longer comfort and soothe you?; how does bingeing make you feel as it goes on?

Patient: After five minutes I stop tasting the food and go onto automatic pilot. I'm not really aware of having any thoughts or feelings while eating. However, when I stop I don't feel very good, I feel sick, miserable, and most of all angry with myself knowing that I've done it again and let myself down.

Therapist: So eating initially provides comfort and momentarily reduces painful feelings, but then it becomes a source of distress and leads to self-critical thoughts. Have I understood you correctly?

Patient: Yes, that's exactly it. Food is comforting, it's just that ultimately I hate how it makes me feel.

Therapist: On balance, stepping back and taking a long-term view, how useful is bingeing as a strategy for coping with painful feelings; what does your experience tell you?

Patient: I know that it doesn't help and makes me feel worse. I have regrets every time I do it, but I feel if I don't binge I'll just go crazy and wouldn't know what to do with my feelings. I might become hysterical and start screaming and make a fool of myself. I don't feel as though I have any option.

Therapist: It's as though you are describing feeling trapped; you can either binge and feel bad, or don't binge but also feel bad. Perhaps it might be useful to understand a bit more about your fears of not bingeing, especially your fear of going crazy; what do you think?

The therapist then proceeded to discover exactly what the fears would involve for the patient and, with the collaboration of the patient, proceeded to challenge this belief as well.

Some useful questions for introducing a longer term perspective can be seen in the following box.

USEFUL QUESTIONS TO INTRODUCE A LONGER TERM PERSPECTIVE

Although in the short term eating appears to be helpful, what are the longer term consequences?

How do you feel later, say when you have actually had a binge?

What are the long-term consequences – do these outweigh any short-term relief?

Introducing alternative strategies for self regulation (increase flexibility)

Patients who have positive beliefs may have few alternative strategies for coping with the cognitive and emotional distress that they are likely to experience when these are discarded. On occasions patients may even substitute bingeing for other dysfunctional compensatory strategies such as drinking alcohol. Patients with positive beliefs may need considerable help to devise and implement alternative ways of coping and managing their distress. Useful questions to introduce flexibility into thinking can be seen in the box below.

USEFUL QUESTIONS TO INTRODUCE FLEXIBILITY INTO THINKING

How else can I think about that?

What alternative way of thinking about that would be more or most useful?

What would someone else think about that; what would one of my friends think, say or do if I told them about that thought?

What would I advise someone else to do, say or think in that situation?

What about the longer term – what's most useful when I think about that, is this going to be just as useful to me in a year's time?

How could I start to try and change my belief?

What could I do as a first step?

BEHAVIOURAL EXPERIMENTS

As with negative beliefs, it is usually helpful to follow verbal restructuring (fairly quickly) with behavioural experiments designed to reinforce and extend what has been learned from the verbal thought challenging. The reasoning behind this advice was outlined in more detailed in Chapter 8.

The main reasons for conducting behavioural experiments at this stage should be carefully reiterated, if necessary, to the patient.

As before, the patient's idiosyncratic meaning of the key negative automatic thought needs to be elicited and key cognitions identified that are to be challenged in the experiment. The main cognitions are then operationalised in terms of clear observable behaviour, asking questions such as 'What would that look like in practice?' Based on the thoughts elicited, a testable prediction is then established.

The sequence of steps involved in planning and conducting behavioural experiments should be carefully explained. The PETS (prepare, expose, test, summarise) model (Wells 1997) is useful here, just as it was for negative beliefs. The steps in the PETS model can be seen in Appendix 9.

A behavioural experiment to test positive beliefs

Below is a sample experiment, presented in the PETS framework and designed to challenge a positive belief about eating. It is important to note that the most useful way to derive predictions from positive beliefs is, in general, to rephrase them, using questions such as 'What do you think will happen?', 'What is the worst that could happen in this situation if you don't go ahead and binge?'

Prepare (P)

(Use a revised DTR to focus on the patient's key positive belief about eating.) Key cognition: 'If I don't binge, then I'll go crazy'. Identify evidence for and against the thought. Use verbal challenging of the evidence that supports the thought.

As noted above, behavioural experiments need to be specific with measurable behavioural targets or outcomes. The prediction needs to be defined and described in the patient's own words. For example, Emma's specific prediction around the above thought might be 'If I don't binge, then I will feel really bad, my head will explode, I'll lose it and completely embarrass myself'. The patient should then be asked to rate her belief in this thought. A scale from 0 = 'I do not believe this at all' to 100 = 'I am completely convinced that this is true' is useful here.

Expose (E)

The patient then exposes herself to the difficult situation or feeling (not bingeing).

Test (T)

She is asked to refrain from bingeing, for a predetermined amount of time (which can be increased in graded steps up to the maximum the patient believes will provide disconfirmatory evidence for her belief). Later on this can be coupled with a paradoxical manoeuvre, for example, trying to make the situation worse, during exposure to a situation that has often triggered bingeing, thus providing an even more stringent test of the belief.

Summarise (S)

The patient and therapist should then discuss the results of the experiment in terms of the case conceptualisation. The belief should also be re-rated by the patient using the same (0–100) rating scale as before.

Further experiments

Together, therapist and patient should then plan further experiments for homework. The aim is to challenge the negative prediction that maintains the positive belief and discover disconfirmatory evidence. Thus further experiments should be targeted at achieving this (and with the aim of decreasing belief in the positive belief). Further experiments can involve repeating the same experiment, as suggested above, with increasing time delays.

As noted in previous chapters, it is also important to reflect on the process, help the patient to develop the skill of setting up their own experiments, and prepare for the unexpected.

Ideas for experiments to test positive beliefs

Some ideas for behavioural experiments to test positive beliefs that can be conducted either in the session or by the patient for homework are shown in the box overleaf.

IDEAS FOR BEHAVIOURAL EXPERIMENTS TO CHALLENGE POSITIVE BELIEFS

Prediction

Eating will help me feel better when I'm upset.

Experiment

Test out and compare the effects of two ways of behaving when upset – eating (what I do normally) and an alternative activity that will engage and occupy me (e.g. solving complex puzzles such as crosswords or Sudoku, counting backwards in 7s for 10 minutes). Monitor and record distress levels before, during and after engaging in the two activities. Compare the results from the two behaviours.

Prediction

If I don't eat when I'm miserable, I'll lose control.

Experiment

Define 'losing control' carefully and in a form that can be measured. Plan not to eat next time I feel miserable. Ask what's the very worst thing that could happen? If that did happen how would I deal with that? Monitor and record the behaviours/feelings that constitute 'losing control'. What happens in the short term and in the longer term? Does the very worst thing happen? If it does, how did I deal with that?

Using distraction (behavioural or cognitive) of some kind can be very useful as an alternative activity but it is important to remember that the task should engage attention in order to be successful. Activities must engage attention/memory sufficiently to break any attentional or cognitive bias. Some ideas for appropriate distracting activities can be seen in the box opposite.

IDEAS FOR DISTRACTION

Count backwards from 100 in 7s.

Recite a poem from memory.

Focus on an object in the environment and describe it in detail out loud.

Ask questions or 'interrogate' events or objects outside the self.

Complete complex puzzles – crosswords, Sudoku.

Play a demanding video game.

A behavioural experiments worksheet

The specially designed worksheet presented in Chapter 8 can also be used when planning and recording the outcome of behavioural experiments with positive beliefs. A completed example of such a sheet, completed with a positive belief, can be seen in the box overleaf.

TROUBLESHOOTING

Tackling positive beliefs using verbal restructuring and behavioural experiments is not always straightforward. Some of the potential problems and suggestions for ways to deal with them in relation to negative beliefs presented at the end of Chapter 8 are also applicable to positive beliefs. These include ways to deal with 'yes but' statements, and ideas for troubleshooting when experiments do not go to plan.

Managing potentially dangerous behaviour

Patients with BN are sometimes tempted to engage in potentially harmful behaviour towards themselves (e.g. cutting). This is never helpful, and such patients may benefit from learning how to use potentially distracting strategies and activities, including some of those outlined in Table 8.11, that are sufficiently demanding to engage attention or memory and thus interrupt the cycle of self-focused attention that maintains distress about eating, weight and shape concerns.

A COMPLETED BEHAVIOURAL EXPERIMENTS WORKSHEET FOR A POSITIVE BELIEF

Thought I want to test (Belief 0–100)	Situation in which I'll test it	Test strategy (what I will do)	Outcome (Belief 0–100)
The things I used to enjoy when upset won't help me now. When I feel bad only food helps 95%	Draw up a list of engaging activities that I used to find comforting when upset. Compare carrying out one of these when I feel bad with eating (what I normally do). Monitor and record the effect of both behaviours.	Try playing a computer game for 20 minutes – choose one that needs a lot of concentration – as my engaging activity.	Worked well. Re-rated belief as 30%, compared to no change in belief when I compared this to a condition in which I engaged in my usual behaviour (eating).

It is always important to make a careful risk assessment when patients describe fears of engaging in extreme and harmful behaviours. Although these are often primarily fears made worse by worry that they will be acted on, in a small minority of cases patients will have previously carried out such behaviours – it is important to assess the future risk carefully, before carrying out behaviour experiments related to such fears.

CHAPTER SUMMARY AND KEY POINTS

This chapter has outlined strategies to identify and challenge positive beliefs.

Key points to remember include the following:

◉ Positive beliefs play an important role in maintaining binge eating and other problematic eating behaviour-related behaviours.
◉ Positive beliefs can usefully be recorded on a modified dysfunctional thought record, and challenged initially using verbal reattribution.
◉ Useful strategies include examining the advantages versus disadvantages, reviewing the counter-evidence, taking a longer term perspective and introducing flexibility into thinking.
◉ Behavioural experiments have an important role, and a worksheet to record these can be helpful.
◉ It is important to undertake a risk assessment when a patient describes fears of engaging in extreme and harmful behaviours.

Negative self beliefs

This chapter outlines ways to introduce negative self belief work in bulimia nervosa and how to help patients create an alternative to their negative self beliefs. It introduces Padesky's prejudice model (Padesky 1990) as a useful metaphor for understanding how negative self beliefs are maintained and suggests ways to build or construct a new, alternative belief. A number of general strategies as well as some specific to BN for challenging old negative self beliefs and/or building up new beliefs are discussed, including strategies that draw on schema theory. These include use of the core belief worksheet, cognitive continua, historical tests of belief, a positive data log, behavioural experiments and flashcards. The use of imagery modification is also described.

Challenging negative and positive beliefs about eating may well lead to some initial shift in negative self beliefs. For example, examining evidence against negative automatic thoughts may impact on negative self beliefs in reducing the degree of belief. At the point of starting core belief work the patient might have already made changes in this area. However, the early work is not usually sufficient in itself; many patients benefit from focused core belief work.

LEVELS OF BELIEF CHANGE

Schema may be tackled at different levels. Freeman and Dattilio (1992) identify a change continuum from greatest to least schematic change. In this model, restructuring involves destruction of dysfunctional schemas and building of adaptive schemas. Likened by Freeman in conference presentations to 'urban renewal' (e.g. Freeman 2001), this is not always practical or possible. Modification involves attenuating old and strengthening new schema. This is often a more practical option. Schema reinterpretation involves helping patients to reinterpret their lifestyles and schemas in more functional ways. For example, patients might recognise that being a perfectionist was part of their make-up but choose to meet this need by employment that values this skill, rather than being driven by compulsive beliefs that result in distress. Finally, schema camouflage consists of helping the patient to acquire the skills that will cover up the schematic problems.

INTRODUCING CORE BELIEF WORK

Core belief work can be complex, difficult and emotionally painful for the patient. The shift to core belief work needs to be introduced appropriately, so that the patient understands that the focus and strategies will be changing. In particular, patients need to understand the different ways in which schema can function, and contribute to their problems. Three main processes have been identified: schema avoidance, schema maintenance and schema compensation (Young and Klosko 1994; Young et al. 2003).

Schema avoidance refers to cognitive and behavioural strategies used by the patient to avoid experiencing emotion as a consequence of the presence of an associated core belief.

When Jody felt distressed her main cognitive strategy involved using thought suppression or trying not to think about the thought. An example of behavioural avoidance would involve avoiding a situation that has become associated with the activation of negative self beliefs. Jody would avoid trying on clothes in a communal changing room.

Schema maintenance refers to strategies which reinforce or keep the emotions and beliefs alive and active.

Georgia was training as a dancer and was in a competitive environment where slimness was valued. Her tutors would draw attention to any observable changes in weight and shape, which reinforced her belief 'I can only succeed if I'm thin/If I gain weight then I've failed'.

Schema compensation refers to the ways in which the patient may seek to overcome or 'make up' for a belief and its emotional consequences. Clues for schema compensation behaviours are often reflected in conditional assumptions.

Becky believed, 'To be successful is to be slim: unless I'm slim I've failed'. Dieting was Becky's strategy for compensating for the belief, 'I'm a failure'. This may result in behaviour that seems to be directly opposed to the actual belief.

Glenn Waller has written widely on the application of Young's model to eating disorders, including on how schema driven processes may differ in BN when compared to anorexia nervosa (e.g. Waller et al. 2007).

THE PREJUDICE MODEL

We have found Padesky's prejudice model (Padesky 1990) helpful in introducing the concept of schema driven processing to patients with bulimia nervosa. This strategy provides a metaphor, elicited through guided discovery to help patients understand the schema driven processes that maintain negative self beliefs. Below is an example of one way of introducing this that we have found useful.

Therapist: I'd like to talk to you about prejudice. Can you think of someone you know who has a prejudice that you can see is wrong?

The patient chooses an acquaintance, Matt, who believes that fat people are lazy. The therapist, using guided discovery, then asks for examples of times when her friend has expressed his prejudice and several examples of situations are provided.

Therapist: If Matt was introduced to an overweight person who didn't conform to his view, what would he say about them?

Patient: Well, he wouldn't believe it and say, that can't be true. Or he'll say that person is different from the rest and not typical of most fat people. He would then get on his soap box and go on about all the lazy fat people he has encountered.

The therapist should aim to elicit several of the processes that may operate to distort information that contradicts a schema (e.g. distortion, discounting the positive). More information on the types of biases that patients with eating disorders may have can be obtained from Waller et al. (2007), Beck et al. (1979) and Burns (1980).

Therapist: What do you think would happen if we tried to change his prejudice?

Patient: He's so convinced that he's right, it would be impossible.

Therapist: How could we start to help him view his belief differently?

Patient: Perhaps by making him notice the fat person who is doing well more, telling him he is not looking at the full picture?

Therapist: What do you think are the similarities between prejudice and core beliefs?

Patient: Yeah, when you believe something it's hard to believe anything else. When someone gives me a compliment I think they are just saying it and don't mean it, or if they say I look healthy I immediately assume they are saying, you're fat.

By now patients have often grasped the idea that their core beliefs act as some kind of prejudice. The therapist then checks out whether the patient's idiosyncratic beliefs do indeed act in this way, using examples of situations previously discussed in which the client has distorted, discounted, made an exception or not noticed relevant information.

HOW TO BUILD OR CONSTRUCT A NEW BELIEF: SOME RULES AND TIPS

Although negative core beliefs are associated with high levels of emotional distress, many patients derive comfort from their familiarity. Modifying these beliefs in the absence of constructing a new positive and adaptive belief might increase levels of distress. It is important to construct a new belief before or in parallel with attempting to challenge the old belief. Below are some ideas for doing this.

Positive Core Belief Questionnaire

A useful first step can be to ask the patient to complete the Positive Core Belief Questionnaire (PCBQ: Noad et al. 2006). This measure is similar in format to the Negative Self Belief subscale of the Eating Disorder Belief Questionnaire (Cooper et al. 1997). The PCBQ, and its scoring details, can be seen in Appendix 14. It can provide a general idea of the sorts of beliefs the patient might learn to endorse.

Creating a positive or alternative belief

It is, however, very important to identify any idiosyncratic beliefs that the patient (in her own words) might accept as an alternative to her negative core belief(s). Below is an example of a dialogue which aims to achieve this for the negative core belief 'I'm not good enough'.

Therapist: If you no longer believed that you are not good enough – how would you like to see your self?

Patient: I don't know, it's difficult to see myself any other way.

Therapist: How about if we explore possible options for developing an alternative belief; we could brainstorm some ideas, is that all right?

Patient: OK, but this feels really uncomfortable. I'm not used to thinking about myself in a positive way.

Therapist: You don't have to have a high degree of belief in whatever new belief we come up with right now, what we need to do over time is to collect evidence that supports it. How about if you just say the first thing that comes into your mind when I ask you the question – how would you like to think about yourself if you no longer believed that you were not good enough?

Patient: Worthwhile, popular, liked, accomplished, a good person, loved, good enough.

Therapist: That's great, you did really well to come up with all those ideas. Which belief shall we go with?

Patient: I'm good enough.

Therapist: OK – so how much do you believe I'm good enough right now out of 0 to 100 per cent, if 100 per cent is that you're completely convinced its true?

Patient: 20 per cent.

Some examples of typical old and new core beliefs from patients with BN can be seen in Table 10.1. These range from beliefs that are clearly positive (and direct opposites to the negative) in tone, to beliefs that are more qualified. In many cases the latter are more realistic for patients to aim for as such beliefs tend to be more adaptive in everyday life.

Some questions are particularly helpful when generating alternative or new core beliefs. Questions we have found useful can be seen in the box opposite.

Table 10.1 Examples of old and new core beliefs

Old beliefs	New beliefs
I'm worthless	I'm worthwhile/I'm a good person
I'm weak	I'm resilient/strong
I'm a failure	I'm good enough
I'm unlovable	I'm lovable
I'm inadequate	I'm capable and able
I'm boring	I'm compassionate/interesting
I'm stupid	I'm intelligent/bright enough
I'm ugly	I'm attractive

USEFUL QUESTIONS TO GENERATE NEW CORE BELIEFS

1. If you no longer believed that you were (name core belief) how would you like to see yourself or think of yourself?
2. What would be a more accurate belief to have as an alternative to . . .?
3. What word(s) capture how you would like to see yourself (the patient can be encouraged to brainstorm here)?
4. What comes to mind when you think of positive alternatives?
5. Which of these words would be a realistic new view of you? (Occasionally patients might come out with a hyper-positive new belief (e.g. I'm totally amazing) which is usually in jest because they feel embarrassed and find it difficult to consider viewing themselves in any other way but negative.)
6. How much do you believe the belief (new belief) right now? Rate intellectual and emotional belief. How much do you believe it to be true intellectually? How much do you feel it to be true?

Sometimes patients struggle to generate a new or alternative belief. If this is the case, it can be useful to ask them to conduct a survey, for example among their friends, to find out what three things their friends value about them. A new or alternative belief can then usually be constructed using this information.

WEAKENING OLD BELIEFS AND BUILDING NEW BELIEFS

Strategies and exercises to weaken old beliefs and build new beliefs will now be described. They include the core belief worksheet (Beck 1995), cognitive continua (e.g. Beck and Freeman 1990; Padesky and Greenberger 1995), historical tests of beliefs (Beck and Freeman 1990), positive data logs (Beck and Freeman 1990), behavioural experiments (Wells 1997) and the development and use of flashcards (e.g. Padesky and Greenberger 1995).

Core belief worksheet

This is a useful first strategy that is not dissimilar to the strategy outlined in Chapters 8 and 9 where evidence was gathered against negative and positive beliefs about eating. The difference here is that the therapist also encourages the patient to reframe, or think in a slightly different (more helpful or realistic) way about the evidence that the patient identifies in support of his or her negative core belief.

The new core belief should be identified using the strategies and questions listed above. Both old and new beliefs should be rated for degree of belief (to enable change in belief to be determined after the exercise has been completed). As before, a scale from 0 to 100 per cent is useful, with 0 anchored at 'I do not believe this thought at all' and 100 at 'I am completely convinced that this thought is true'. The focus of the exercise is on the positive – with the initial identification of evidence contradicting the old belief and supporting the new belief. Any evidence for the old belief is then reframed. The exercise may lead to some modifications in the actual beliefs – these should be recorded, together with belief in them at the end of the exercise. A completed core belief worksheet for a patient carrying out this exercise can be seen here (see also Appendix 15, p. 242).

COMPLETED CORE BELIEF WORKSHEET

Old core belief	New core belief
I'm a failure	I'm good enough
What is the most you've believed this belief this week (intellectually and emotionally 0–100%?)	**What is the most you've believed this belief this week (intellectually and emotionally 0–100%?)**
Intellectually 70% Emotionally 100%	Intellectually 40% Emotionally 10%
What is the least you've believed it this week (intellectually and emotionally 0–100%?)	**What is the least you've believed it this week (intellectually and emotionally 0–100%?)**
Intellectually 50% Emotionally 70%	Intellectually 10% Emotionally 5%

Meaning of the old belief (ask patient to operationalise the belief)	Meaning of the new belief
Unless everything I do is faultless I see it as a failure. It is my fault when things go wrong because I should know better. You can always improve and do better, there is no excuse. The moment I succeed in something I do the pleasure is short lived because I'm striving and working towards my next goal. When people praise me for what I've accomplished I feel uncomfortable because I just don't see it that way. I need to be critical of myself because it's motivational and helps me get things done, otherwise I'd be lazy. I constantly feel that I don't live up to other people's expectations, especially my father's. I know that I'm not stupid and can't bear the idea of being ordinary. I have to achieve something special to be recognised. Failure is not an option.	Good enough some of the time would mean that I would be able to relax the high standards that I apply to everything. Letting myself off the hook would give me more time, I might even learn to relax some of the time. Learning to recognise and make a realistic judgement that some things are less important than others and to prioritise what I do. Not beating myself up for the slightest mistake and learning to let some things go.
Evidence against old belief (in the last month)	**Evidence to support new belief (in the last month)**
Dinner party went badly, but didn't blame myself for the one hour delay in serving the main course. People seemed to enjoy themselves anyway. Got a 2:1 for an essay, was expecting a first but was able to cope with this. On the two occasions that I binged I was able to eat less food and didn't vomit. I didn't see this as the end of the world and didn't blame myself.	When I couldn't get into my jeans I was calm and didn't panic and didn't immediately want to restrict or binge. I was criticised by my tutor and able to put my mistake down to experience instead of going on a mad binge. I said no to going out with friends because I had work to do and didn't worry about what they thought of me.

Some useful questions to help a patient complete the core belief worksheet can be seen in the box.

USEFUL QUESTIONS TO HELP COMPLETE A CORE BELIEF WORKSHEET

1. How much do you believe the old belief (both intellectually and emotionally) out of 0–100%, if 100% is that you are convinced that it's true?
2. What does the old belief mean to you?
3. How much do you believe the new belief (both intellectually and emotionally) out of 0–100%, if 100% is that you are completely convinced that it's true?
4. What does the new belief mean?
5. In the last month what evidence do you have against the old belief (identify situations/events)?
6. In the last month what evidence do you have that supports the new belief (identify situations/events)?
7. If you were to ask a good friend/partner for reasons why this old belief isn't true in the last month what would they put on the list?
8. If you were to ask a good friend/partner for evidence to support the new belief in the last month what would they say?

Note: when doing this exercise it is important to agree to stay with the facts of the situation and not with the patient's distorted interpretations.

Cognitive continua

Cognitive continua can be used in several different ways when working with core beliefs. We describe one way (use of dichotomous labels) that we have found particularly useful with BN patients.

Each end of the continuum should be labelled, one end with the patient's negative core belief, and the other with an agreed opposite. The patient then marks where she thinks she currently falls on this continuum. Using guided discovery the therapist asks if there has been a time recently when the patient has been somewhere else on the continuum. The therapist might need to prompt, for example, what about the time when (the therapist then refers to past situations that the patient has described). The therapist might also ask, 'Where would X [name a good friend] put you on this continuum?' Other people can also be plotted on the continuum. The aim is to help the patient recognise that her degree of belief changes over time and is not set in stone. This is followed up by asking the patient for the most extreme meanings or examples of the beliefs at each end of the continuum, by asking, for example, 'Hypothetically, what quality/personality trait might someone of that description have (at each end of the continuum separately)', and creating a list of dichotomous variables on a series of continua that mirror the original two beliefs.

Isobel's original continuum was labelled 'I'm unlovable' at one end and 'I'm lovable' at the other end. Traits she identified as characteristic of someone who was extremely unlovable included being fat and unattractive, and not having a boyfriend or husband.

An example of extreme labels on a cognitive continuum can be seen here.

in control	out of control
0%	100%
Sticking to diet	Bingeing
Slim	Fat
Popular and liked	Criticised
Never gaining weight	Weight escalating
Perfection	Slob

Useful questions to generate a list of these extremes (or anchors) after having identified the original two anchor points (or ends of the continuum) can be seen in the box.

USEFUL QUESTIONS TO GENERATE A LIST OF EXTREME QUALITIES

1. What does *I'm worthless* (or other belief) mean to you?
2. What would someone who's *really worthless* look like and how would they behave?
3. What does *worthwhile* (or other belief) mean to you?
4. How would someone who was a *worthwhile* person behave and what would they look like?

After generating the two lists of extreme labels, the patient rates herself on each one. Finally, after considering what she has done, and where these ratings fall, she goes back and rates herself again on the original dichotomous continuum (see Appendix 15, p. 243). The completed example is shown here.

different			fit in
	Rating 1	Rating 2	
	X	X	

0%			100%
No friends			People to go out with
		X	

0%			100%
Don't share others' interests			Like some things others do (e.g. bands, music)
	X		

0%			100%
Hated by others			Has some friends
	X		

0%			100%
No personality (e.g. is boring)			Can have a good conversation
	X		

0%			100%
No shared values			At least two common values/goals
		X	

0%			100%
Looks weird – very unusual dress style, stands out			Dresses similarly to others, own style
	X		

0%			100%

The lists of variables or mini continua created breaks down the meaning of the extreme labels. After completing the rating it is typical to find some shift is evident, and the patient has moved a little towards the more 'positive' end. It is helpful to reflect with the patient on how and why any change has occurred. Recording this, using the patient's own words, at the bottom of the exercise can be useful. An example of one patient's conclusion after completing such an exercise can be seen in the box.

CONCLUSION FOLLOWING CONTINUA EXERCISE

I was pretty much completely convinced that I was a bad person at the start (belief = 90%). It's gone down now (belief = 60%). I think breaking it up like that made me see how complicated it all was – not just black and white. When I thought what a really bad person would be like, then I could see that I'm not like that. I was surprised in fact that when I thought about what others would say – they'd say I was more at the other end. I don't always believe them, but then I'm never like the really bad person so I guess I need to rethink how I see myself a bit.

Historical test of beliefs

This exercise can be helpful for those who have experienced negative experiences in early life, but have not necessarily connected them with their current distress or managed to reframe them into more manageable memories. Both old and new beliefs are identified and the patient makes a prediction about what she expects to find if she reviews her past. Evidence consistent with the old belief is identified and reframed. Evidence is also collected that contradicts the old belief. The exercise is split into different periods of time, so that evidence can be linked to developmental milestones; for example, it would be unreasonable to expect a 4 year old to possess abilities and knowledge more typical of a 12 year old. This can help shift blame away from the child. Useful questions to help with this exercise can be seen in the top box overleaf.

As with the other exercises described in this chapter core beliefs are rated before and after the exercise, and mini summaries are sought during and at the end of the exercise. Patients may need help with these: useful questions to ask to help the patient summarise the results of the exercise are included in the bottom box overleaf.

USEFUL QUESTIONS TO REFRAME EVIDENCE CONSISTENT WITH OLD BELIEF AND TO ELICIT INCONSISTENT EVIDENCE

1. Where do you think the idea that you are *unlovable* (or other belief) first started?
2. Where were you, how old were you, what were you doing at that time (setting the scene)?
3. How did you make sense of that experience or event etc.? What did that mean to you?
4. How did you think and feel about yourself at that time?
5. How were you viewing that situation as a child?
6. If you were observing another child in a similar situation now how do you think the child would view the situation?
7. As an adult looking back at that situation what do you know now that you didn't know then that could help you understand more about what was happening?
8. What do you think the reasons might be for why X (person) behaved in that way?
9. If you were to give an alternative explanation to the child based upon what you know now, what would you say?

USEFUL QUESTIONS TO SUMMARISE THE RESULTS OF THE EVIDENCE ON HISTORICAL TESTS OF BELIEFS

We've tried to understand the reasons why you believed X during the ages of Y to Z. We've also looked at the evidence against the belief, as well as evidence that might support an alternative view. What have you learned or discovered? In what way is this new information helpful? How have you been behaving in ways that are consistent with your old beliefs? How might you behave in ways that are consistent with your new beliefs? What impact will this knowledge or new ways of behaving have on your bingeing and vomiting, your relationship with others, your view of yourself?

The positive data log

This is a long-term strategy that takes place over several months. It was used by Beck (e.g. Beck et al. 1979) and has been termed a 'positive data log' (for example, by Padesky 1994). Once new or alternative beliefs have begun to be developed then patients can be encouraged to keep a small diary in which they record any experiences that they have which are consistent with the new beliefs that they are trying to develop or build up. An example page from a positive data log can be seen in the box.

SAMPLE PAGE FROM A POSITIVE DATA LOG

Evidence to support the belief that people accept me for me and not because of how I look:

- I was invited to a party on Friday. People seemed interested in what I had to say. Dan asked if I wanted to go out and see a film later in the week.
- Was approached by my supervisor to teach undergraduates. My supervisor must value my academic abilities.
- Did a survey to find out the five most important characteristics that people valued in me. No one mentioned weight or shape. People said lovely things about me – that I was fun to be with, and a good, kind friend.
- My jeans were tight and I didn't panic. Even though I was convinced that I'd gained weight and felt that my stomach was sticking out it didn't stop me from going out clubbing. I was chatted up twice.

It is usually important to review the log each therapy session, and to look over with the patient what kinds of things she has been recording. Patients sometimes need practice in learning how to use the strategy effectively. Initially, for example, they may need some time with the therapist to identify the kinds of things that have happened, or that they have done over the week, that it might be useful to record.

A variant on this, which incorporates the positive data log, is to suggest that the patient keep a scrapbook in which they put evidence that helps to support their new beliefs in a range of different media. This might include copies of emails, cards or notes that they have received, as well as the usual written, reflective record used in a straightforward positive data log.

Behavioural experiments

Behavioural experiments have a crucial role. The exercises described so far in this chapter will be most effective if they are followed up by behavioural experiments to test an aspect of the issue that has been discussed. Most importantly, a test of predictions derived from a negative core belief will be particularly valuable.

Exactly the same principles apply as were outlined for behavioural experiments in Chapters 8 and 9. An example of an experiment, developed using the PETS framework, can be seen in the box.

A BEHAVIOURAL EXPERIMENT TO TEST OUT PREDICTIONS FROM A NEGATIVE CORE BELIEF

Prepare

Key cognition/prediction: I'll look silly, drop my papers all over the floor, stumble, people will laugh (prediction from core belief – I'm an embarrassment).

Expose

Go to the meeting, stay until the end (avoidance), don't drink more than one cup of coffee (safety behaviour). Use an external focus of attention.

Test

Carry out plan – and ask two questions (disconfirmatory manoeuvre).

Summarise

I was really nervous, but I didn't drop anything. I asked three questions (disconfirmatory manoeuvre), one more than I had planned, and decided to have a glass of juice not coffee. I also focused on what was happening outside of me. No one laughed when I asked my questions – people seemed pleased that I had raised the points. I did leave a bit earlier than I had intended – and I need to work on that – maybe repeat the experiment after trying to work out what might help me stay right to the very end?

Flashcards

These can be useful reminders of important points learned or understood in treatment, or summaries of information that patients may find useful in particular situations. Index cards or self-adhesive notes can be useful for these, depending on whether they are to be kept in a handy drawer or bag, or affixed to a cupboard or fridge. Ideally, they should be·hand-written by the patient so that they are participating fully in the process, and having the flashcard written in their own handwriting will help make it harder to dispute. A sample flashcard template is in Appendix 15 (p. 244) and an example of one used by our patients can be seen in the box.

SAMPLE FLASHCARD TEMPLATE AND EXAMPLE

When my core belief (e.g. I'm unlovable) is triggered I start to think . . . (e.g. no one likes me).

This makes me feel . . . (e.g. sad, depressed).

When I'm thinking and feeling like this my way of coping is to binge eat . . .

However, while binge eating helps in the short term, in the long term I feel . . . (e.g. worried, panicky).

List all the evidence against the core belief (e.g. I'm unlovable).

(There are people who like me; I have a good relationship with my cousin; I get asked to social occasions.)

Right now, what I need to do is (for example):

- Distract myself
- Self-soothe
- Examine my positive data log
- Look over my notes on 'evidence against' this belief.

IMAGERY MODIFICATION

Some negative core beliefs are very resistant to change. Strong 'emotional' belief can be particularly hard to shift, and may remain relatively high even after 'rational' belief has reduced. Typically, patients may say, of such a belief, 'I know it's not really true, but it still feels like it is'.

One way we have found useful in modifying emotional belief, especially when rational belief has been significantly reduced using some of the strategies described earlier in this chapter, is to use imagery modification. We have some preliminary experimental evidence for the efficacy of this procedure in patients with BN (Cooper et al. 2007b). The procedure involves identifying a relevant memory from early childhood that encapsulates the patient's negative core beliefs, and then working actively with the patient using imaginal strategies on the memory to restructure and reinterpret the beliefs at the heart of the memory.

The mechanism involved in producing belief change in this procedure is not well understood. Self beliefs often resemble memories or events from the past and are closely associated in meaning (Somerville and Cooper 2007; Somerville et al. 2007), suggesting that they may be 'fused' with them in some way. One possibility is that imaginal strategies such as those we describe here have a metacognitive function, that is, they enable patients to see their beliefs and memories as representations rather than events. As such they may alter the way in which the patient relates to them.

A proforma, based on that described in Wells and Hackmann (1993) and containing useful questions for conducting this type of intervention, can be seen in the box.

PROFORMA FOR IMAGERY INTERVENTION

What's your earliest recollection of having the thoughts and/or feelings associated with the thoughts?

What's your most upsetting or worst memory of having the thoughts and/or feelings associated with the thoughts and/or feelings associated with the thoughts when you were a child?

Can you tell me a bit about the memory?
How old were you?

What did you think about yourself as a result of this event? What did it say or mean about you?

When you think and/or feel X is there anything you can do to change how you think or feel?
Do you think the thought/feeling is connected to your bingeing/dieting (and/or other eating disorder-related behaviours)?
Is that (eating disorder-related behaviour) helping with this thought/feeling?
If it makes you feel worse what keeps it going?

What would happen if you didn't do this?
What's the worst that could happen?
How do you think that works?

Do you still believe these things? Do these thoughts reflect your general beliefs or feelings about yourself?

What are you (the child) thinking?
What are you feeling?
What meaning do you draw from what is happening/the situation?
Why do you think this is happening?
What do you think about yourself as a result of this event?
What rules for living are you constructing?
What interpretation are you making about (for example) your sense of control, safety, lovability, worthiness, sense of belonging/connectedness to others etc.

Do you believe these things now as an adult?

Is there another view?
What do you think others would say?
What would you as an adult now say about someone else/a child in that position?

Who would you like to communicate with?
What would you like/do you need to hear from them?
Is there anything else you need or want?
What would the adult/safe person say or do in response?
What would you like to do now?
What would you like to say to the adult/safe person?
What would help with this?
What would you like to happen?

Identifying an early memory

The first step is to identify an early memory closely associated with or linked to the negative core beliefs. Clinically, the relevant beliefs should be clear to both the therapist and patient by now, so the first task is to ask the patient to bring the beliefs, and any associated feelings, to mind. This is often best done by asking the patient to close their eyes and concentrate hard on getting themselves into experiencing the beliefs.

Questions should then be used to help the patient identify the earliest and/or worst early memory that they can recall that is linked to these beliefs.

Once a specific example has been identified, it is helpful to obtain a general idea of what the memory is about, and how old the child in the memory is.

The memory should be detailed and as 'sharp' as possible. Some useful tips for sharpening memories that are initially only vague in content or intensity are described in the box.

USEFUL STRATEGIES TO SHARPEN THE IMAGE OF THE EARLY MEMORY

If the patient has difficulty identifying their earliest or most upsetting/worst memory then it might be useful to focus on a specific emotion and intensify that emotion by focusing on bodily sensations and allowing an image/memory to arise from the feeling. If the image/memory is vague and needs sharpening further then it can be useful to focus on the experience through difference senses and work initially on a specific sensory experience (e.g. an associated sound or smell), allowing the image/memory to come into focus by concentrating on that. The latter has been referred to as 'multisensory evocation' (Edwards 1990).

Identifying and rating beliefs

The core beliefs encapsulated in the early memory identified should then be clarified. Although they may be relatively well understood, imagery can identify additional relevant beliefs, or result in useful idiosyncratic interpretation or phrasing of known beliefs.

In all cases the phrasing and interpretation identified here should be the focus of the intervention, as this is where the most emotion in relation to the beliefs is likely to be located. If there is any doubt at this stage it can be useful to check that the beliefs identified in this way are connected with the patient's problem eating behaviour.

It is important to check that the adult still believes the thoughts identified, and that the beliefs reflect their general view. The beliefs should be recorded in the patient's exact words. Each belief should then be rated on a scale from 0 to 100, for 'rational' and 'emotional' belief, using the scale and instructions in the box opposite.

Most of the relevant beliefs are likely to be strongly held emotional beliefs about the self, although occasionally beliefs about others, the future or the world in general will be identified. These can be treated in exactly the same way as self beliefs.

SCALE FOR RATING BELIEFS

Use the scale below to rate how much you believe each of the thoughts right now. Base your first rating on what you rationally believe or know to be true when you consider the evidence logically. Base your second rating on what you emotionally feel deep inside, regardless of what your rational side knows to be true.

0	10	20	30	40	50	60	70	80	90	100

I do not believe this thought at all

I am completely convinced that this thought is true

Introducing imagery modification

Imagery modification can be introduced as follows:

It seems that you have had these beliefs for a very long time and that you may have come to believe these things because of upsetting things that happened to you as a child. One way to change these beliefs and the feelings that go with them is to return to your first memory of having them and try to give the child you were then some of the knowledge, compassion and ability to think rationally that you may not have had access to as a small child. We've found that a good way to do that is to use imagery. This involves getting a clear picture of yourself as a child in the early memory you have talked about that seems to be linked to those beliefs and then working with me to change things. The aim is to see whether some of the conclusions you came to as a child are ones that you would come to now, as an adult. That's what I'm going to suggest we try now. Does that make sense to you? Do you have any questions? How do you think that will turn out? Do you have any worries or fears about trying that?

The patient should be asked to return to and focus on the memory and to describe what she experiences in the first person, as if she is the child present in the situation now. This should include a detailed description of thoughts and feelings.

At this point it may be useful to summarise the personal meaning the patient identifies, and check that this is still something that the adult believes or feels.

At this stage, it can be useful to engage in some rational responding with the patient in order to try to introduce some flexibility in thinking.

Modifying the early memory

Once some flexibility has been introduced then the child's beliefs should be modified directly. The first step here is to bring either the adult self and/or a safe person (e.g. teacher, relative, therapist) into the image as an 'understanding adult'.

The patient should then, as a child in the memory, use their imagination to create a vivid experience of the adult or safe person interacting with the child and communicating these things or carrying out any requests directly. The patient should describe the process and what is happening as she creates it. The therapist should prompt as necessary to ensure that the procedure is focused on modifying the core beliefs that the child has previously expressed, and that have been identified as beliefs currently held by the patient as an adult. At intervals the therapist should check the impact of the procedure on the child's beliefs and feelings, to ensure that the procedure continues to focus on modifying the core beliefs identified. If necessary the procedure and questions should be adjusted and always tailored towards reducing the key beliefs identified as much as possible. This may involve asking the child to rate how much she believes specific beliefs to be (particularly emotionally) true at various points. The ultimate aim is to try to reduce the emotional belief as much as possible. Nurturing or changing the child or other people's behaviour, or a combination of the two, may be most appropriate. It is important to be flexible, depending on the needs of the patient and clinical judgement.

Re-rating the beliefs

At the end of the procedure the beliefs that were the target of the procedure should be re-rated using the scales on p. 162. Finally, it is important to debrief the patient, and spend time reflecting on the process and the impact it has had on them more generally.

A summary of Rebecca's experience and progress through an imagery modification session now follows.

REBECCA'S PROGRESS THROUGH IMAGERY MODIFICATION

Early memory

Being bullied at school age 8–9
Mum very ill and in hospital – too frightened to tell anyone
Refused to attend school, eventually changed to a new school

Beliefs

	Rational belief	Emotional belief
I'm all alone	60	100
I don't fit in	60	100
I'm different	50	95
I'm not clever	60	90
I'm not understood	70	100

Modifying Rebecca's early memory

Rebecca generated a vivid image of her most distressing memory of being bullied, using as many senses as possible

She was encouraged to get back into the situation, as if she were actually there, and the events in the image were currently happening to her

Rational responding was used (what would someone else say, what would you say now as an adult to a child in that position?), and Rebecca commented: 'Someone should have noticed, seen that I was unhappy and done something'

The image was modified

(Who would the child like to talk to, what would they like to say, what would they need?) Rebecca stated: 'My auntie, she was always kind to me, she gave me good birthday presents – things I wanted; I stayed with her when my mum was ill and in hospital – she always had time for me'; 'I wanted someone to ask her if anything was wrong, give me some space and time, notice that I was suffering, then listen, understand how upset I was, how much I wanted to join in with others, and not be left out, how alone I felt'; 'I wanted someone to speak to the other children

– so they understood how cruel they were being, and how I felt; I wanted to feel loved, special and wanted and included'.

(What would your auntie say and do?) 'Just having auntie notice would be great, and say "it's not your fault, there's nothing wrong with you, this can be sorted out, you will make friends".'

Rebecca then imagined her auntie sitting down with her in the evening at home by the fire, and asking her if she was OK. She imagined explaining it all to her auntie, about what was happening and how she felt, auntie coming into the school playground, making a huge fuss of her, giving her a great hug, and taking her away from the bullies. She imagined auntie speaking to the school – and after that the bullying stopped.

Change in beliefs

Rebecca's rational beliefs decreased overall 5–10 points, while her emotional beliefs decreased overall by 30–40 points after a single session.

The main steps in undertaking the imagery modification procedure are summarised in the box below.

STEPS IN IMAGERY MODIFICATION

- ⊙ Identify early memory
- ⊙ Identify and rate beliefs
- ⊙ Modify early memory
  - ⊙ Get back into the situation
  - ⊙ Use rational responding
  - ⊙ Employ imagery to modify beliefs
- ⊙ Re-rate beliefs

While one session can produce a significant change in beliefs, especially emotional belief, it is usually helpful to repeat the exercise to ensure greater change in beliefs. It is also worth remembering that a session in which beliefs are modified using imagery can take rather longer than the average session length, and it is important to make sure that sufficient time is allocated or time is used effectively so that the patient does not have to stop the exercise at a point when she feels upset or distressed.

TROUBLESHOOTING

Core belief work rarely proceeds smoothly; the therapist and patient should be prepared for ups and downs. Below are some tips that we have found useful to keep in mind when difficulties arise.

- *Beliefs are rarely realistic*. However, the patient behaves as though they are true and as a consequence she may not have modified her behaviour. For example, this may mean that she has not developed the ability to commit to a job or relationship, or the persistence needed to stick at a course of study or training.
- *Need for social or environmental change*. Patients may be maintaining or reinforcing their core beliefs daily: they may be being abused, or ill treated by a partner, family or friends, or experiencing bullying by continuing in unsuitable employment.
- When an eating disorder has an early onset and is longstanding, *patients may lack relevant developmental experiences*. This is particularly a problem for those with a past history of AN who have later developed BN. This can mean that the patient is behind her peers in life and emotional development. Sometimes this has been encouraged or perpetuated by the family because the patient was not well (it is possible she may have been overprotected, and/or not expected to do things appropriate for her age because of her perceived vulnerability). The patient may have missed out on forming appropriate peer relationships or intimate sexual relationships. Such patients often need help to get into the habit of taking responsibility for themselves, or forming appropriate relationships. This may need to be a treatment goal.

CHAPTER SUMMARY AND KEY POINTS

This chapter has outlined ways in which negative self beliefs can be identified, and how old beliefs can be challenged and/or new alternative beliefs built up or constructed.

Key points to remember include the following:

- Focused core belief work is usually necessary to achieve maximum change in negative self beliefs.
- The prejudice model is useful as a way to introduce this work.
- It is important to develop or construct a new or alternative belief as a first step.
- Strategies that aim to decrease belief in old beliefs and strategies that aim to increase belief in new beliefs can both be useful. These include

use of the core belief worksheet, cognitive continua, historical test of belief, a positive data log, behavioural experiments and flashcards.

⊙ The use of imagery modification can be particularly useful for challenging strongly held emotional beliefs.

CHAPTER 11

Ending therapy

This chapter considers how to end treatment and the tasks that need to be undertaken at this stage. These include dealing with any residual problem behaviours and beliefs, devising a blueprint to highlight successes and the reasons for these, and developing a relapse prevention strategy.

Once bingeing and vomiting have substantially reduced or stopped, and the different elements of treatment have been successfully completed, then ending treatment should be considered. From the beginning of therapy the patient is made aware of the time-limited nature of cognitive therapy and the number of completed sessions is tracked collaboratively. However, the impact of ending therapy on the patient should not be underestimated and needs to be approached with sensitivity and care, in order that it is not experienced negatively by the patient, and so that the chances of later relapse are minimised.

Anna was anxious about ending therapy and worried how she might cope in the future without regular sessions. She had also appreciated the relationship she had with her therapist and said that she would miss her. Although Anna had made good progress and acquired skill in managing her problems, the therapist was sensitive to Anna's need for dependence and was aware of the benefits in preparing for ending early on in therapy. In parallel to this the therapist worked on helping Anna to increase her sense of self-efficacy. At the end of therapy Anna understandably felt some anxiety about the future and was sad to be saying goodbye to the therapist, but she stated that she felt much better prepared for both the ending and the future than she had imagined she might be early on in therapy.

Four things are important when considering ending therapy. First, a check must be made for any residual problem behaviours and cognitions. Second, a blueprint should be developed with the patient so that she can take away a summary of her progress and what has contributed to her success. Third, strategies for dealing with any relapses or signs suggesting relapse might be likely should be covered with the patient. Finally, the impact of ending a therapeutic alliance needs to be considered.

RESIDUAL BEHAVIOURS AND COGNITIONS

As well as self-report, any remaining cognitions or problematic behaviours can be identified by readministering the relevant cognitive and behavioural measures used when the patient was first assessed. Indeed, it is usually useful to repeat the majority of the measures administered during the assessment phase in order to monitor, in a more objective way, the progress that has been made.

We usually repeat the self-report measures that are listed below:

Eating Attitudes Test
Eating Disorder Examination – Questionnaire
Beck Depression Inventory
Beck Anxiety Inventory
Rosenberg Self Esteem Scale
Eating Disorder Behaviours Questionnaire
Eating Disorder Thoughts Questionnaire
Eating Disorder Belief Questionnaire

These include measures of eating disorder symptoms and psychopathology, and general symptoms and psychopathology. We also repeat the specific cognitive and behavioural measures that are more closely related to the model and this enables us to identify residual cognitions and behaviours that may still be problematic.

The Eating Disorder Thoughts Questionnaire (EDTQ: Cooper et al. 2006) can be useful in identifying any positive and negative beliefs that the patient may continue to believe. It gives information on the presence and relevance of positive (and other) beliefs about eating.

The Eating Disorder Behaviours Questionnaire (EDBQ: Cooper et al. 2006) is useful in identifying any characteristic behaviours that may continue to play a role in maintaining the beliefs that are important in BN.

It is also important to track changes on idiosyncratic (e.g. 0–100 belief) ratings that have been used in treatment to assess the patient's specific concerns and issues and that are not necessarily captured completely on the self-report measures.

For assistance in understanding what a 'normal' score looks like on each of the self-report measures we recommend that at the end of treatment Table 2.2 (p. 42) can be consulted. Where these are available it lists 'cut-off' scores for identifying potential cases of eating disorders. It also contains ranges of scores on representative samples obtained by non-eating disordered participants (all female) in some of our research, together with comparison scores or ranges (if available) for women with BN who fulfil DSM-IV diagnostic criteria for BN.

One helpful way to encourage patients to view their change with treatment is to suggest, if possible, that they produce a visual representation of their self-report questionnaire, and also weekly ratings, using a software package such as Excel, which will allow them to create and plot their scores on a graph. They can also add in the cut-off scores from Table 2.2 (p. 42) to see how their scores now compare to 'normative scores'.

Elevated scores

If, at this stage, the patient has scores on any of the cognitive or behavioural measures that are significantly higher than those for non-eating disordered women, then the reason for this needs to be discussed. The patient's motivation to change might have reduced and there might be some fears about recovery. Another possibility is that the patient has changed her criteria for responding to the measures, and is underestimating progress. Since key cognitions and behaviour are measured on a session by session basis, using the Eating Disorder Rating Scale (see Appendix 1), and stuck points are normally identified at an early stage through session feedback and homework review, including the Weekly Evaluation Sheet (see Appendix 2), the chances of this happening are likely to be relatively small. Nevertheless, if some problems remain, the therapist needs to consider whether the patient has acquired the necessary skills to continue to work on these between ending therapy and the first booster session.

In research that has evaluated cognitive behaviour therapy for BN there is some suggestion that patients may continue to make progress post-treatment (Fairburn et al. 1991), which suggests that patients do not need to be completely symptom free at the end of treatment. Additional sessions are normally unnecessary, as many residual symptoms continue to improve after treatment. However for patients with more complex needs, a longer course of therapy, 20–24 sessions, might be offered from the outset.

Often therapists feel anxious and responsible if their patient has not made a full recovery and can slip into offering additional therapy sessions, which in some cases is unlikely to make any difference to the final outcome. Provided that the treatment programme has been covered following formulation in the context of a collaborative relationship it is useful to remember that it is normally best for the patient to take responsibility for continuing to work on any residual problems. A discussion about the pros and cons of additional or alternative treatments can be useful, including discussion of the patient's care-seeking behaviour. Overall, it is important to convey that the patient is not being 'dismissed' and there should be an open and explicit discussion about the reasons for ending the treatment at this point.

Although further therapy sessions are likely to be unhelpful for most patients, it is good practice to offer follow-up appointments, known as booster sessions, which provide an opportunity to review the blueprint and any progress made by the patient since ending treatment.

BLUEPRINT

A blueprint, outlining the patient's successes in treatment, and what has contributed to these, should be developed. This must be done in collaboration with the patient; by this stage in treatment it is expected that the patient will contribute most of the material for this, assisted by prompts from the therapist.

A series of useful prompts and related questions that can be used by the therapist are listed in the box (see also Appendix 15, pp. 245–246).

PROMPT QUESTIONS FOR THE BLUEPRINT

General questions

What have you learnt in our therapy over the last few months?
What have you found useful or helpful?
What cognitive therapy skills have you developed?
What has been difficult?
What problems are remaining?
How might you work on these? Develop a plan.

Specific questions

The cognitive model: understanding what keeps the problem going

What beliefs and thoughts are important in maintaining binge eating?
How do these beliefs and thoughts play a role in maintaining BN symptoms?
What beliefs make you vulnerable to BN?

Detached mindfulness

What is the aim of detached mindfulness?
What specific DM strategies did you find most helpful?

Fears associated with change

What fears did you have about changing?
How did you overcome these?
What was most helpful here?

Challenging negative and positive beliefs about eating

What helped you overcome your negative beliefs about eating?
What was most helpful here?
What helped you overcome your positive beliefs about eating?
What was most helpful here?

Challenging other problem behaviours

What helped you to decrease any other problem eating-related behaviours?
What was most helpful here?

Negative self beliefs

How did you challenge your negative self beliefs?
What strategies were most helpful?

When developing a blueprint it is useful to start with a general therapy review and then to move on to more specific questions. The following specific areas should be covered, corresponding to the different stages of treatment.

1. Fears associated with change.
2. The cognitive model – understanding what keeps the problem going.
3. Detached mindfulness.
4. Challenging negative and positive beliefs about bingeing and eating-related behaviours.
5. Negative self beliefs.

A completed worksheet covering these topics and including some useful prompt questions, and which has been completed by Jenny, can be seen in the following box.

COMPLETED BLUEPRINT

I've learnt that binge eating was my way of coping with feeling upset, and with problems rather than something that controlled me. However, it only helped in the short term; when eating for a brief yet blissful moment, I was not aware of my thoughts or feelings only to feel horribly depressed later. It was so easy to slip back into the binge vomit cycle, like a reflex reaction. I felt so ashamed of the bulimia and didn't like myself very much and feared that people would not want to know me if they knew what I did to myself, or if I gained weight. I believed that throwing up after bingeing stopped me from getting fat and felt compelled to continue doing it even after eating normal meals, just in case; it was my security blanket. The other side was that I didn't have to restrict my eating and would tuck into three course dinners knowing that I'd get rid of it later. Vomiting did control my weight to some extent and I didn't become fat although I constantly moved between two dress sizes and felt horribly bloated most of the time. I learnt that I could eat normally without over-controlling what I ate and not gain weight, just like most other people do. I feel more confident and positive about myself, and less concerned what others think of me.

Just coming here every week and talking to someone about my problems was helpful; I felt you really understood me. I'd lived with the shameful secret of bulimia for years and worried that you would think my behaviour was disgusting and found it reassuring that you didn't judge me. I liked the fact that I wasn't expected to make changes immediately and how you helped me think about what bulimia meant to me. I hadn't considered the advantages of having bulimia and addressing my fears about changing was helpful. I found drawing several examples of the bingeing cycle helpful, which helped me to recognise what my positive and negative beliefs about eating were. Once I understood what was going on I was able to make changes. The lists of questions to challenge the beliefs were useful. The behavioural experiments really made a difference; I liked the idea of gathering new evidence that on most occasions disconfirmed some of my negative predictions. I'd spent years counting calories believing that I needed to do this to prevent losing control and found out that this behaviour increased my sense of loss of control. The core beliefs work was good although painful at times. The continuum work helped me challenged my black and white thinking style and I'm now able to see shades of grey. The imagery work was really useful.

I've learned how to question positive and negative beliefs about eating. I've used the PETS framework for experiments.

Early on I was really undecided about changing and wanted you to make everything okay. The realisation that only I could make the changes and take responsibility for doing the work was difficult, though I'm glad that I did. When I discussed my family it felt as if I were blaming them for my problems which made me feel disloyal and guilty.

> I can't think of anything specific that's still a problem other than I'm worried about bulimia coming back in the future. I'm also worried about how I would cope if I gain weight in the future.
>
> I need to spot when I'm worrying and remind myself that there is no point worrying about something that hasn't happened, it's a waste of time. If I do experience problems in the future I can address them as and when. I have new skills and my therapy notes that I can refer to.

RELAPSE PREVENTION

Although many patients with BN make a full recovery, there are no guarantees that an eating disorder will not recur. However, there are ways to try to minimise the chances of this happening.

Early warning signs

All patients should be asked to identify their vulnerability and personal signs that they may be starting to fall back into the eating disorder trap. Thinking about when or how it first started can be helpful here, as well as any signs that it might be returning after a good, long spell free from it. Signs identified by Jenny can be seen in the box below.

EARLY WARNING SIGNS IDENTIFIED BY JENNY

Ruminating about my appearance, e.g. questioning myself, why I feel this way, what is happening to me, thinking 'I should cut down a bit on my eating, I'm looking a bit fat' and feeling consumed by my thoughts.

Turning down invitations, avoiding friends because of feeling self-conscious and low in mood.

Getting irritated and easily annoyed by little things that don't really matter.

Planning to diet and making endless lists of goals for what to eat and how much weight to lose.

Obsessively reading food labels in the supermarket.

Worrying about what I might be given to eat if I go out – and whether it will be full of fat and calories.

Feeling tempted to skip meals, even though hungry.

Relapse prevention

Having done this, patients should identify what they can do to prevent these early warning signs from developing into a full-blown problem. Jenny made a plan to deal with her personal early warning signs. This included using her blueprint and also some of the strategies that she had used successfully in treatment, as shown in the box.

JENNY'S PLAN TO DEAL WITH HER EARLY WARNING SIGNS

Stop and think about what is happening – consider what type of thoughts I am having, e.g. worry, rumination.

Stop ruminating – use detached mindfulness, worry postponement etc.

Remind myself of what helped in therapy by looking at my therapy notes.

Develop a plan for coping, which might involve challenging my style of thinking, problematic cognitions and behaviours.

Use problem-solving strategies.

Plan a mini cognitive therapy session to review progress in three days' time.

Future stressors

Patients may also find it helpful to think ahead to any stressful situations or events that they know they will have to deal with in the next few months, and formulate some plans for how to deal successfully with the additional stress these may create, without reactivating their BN.

LIFESTYLE CHANGES

As a result of successful treatment, patients with BN may decide that they would like to make some major lifestyle changes, or discover that they have some additional problems that were not entirely clear at the start of their treatment for BN. Depending on the patient and the particular problem, further treatment for this may be indicated. In most cases, however, it is usually best to take a break from treatment, as patients often continue to resolve their problems themselves after successful BN treatment, and/or direct the patient to good self-help materials or support groups as appropriate.

CHAPTER SUMMARY AND KEY POINTS

This chapter has outlined the tasks to be completed towards the end of treatment.

Key points to remember include the following:

⊙ Ending treatment should be built into the whole of treatment.
⊙ Assessment measures should be readministered to monitor degree of change and need for further or additional work.
⊙ Any residual problem behaviours and beliefs should be addressed.
⊙ A blueprint outlining the patient's successes, and what has been particularly useful in treatment, should be written.
⊙ Signs of relapse should be identified and a plan devised to deal with them.

Therapist resources

APPENDIX 1

EATING DISORDER RATING SCALE

1. How distressing/disabling has your eating disorder been in the last week?

0	1	2	3	4	5	6	7	8

Not at all   Moderately   Extremely
The worst I have
ever been

2. How often in the past week have you tried to diet or restrict your food intake?

0	1	2	3	4	5	6	7	8

Not at all   About half   All the
the time   time

3. How often in the past week have you binged?

0	1	2	3	4	5	6	7	8

Not at all   About half   All the
the time   time

4. How often in the past week have you vomited to lose weight or prevent weight gain?

0	1	2	3	4	5	6	7	8

Not at all   About half   All the
the time   time

5. How often in the past week have you taken laxatives to lose weight or prevent weight gain?

0	1	2	3	4	5	6	7	8

Not at all   About half   All the
the time   time

6. How often in the past week have you taken exercise to lose weight or prevent weight gain?

0	1	2	3	4	5	6	7	8

Not at all   About half   All the
                   the time   time

7. Below are a number of the thoughts that you may have, at times, about eating, weight and shape and about yourself. Indicate how much you believe each thought by placing a number from the scale in the box next to each item.

0	10	20	30	40	50	60	70	80	90	100

I do not   I am
believe this   completely
thought is   convinced that
true   the thought
                              is true

Negative beliefs – uncontrollability

- ☐ Once I've started bingeing I can't stop
- ☐ I have no control over my weight concerns
- ☐ I can't ignore my worrying thoughts about my shape
- ☐ I can't stop myself thinking about food

Negative beliefs – negative consequences

- ☐ Eating will make me fat
- ☐ Eating fat will make me fat
- ☐ If I get fat or gain weight people will reject me
- ☐ If I eat normally I'll gain weight and become obese

Positive beliefs – bingeing

- ☐ Bingeing will make me feel better
- ☐ Bingeing will stop my painful feelings
- ☐ Bingeing will take my mind off my problems
- ☐ Bingeing helps me control my thoughts

From Treating Bulimia Nervosa and Binge Eating by Myra Cooper, Gillian Todd and Adrian Wells – published by Routledge

Positive beliefs – covert behaviours

- ☐ Concentrating on my shape stops me getting fat
- ☐ Worrying about my shape stops me getting fat
- ☐ Checking my appearance stops me getting fat
- ☐ Paying close attention to what I eat stops me getting fat

Positive beliefs – vomiting and purging

- ☐ Being sick stops me gaining weight
- ☐ Being sick stops me worrying about myself
- ☐ Being sick calms me down
- ☐ Being sick makes me feel better

Self beliefs

- ☐ I'm stupid
- ☐ I'm no good
- ☐ I'm all alone
- ☐ I'm unlovable

APPENDIX 2

WEEKLY EVALUATION SHEET

Date:

What have I achieved this week?

What have I learned?

What has been difficult for me?

What areas do I need to work on over the next week?

What realistic, achievable goals can I set myself?

What problems am I likely to have?

How might I overcome these?

What do I want to work on in therapy this week?

Comments:

APPENDIX 3

A CLIENT'S GUIDE TO COGNITIVE THERAPY FOR BULIMIA NERVOSA

Introduction

This Guide will provide you with information about cognitive therapy (CT) for bulimia nervosa (BN) and what it involves, using a question and answer format. Your therapist is interested in your views and reactions to the Guide. If you have any questions or comments then please feel free to mention them. You may wish to underline key sentences, or write notes on the Guide, to remind yourself of points you would like to comment on or discuss in more detail.

What is cognitive therapy for BN?

Cognitive therapy is a psychological treatment that has been found to be effective in treating a range of problems including bulimia nervosa.

After conducting a detailed assessment of your eating problems, your therapist will help you to understand your BN, particularly what keeps it going and why it might have developed. You will then be in a better position to make some changes and to overcome bulimia nervosa.

Treatment will help you address uncertainty and anxiety about changing your problem. You will learn a range of strategies and techniques that will help you to stop binge eating. These involve questioning negative and positive beliefs about eating, and challenging unhelpful behaviours. Finally a 'blueprint' or plan will be developed that will help you to prevent slipping back into bulimic behaviours.

What are the aims of CT for BN?

The main goal of treatment is to teach you strategies and techniques that you can apply by yourself, at home, to overcome your problems. You will learn strategies that will continue to be useful once treatment is over for some time to come. Overall, cognitive therapy aims to provide you with the skills to be your own therapist

What does it involve?

Treatment is usually short term (normally up to 16 sessions) and structured.

Each session lasts approximately 50 minutes, and the discussion will focus on specific aspects of your BN, and how these might be addressed.

More specifically it involves the following:

Agenda setting

Sessions will be structured round an agenda in order to make the best use of the time available. The agenda will be drawn up at the beginning of the session. Priority items will be identified and time budgeted so that these are dealt with first. Your therapist will select items for discussion but will also expect you to bring items, particularly in the later stages of treatment. An agenda ensures that items that are important to you, as well as items that your therapist believes to be important, are covered. It also helps to avoid an 'end of session rush', a tendency to deal with important items in the last few minutes of the session. It is important to be realistic about the number of items that can be tackled comfortably in one session. Try to avoid the temptation to cover too many items. Patients also find that it is usually most helpful to deal with items one at a time rather than jump from item to item. You will gain a sense of achievement and closure by settling issues one at a time.

Feedback

Your therapist will encourage you to contribute your own ideas and suggestions and will welcome questions. During sessions you will be encouraged to provide mini summaries of what you have learned, and to give feedback on your progress with trying out the strategies and techniques discussed and agreed upon in sessions.

Working as a team

Cognitive therapy involves working together with your therapist to make changes and overcome your eating problem. The goals of treatment, understanding of your problem, the skills you learn, the strategies and techniques you employ will all be developed and agreed jointly with your therapist.

Evaluation

To give you the best chance of getting better, your therapist will be evaluating your progress in treatment very carefully. It is very important to know whether or not this approach helps you.

Diaries and questionnaires

You have probably already filled in some questionnaires to help your therapist assess your current problems. At the beginning of each session you will be asked to complete one brief questionnaire. This will help your therapist to assess how you have been in the past week. At the end of treatment you will be asked to fill in the initial questionnaires again. These questionnaires will enable your therapist to see what progress you have made at the end of treatment. There will be additional questionnaires to be completed in some sessions, or for homework. These will give your therapist more information about specific problems that you may have. They will help identify problems that may need to be worked on in treatment.

Homework

Discussion of your problems is likely to be helpful but will not usually be enough, by itself, to help you overcome them. Putting ideas into practice in everyday settings is essential. To help you do this, you will be expected to carry out weekly homework. Homework assignments will be agreed in collaboration with your therapist. They will be designed to try out strategies and test ideas discussed in sessions. If you are unable to complete any of the assignments agreed, for whatever reason, then it is important that you let your therapist know this at your next meeting. Your therapist will then be able to help you resolve any difficulties.

What will I have to do?

Therapy involves a number of things. For example, it might involve completing diaries and record sheets, reading information about BN, taking part in exercises in the session and planning and carrying out a range of different tasks, both in sessions and on your own at home.

You will have to make a commitment to treatment. A full course of treatment is likely to be of most help to you. If you do stop treatment before the end, you may well lose out on any progress you have made. You may also miss out on the chance to get better and stay better. If you are thinking of stopping treatment please discuss this with your therapist before you come to a decision.

You will have to set aside time, not only to attend sessions, but also to complete homework assignments. Treatment is also likely to require effort, hard work and persistence. For treatment to stand a good chance of success you will have to give it a high priority. However, if you are willing to invest the time and effort then the payoff, overcoming your eating problem, is likely to be considerable.

What happens after treatment?

Depending on your progress and the resources available locally, your therapist may arrange one or more follow-up or booster sessions after the end of treatment.

I have lots more questions; what should I do?

It is not unusual to have lots of questions about eating disorders and therapy particularly when first starting treatment. Your therapist will not be at all surprised if you do have concerns and questions, and will always be willing to discuss these with you. As a first step, if you have questions and concerns right now, then make a note of them, and take them with you to your next session. Your therapist will be pleased to discuss them with you.

Recommended reading

Cooper, M.J., Todd, G. and Wells, A. (2000). *Bulimia Nervosa: A Cognitive Therapy Programme for Clients*. London: Jessica Kingsley.

APPENDIX 4

EXAMPLE ASSESSMENT LETTER

Dear Alice

Thank you for attending the outpatient clinic for an assessment on 27 November 2006, it was a pleasure to meet you. This letter attempts to provide a summary of the assessment. If there is anything in this letter that is factually incorrect or is expressed in a way that does not reflect what you told me, then please do not hesitate to contact me and I will make the necessary changes.

As you know you were referred by your GP Dr Smith for an assessment of your eating problems. You told me that your main problem was binge eating, which you felt was uncontrollable. You described having large binges that involve eating up to 6000 calories, after which you induce vomiting. In the last 28 days you binged on 26 days. On 16 of those days you binged three times a day, and on the remaining 10 you binged daily, which makes a total of 58 binges over 28 days. You said that when you are not bingeing you try to restrict your food intake and will often try and follow a specific diet, for example the South Beech diet. While bingeing you described feeling a sense of being out of control and find it difficult to stop eating. You feel compelled to eat the whole cake, tub of ice cream or the whole loaf of bread and will not be able to put your mind at rest until all the food has gone. You told me that you are spending in excess of £200 a week on food and feel worried that you are getting into debt. On occasions you have taken food from friends' cupboards and feel extremely guilty about this and worry this behaviour might cost you friendships if they find out.

We discussed triggers for bingeing, which tend to be when you are feeling stressed and anxious or low in mood. This usually occurs when you are sleep deprived because of worrying about your course work and thinking about not being liked by your friends. A further trigger you observed is when you feel fat or worried about your figure. There are also occasions when you will binge when feeling bored. On reflection, you noticed that bingeing was a way of coping with negative critical thoughts you have about yourself, and in the short term eating provides a sense of relief from your distress only to be followed by greater distress, which makes you want to eat again.

As a way of compensating for binge eating, you induce vomiting 100 per cent of the time, and to compensate for the calories absorbed during a binge you exercise hard at the gym on a daily basis. Your regime usually includes attending 2–3 studio classes, for example yesterday you did a 45 minute cardio-cycle class followed by a 1 hour pump class after which you did 30 minutes of weight lifting, and ended with a 1 hour step aerobic class. You told me that you would feel guilty if you do not exercise and will not allow yourself a day off. After bingeing you described having a bloated and painful stomach and on 1–2 occasions a week you will take laxatives in normal amounts to reduce the bloating. You were very clear that your use of laxatives was not as a weight control strategy.

You described a typical day for eating as yesterday. You got up at 7.30 a.m. feeling starving hungry and binged. The binge initially started with healthy food that included two bowls of porridge with banana and a fruit smoothy, which degraded into eating junk food. After bingeing you went back to sleep until 11.00 a.m. Between the hours of 11 and 1 p.m. you binged for the second time on doughnuts, bread and chocolate. The next time you ate was 8.30 p.m. at a friend's house, and then at 11.00 p.m. you binged for a third time on crisps, cake and chocolate.

You told me that you were concerned about the effect of binge eating on your physical health. You suffer with heartburn and tend to have pain in your stomach following bingeing for which you take milk of magnesia. You feel exhausted most of the time and have no energy. You have regular sore throats and mouth ulcers and said that your voice is so husky it sounds as though you smoke 40 a day. You have been taking fluoxetine 60mg a day for the past 9 months, which has had no impact on reducing bulimic behaviours.

You described being extremely concerned about your weight and shape. You said that your shape is more important than your weight and worry that your thighs, hips and stomach are disproportionate to the rest of your body. You are worried that your breasts are too small and would ideally like a flat stomach. In the company of other young females you often compare yourself negatively to those who you perceive as beautiful and better looking than you, which causes distress. You say to yourself, 'I'm so ugly, no one would want to take notice of me'. You told me that your weight fluctuates a lot within a 3 stone range, which is noticeable to other people, which you find humiliating and leaves you feeling concerned about what other people think of you.

You told me that during phases of excessive bingeing you gain weight rapidly, between 8 and 12kg at a time. The first 8kg goes on over 3–4 weeks and the remaining 6kg more slowly. When your weight gets too high you will then try and lose weight through exercising excessively and through restricting your food. You said that you tend to lose weight quite quickly and that your most typical weight is 68kg (BMI – 20.9). Your highest weight was 82kg (BMI – 25.3) in June 2004, and your lowest weight was 59kg (BMI – 18.2) in August 2005. Your weight in the Clinic today was 64kg, with a height of 1.8m. I calculated your current Body Mass Index at 19.7, which is at the bottom end of a normal healthy weight range. You told me that you do not weigh yourself and feel scared to have scales around you because in the past you have compulsively checked your weight several times a day.

You described feeling preoccupied with food to the point where it makes it difficult to concentrate. Your college work had been badly affected and your exam result at the end of your second year was lower than predicted. This has been very upsetting for you, which has made you determined to do something about your eating disorder.

You described feeling stupid and compare yourself negatively to other people and think, 'They cope and do well, why can't I?' This make you feel angry and critical of yourself. You said you associate pain with feeling happy and that eating to the point of distension is painful and serves as a punishment. You also felt that one side of you wanted to make yourself fat and ugly as a way of pushing people away and protecting yourself from getting hurt.

We discussed some of the reasons why you felt the need to punish yourself. You told me that you were sexually abused as a child until the age of 16 and one way of coping with the abuse was to binge eat because the pain took away the painful thoughts and made you feel happy. You felt that after a period of counselling that one side of you has come to terms with the abuse yet currently find that any negative emotion is intolerable and use binge eating as a way of coping. As a child you wanted to make yourself fat as a way of trying to protect yourself from being hurt. However, the abuse continued and you were teased and bullied at school because of your weight. During this time you had few friends and felt lonely and isolated. In your later teenage years you desperately wanted to lose weight so would starve yourself and exercise; you also continued to binge eat and found that inducing vomiting helped to keep your weight down.

You were brought up in a large Catholic family in Northern Italy. You described your upbringing as very strict and restrictive. Your father is 60 and works as a physician. Your mother is 55 and is a housewife. You have six siblings, two sisters and four brothers, two of whom are identical twins. You are the youngest in the family. You said that you get on well with everybody and feel particularly close to your second eldest sister, Gabriella. You described your family as not being very open emotionally although supportive in a practical sense. You enjoyed junior school and made friends. At secondary school you excelled academically and were picked on by your peer group and teased about your weight. In hindsight you recognise that the bullying was probably unrelated to your size and probably about other factors such as showing vulnerability. You came to University in London to read Veterinary Science.

It was our impression that you have bulimia nervosa, purging subtype. We discussed how cognitive therapy is the treatment of choice and that many people manage to make a full recovery. We think that you would greatly benefit from this therapy and will place you on our waiting list. It is likely to be 4–6 months before a place becomes available and would recommend that in the meantime you read and work though some self-help material. I suggest that you read *Bulimia Nervosa: A Cognitive Therapy Programme for Clients* by Myra Cooper, Gillian Todd and Adrian Wells (Jessica Kingsley).

We will write to you once a place for individual therapy becomes available.

Yours sincerely

From Treating Bulimia Nervosa and Binge Eating by Myra Cooper, Gillian Todd and Adrian Wells – published by Routledge

APPENDIX 5

EATING BEHAVIOUR QUESTIONNAIRE

Name:		Date:	

Instructions

Listed below are some statements about different behaviours. They all describe ways in which people sometimes behave. Please read each statement carefully and decide how often you find yourself behaving in the way described. Use the rating scale to describe how often you engage in each behaviour. Write the number in the box before the statement.

Rating scale

0	10	20	30	40	50	60	70	80	90	100

Never   Always

1. ☐ Diet to lose weight or prevent weight gain
2. ☐ Eat large amounts of food only when you're on your own
3. ☐ Wear baggy clothes that hide your shape from others
4. ☐ Collect recipes
5. ☐ Visit food shops or supermarkets primarily to look at food rather than to make a purchase
6. ☐ Put only small amounts of food onto your fork or spoon at a time
7. ☐ Talk about food
8. ☐ Fill up on lots of low calorie food
9. ☐ Avoid weighing yourself
10. ☐ Chew food and spit it out without swallowing
11. ☐ Avoid communal changing rooms
12. ☐ Cook elaborate meals
13. ☐ Eat more than you intended
14. ☐ Buy lots of food that is high in fat, sugar and carbohydrate
15. ☐ Eat only 'safe' foods (i.e. low calorie or familiar foods)

16		Hoard food
17		Eat slowly
18		Read cookery books and cookery magazines
19		Check your weight with average weights in books and magazines
20		Wear loose clothes
21		Watch food programmes on television
22		Eat diet foods
23		Visit shops to look at cooking utensils rather than to make a purchase
24		Eat large quantities of high calorie food
25		Go on eating binges in which you lose control of your eating
26		Take only small mouthfuls of food at a time when eating
27		Avoid drawing attention to your weight and shape
28		Spend hours preparing a meal
29		Eat until you feel sick
30		Avoid wearing tight fitting clothes
31		Eat only when you're by yourself
32		Buy unusual cooking utensils that you are unlikely to use a great deal
33		Avoid looking at your body when taking a bath or shower
34		Eat more than others would eat in similar circumstances
35		Make rules about what you should or shouldn't eat
36		Wear large chunky jumpers
37		Avoid food if you don't know how many calories are in it
38		Chew your food for a long time before swallowing
39		Spend a long time searching for ingredients that are hard to find
40		Set yourself a strict calorie limit for each day
41		Eat little in front of other people but eat large amounts when they have gone
42		Visit specialist food shops
43		Avoid looking at your body in the mirror
44		Check the calorie content of food before you buy it
45		Eat food, when you're on your own, that has been thrown away
46		Wear clothes that are a size or more too big
47		Go to several shops, hoping you won't be noticed, buying small quantities of food in each shop

From Treating Bulimia Nervosa and Binge Eating by Myra Cooper, Gillian Todd and Adrian Wells – published by Routledge

Eating Behaviour Questionnaire Scoring

Add up the scores for each item on each subscale and divide by the number of items in the subscale.

Weight and shape (10 items): 3, 9, 11, 20, 27, 30, 33, 36, 43, 46.

Bingeing (10 items): 2, 5, 10, 16, 25, 29, 31, 41, 45, 47.

Dieting (9 items): 1, 8, 15, 19, 22, 35, 37, 40, 44.

Food (10 items): 4, 7, 12, 18, 21, 23, 28, 32, 39, 42.

Eating (4 items): 6, 17, 26, 38.

Overeating (4 items): 13, 14, 24, 34.

APPENDIX 6

EATING DISORDER BELIEF QUESTIONNAIRE

Name:		Date:	

Instructions

Listed below are different attitudes and beliefs which people sometimes hold. Please read each statement carefully and decide how much you agree or disagree with the statement. Base your answer on what you emotionally believe or feel, not on what you rationally believe to be true. Choose the rating which best describes what you usually believe or what you believe most of the time rather than how you feel right now. Write the number in the box before the statement.

Rating scale

```
    0    10   20   30   40   50   60   70   80   90   100
```

I do not
usually
believe
this at all

I am usually
completely
convinced
that this
is true

1. I'm unlovable
2. If my flesh is firm I'm more attractive
3. I'm ugly
4. I'm useless
5. I'm a failure
6. If I eat a forbidden food I won't be able to stop
7. If my stomach is flat I'll be more desirable
8. If I lose weight I'll count more in the world
9. If I eat desserts or puddings I'll get fat
10. If I stay hungry I can guard against losing control and getting fat
11. I'm all alone
12. If I eat bad foods such as fats, sweets, bread and cereals they will turn into fat

13 ☐ I'm no good

14 ☐ If I eat normally I'll gain weight

15 ☐ If I eat three meals a day like other people I'll gain weight

16 ☐ If I've eaten something I have to get rid of it as soon as possible

17 ☐ I'm not a likeable person

18 ☐ If my hips are thin people will approve of me

19 ☐ If I lose weight people will be friendly and want to get to know me

20 ☐ If I gain weight it means I'm a bad person

21 ☐ If my thighs are firm it means I'm a better person

22 ☐ I don't like myself very much

23 ☐ If I gain weight I'm nothing

24 ☐ If my hips are narrow it means I'm successful

25 ☐ If I lose weight people will care about me

26 ☐ If my body shape is in proportion people will love me

27 ☐ I'm dull

28 ☐ If I binge and vomit I can stay in control

29 ☐ I'm stupid

30 ☐ If my body is lean I can feel good about myself

31 ☐ If my bottom is small people will take me seriously

32 ☐ Body fat/flabbiness is disgusting

Eating Disorder Beliefs Questionnaire Scoring

Add up the scores for each item on each subscale and divide by the number of items in the subscale.

Negative self beliefs (10 items): 1, 3, 4, 5, 11, 13, 17, 22, 27, 29.

Acceptance by others (10 items): 8, 18, 19, 20, 21, 23, 24, 25, 26, 31.

Self acceptance (6 items): 2, 7, 9, 12, 30, 32.

Control over eating (6 items): 6, 10, 14, 15, 16, 28.

APPENDIX 7

EATING DISORDER THOUGHTS QUESTIONNAIRE

Name:		Date:	

Instructions

Listed below are some thoughts which people sometimes have when eating. Please read each thought carefully and decide how much you believe each thought to be true. Choose the rating which best describes how you usually feel rather than how you feel right now. Write the number in the box before the thought.

Rating scale

0	10	20	30	40	50	60	70	80	90	100

I do not usually believe this at all

I am usually completely convinced that this is true

1. ☐ I'll get fat
2. ☐ If I don't eat I'll lose control
3. ☐ My clothes won't fit any more
4. ☐ It doesn't matter if I keep eating
5. ☐ If I eat it will stop the pain
6. ☐ It's not me doing this
7. ☐ I'm going to go on getting heavier and heavier
8. ☐ I deserve something nice
9. ☐ If I eat it will take away the 'all alone' feeling
10. ☐ I'll just have a little bit more
11. ☐ The urge to binge is stronger than my willpower
12. ☐ I've nothing apart from eating/bingeing in my life
13. ☐ I'll gain weight

14	I've no self control
15	If I eat it will comfort me, it's a way of being nice to myself
16	I'll hate myself after eating so much
17	If I eat it will stop me feeling frightened
18	Go on, eat more to punish yourself
19	One more bite won't hurt
20	I'll have to vomit (exercise, take laxatives)
21	If I don't eat then I'll be overwhelmed with distressing thoughts and feelings
22	I'll have to go on a strict diet
23	If I eat it will all hurt less inside
24	If I eat it will stop me feeing bored
25	I'll look a mess after eating so much – fat and disgusting
26	If I eat it means I don't have to think about unpleasant things

Eating Disorder Thoughts Questionnaire Scoring

Add up the scores for each item on each subscale and divide by the number of items in the subscale.

Negative thoughts (10 items): 1, 3, 7, 11, 13, 14, 16, 20, 22, 25.

Positive thoughts (10 items): 2, 5, 6, 9, 12, 17, 18, 21, 23, 26.

Permissive thoughts (6 items): 4, 8, 10, 15, 19, 24.

APPENDIX 8

CONSEQUENCES AND DANGERS OF THE SYMPTOMS OF BULIMIA NERVOSA

Impact of specific symptoms

Bingeing

Bingeing leads to fullness in the stomach, bloating and abdominal discomfort. It may also lead to more general digestive problems including stomach cramps, wind, constipation and diarrhoea.

Vomiting

Vomiting is not an effective means of weight control. Research suggests that self-induced vomiting results in the retrieval of less than half the calories consumed in a typical binge. Since binges usually consist of large quantities of food, this means that a large number of calories are likely to be retained. This explains why people who vomit every time they eat are not necessarily underweight. Vomiting also encourages overeating. The thought that follows bingeing, e.g. the thought 'I'll get fat', and that you may identify later on with your therapist, maintains vomiting, and is likely to be less distressing and less likely to act as a deterrent to bingeing if you believe that vomiting removes most of the calories consumed in a binge.

If vomiting is frequent, and has been occurring for some time, then there may be a variety of physical and physiological effects.

- ⊙ *Teeth damage can occur*. Exposure to acid from the stomach, which occurs during vomiting, will erode dental enamel. Brushing the teeth after vomiting makes the erosion worse: acid in the mouth remaining after vomiting then scours the teeth. Although the damage is irreversible, erosion will stop once vomiting stops.
- ⊙ *Swelling of salivary glands*. Glands around the mouth that produce saliva will swell gradually in some people who induce vomiting. The swelling is painless but may lead to increased production of saliva. The parotid gland (the gland commonly affected most in mumps) often swells the most. As a result the face may take on a round, chubby appearance. This may be particularly distressing as the face may then appear 'fat'. The swelling is reversible and will gradually diminish as eating habits improve.

⊚ *Throat damage*. Most people induce vomiting by manually stimulating the gag reflex. This requires force and may result in superficial injuries to the back of the throat. These injuries may get infected. Recurrent sore throats and hoarseness are also common.

⊚ *Oesophagus*. Rarely, violent vomiting can lead to tearing and bleeding of the wall of the oesophagus, the tube leading from the mouth to the stomach. If this happens, medical advice should be sought. Vomiting repeatedly over several years can weaken the oesophagal sphincter, the set of muscles at the top of the stomach. If this happens the contents of the stomach may return spontaneously into the mouth, a distressing and uncomfortable experience.

⊚ *Hands*. If fingers are used to stimulate the gag reflex then damage can occur to the knuckles on the hand used. Abrasions may appear, then scars form. This injury is commonly known as 'Russell's sign'.

⊚ *Electrolyte balance*. Body fluids and electrolytes can be disturbed in a number of different ways. The most concerning is a low potassium level (hypokalaemia) which can result in heartbeat irregularities. Symptoms of fluid or electrolyte disturbance include extreme thirst, dizziness, fluid retention (swelling of legs and arms), weakness and lethargy, muscle twitches and spasms. Up to half of those with bulimia nervosa have some fluid and electrolyte disturbance but fortunately most have none of these symptoms and in most cases the electrolyte disturbance is only mild. The effects are reversible and disappear once vomiting stops. Chemically inducing vomiting, for example, by using Ipecac or salt water, can also be another cause of electrolyte disturbance.

Laxatives and diuretics

Laxatives have little effect on calorie absorption. It is common for people with bulimia nervosa who take laxatives to find that they become dependent on them, needing to take more and more for the same effect. Taking laxatives can also lead to electrolyte disturbances. People taking laxatives in addition to vomiting regularly are particularly at risk. Fortunately, the effects of taking laxatives are usually reversible. However, stopping laxatives suddenly may lead to rebound water retention and, thus, a temporary increase in weight.

Diuretics

Diuretics or water pills have no effect on calorie absorption. In large quantities diuretics also lead to fluid and electrolyte disturbances. Again, the effects are typically reversible, but stopping them suddenly may lead to rebound water retention and, as with stopping laxatives suddenly, a temporary increase in weight.

Diet pills

There is no evidence that diet pills are helpful in bulimia nervosa. They may have unwanted side effects.

Over-exercising

Excessive exercise can be harmful. It can lead to injury and in extreme cases compulsion to exercise strenuously may mean that injuries are not given adequate time and rest to heal.

Dieting

⦿ *Effect on hormones.* Dieting, with or without weight loss, can affect hormones, resulting in irregular or absent menstruation. The body needs a certain amount of body fat for menstruation to occur. This may be why menstruation is affected when there is weight loss. However, the reason why menstruation may be affected, even when body fat is adequate, is not yet understood. Dieting is also associated with high levels of the hormone cortisol, which in turn is associated with stress, a known trigger for binge eating.
⦿ *Appetite control.* Dieting can disturb certain physiological mechanisms that control eating. The nutritional content of food, particularly the amount of carbohydrate, fat and protein, affects the mechanisms controlling appetite. An unbalanced diet can thus affect hunger, and encourage overeating.
⦿ *Serotonin levels.* Dieting affects certain chemical neurotransmitters in the brain, particularly serotonin. The effect is more pronounced in women than in men. Serotonin is thought to play a role in normal eating and in food selection, thus dieting, by affecting serotonin levels, may exaggerate and increase the risk of developing bulimia nervosa.

Impact of related behaviours

Illicit drugs

These can be very unhelpful. Some encourage overeating, either directly or indirectly by lowering normal psychological resistance to bingeing.

Alcohol

Some people with bulimia nervosa find that they are much more likely to binge when they have been drinking large amounts of alcohol. In some cases heavy drinking can also induce a relapse and a binge after some time without binge eating.

Checking and avoidance behaviour

People with bulimia nervosa frequently engage in a variety of behaviours connected with their weight and shape. For example, they may weigh themselves frequently, avoid changing in communal changing rooms, avoid swimming, avoid wearing tight clothes, check or measure body parts, or engage in extreme dieting. These behaviours are self-defeating; they serve only to increase rumination, i.e. preoccupation and concern with weight and shape. It is easy to see how focusing on weight and shape might increase rumination about these issues. However, the opposite, deliberately trying to avoid focusing on weight and shape, is just as likely to increase preoccupation: try hard not to think about a white bear for a few moments and notice what happens!

General impact of bulimia nervosa

Decreased quality of life

Overall, bulimia nervosa can lead to depression and demoralisation. It can also be a very lonely disorder; the secrecy, guilt and shame felt about it may lead to isolation from other people. Sufferers quite often report feeling lonely and isolated. It often affects many aspects of life and reduces overall quality of life. There may be a tendency to avoid social contact and social occasions, particularly when food is involved. This can be upsetting and puzzling to friends and family. With time, relationships may suffer, either because the eating disorder takes up time and attention or because of the need to hide essential details of the problem from other people. Children may be affected; there may be attempts to restrict their food intake as well or simply a lack of food available for them because of attempts to avoid bingeing by keeping very little food in the house. Some sufferers find themselves unable to meet their child's emotional needs except through food, including by over and inappropriate feeding. Daughters, in particular, may suffer as they get older and may feel under pressure to join in a mother's dieting. There may also be financial difficulties; bingeing can be an expensive burden.

Impaired fertility

Dieting and weight loss can impair fertility, although the effects are typically reversible. Little is known about the effect of bingeing on fertility and pregnancy. The use of vomiting, laxatives and diuretics is more likely to be harmful. Some pregnant women with bulimia nervosa may be at risk of gaining too little weight and of giving birth to underweight babies. Preliminary work, which needs to be confirmed, suggests that the miscarriage rate may be higher in those with bulimia nervosa than in women without eating problems.

APPENDIX 9

STEPS IN THE PETS FRAMEWORK

Prepare

Identify target thought (e.g. 'I'll lose control')

Rate belief in thought

Identify problematic situation

Operationalise target thought as an observable prediction with a 'test strategy'

Clarify the rationale for the experiment

Expose

Expose to the problematic/trigger situation (e.g. eating biscuits)

Test

Test prediction by performing a disconfirmatory manoeuvre, that is, behaviour or actions that will provide a rigorous or 'extreme' test of the prediction (e.g. eat two biscuits then stop)

Summarise

Review outcome – 'What did you discover?'

Re-rate belief in target thought

Refine experiment and repeat

Source: Adapted from Wells (1997).

APPENDIX 10

MYTHS ABOUT BULIMIA NERVOSA AND COGNITIVE THERAPY

There are some myths about bulimia nervosa (BN), eating and food, and cognitive therapy (CT) that are not founded in fact. Below we identify some common 'myths' and discuss whether or not there is any truth in each of them.

Bulimia nervosa

It's not a real illness

BN varies in severity like many other illnesses and problems, but it is a recognised mental health problem. BN (like other eating disorders) is just as much a 'real' illness as any other disorder or disease.

Only adolescents and young women get BN

BN is more common in adolescents and young women, but not all people with BN are adolescents or young women. Other people, including older women and men, can suffer from BN.

It's just dieting a bit too much

There is much more to BN than dieting a bit too much. Many people diet but do not develop BN or any other eating disorder; dieting is not the same thing as BN.

The best thing to do is to 'pull myself together' and try harder to lose weight

BN does not respond to attempts to 'pull yourself together', either trying harder to control your eating or trying harder to lose weight. It is about what you do just as much as how much effort you put in and therapy will help you to focus your efforts in the most helpful way.

From Treating Bulimia Nervosa and Binge Eating by Myra Cooper, Gillian Todd and Adrian Wells – published by Routledge

It's a sign of weakness or serious character flaw

BN has nothing to do with weakness or character flaws. It is easy to blame or criticise yourself for your illness, but this rarely helps.

No one else can possibly understand what it's like

While no one else can have exactly the same experiences as you, not even someone with BN, you may be surprised when you do start to share your experiences with others that you are not alone, and that others have had very similar experiences. Very often this leads to a feeling that others do understand how you feel quite well.

Mothers are to blame for eating disorders

It is never helpful to blame others for your eating disorder; life is never so straightforward or simple that a single person can be 'blamed'. A huge number of factors will have created the circumstances in which your eating disorder has developed – therapy will help you to understand what some of these are, and how they may have worked together.

The media are to blame for eating disorders

It is very fashionable to promote thinness, including extreme thinness (e.g. Size 0), and there is no doubt that images of perfection in appearance do have a very negative impact on how women feel about their own bodies and appearance. Such images also seem to encourage dieting, which is a known risk factor for bulimia nervosa. However, no researchers or clinicians believe that these are the only factor involved. Personal circumstances and individual factors are likely to be equally, if not more, important.

Purging is a good way to lose weight or prevent weight gain

Research indicates that purging, whether vomiting, using laxatives or some other means, will not get rid of all the food that you have eaten, and that, as a weight loss strategy, it is relatively ineffective.

Eating disorder related behaviours are generally harmless

Some people with BN experience medical complications as a result of their eating disorder behaviour, and may need medical management. Fortunately, serious medical complications are rare and most problems that people experience as a result of their BN behaviours are reversible with recovery.

Eating and food

Some foods (e.g. chocolate, butter, sugar) are just 'bad' and you should never eat them

Banning some foods from your diet completely is unlikely to be helpful – there is nothing inherently or morally 'bad' about certain foods, even if you feel that this is the case.

A healthy diet shouldn't include carbohydrates, fat or sugar, and healthy eating means only salad and low calorie food

Healthy eating means a balanced diet, not one that excludes whole groups or categories of food, or that involves eating excessive amounts of one particular type.

Some foods automatically lead to weight gain – it's what you eat, not how much, that matters

There is nothing inherently weight inducing about specific foods – it's how much you eat and how much energy you then expend that matters.

The only way to lose weight is to give up eating all the foods I really like

This is rarely useful or helpful – a balanced diet that involves eating fewer calories is the best way to lose weight.

Cognitive therapy

Talking won't help: people with psychological problems need medication

Some people with BN are helped by medication, and it may be worth considering this in certain circumstances, but the evidence is that many more people are helped by 'talking' treatments such as cognitive therapy.

It's too simple or basic to work

This can be an initial reaction, especially when the treatment is explained or described briefly or by someone who isn't an expert in it. The basic principles are simple (like all good scientific theories) but the practice, as you will find, is more complex.

Everyone with BN needs lengthy psychotherapy, not a short-term treatment

The evidence does not support this – many patients can recover significantly with short-term psychological treatment.

Someone who hasn't had BN (e.g. a therapist) can't possibly understand or help me

It can be very useful to talk to other people who have or who have had BN, but therapists who have no personal experience of BN can be very effective therapists. Would you request that your doctor had exactly the same symptoms or illness before accepting treatment?

The therapist will want to make me eat more, gain weight or get fat

Good therapists have no interest in making patients with BN eat more or gain weight, unless of course the patient is so seriously or dangerously underweight that their health is compromised. Equally, they have no interest in patients becoming fat. Weight gain or eating more is not the principal or even an aim at all in the vast majority of cases, and is certainly not an aim of the treatment presented here.

CT won't deal with how bad I feel inside (especially if it is all about cognition or thoughts)

The word cognitive refers to the means by which change in emotional experience is achieved. Emotional experience is an important topic and focus of attention in CT; as well as becoming less preoccupied or thinking less about eating, food, weight and shape, CT aims to help you feel better.

From Treating Bulimia Nervosa and Binge Eating by Myra Cooper, Gillian Todd and Adrian Wells – published by Routledge

APPENDIX 11

MEDICAL ASPECTS OF BULIMIA NERVOSA FOR FAMILY PHYSICIANS

With increasing evidence for the effectiveness of psychotherapy for BN, patients are more likely than ever before to be seen and treated by therapists whose professional training is in psychological therapy, and who have little or minimal medical training. This is particularly true with the trend towards treatment of less severe mental health issues, including less severe eating disorders, in primary and secondary care settings. In such cases general practitioners (GPs) have an important role in the treatment of BN. Indeed, apart from patients who are being treated in hospital, the family physician is frequently at the centre of medically managing the patient. It is important that the patient's physical health as well as mental health is appropriately monitored and, at various points based on the physician's medical assessment, referral or advice from specialist medical services might be sought. This is equally true of men with BN as it is of women with the disorder.

Bulimia nervosa can be associated with a range of physical problems, some of which are potentially serious if left untreated. It may also be appropriate to prescribe some psychotrophic medication. If this is indicated, and when specialist eating disorder services are not involved, the decision about this and its monitoring often rests with the physician.

Some detailed texts and guidelines have been written about the medical management and risks associated with BN. Our aim is not to replace these; rather we aim to address some of the common issues and questions that GPs experience as the primary medical practitioner for a patient with BN who is also receiving psychological treatment.

Baseline assessment

It is recommended that the physician check height and weight and calculate Body Mass Index (BMI), provided of course that the patient is willing to agree to this. If the patient has a low BMI it can be helpful to check core temperature and carry out a squat test (see below). The physician would normally ask about general health and well-being, menstruation, nutritional intake and physical activity. Blood pressure and pulse rate should be taken, as part of a full physical examination, looking particularly for signs of nutritional deficiency, such as muscle weakness or yellowing skin and sclera. If the patient is engaging in purging behaviours, an assessment of any symptoms associated with the purging needs to be made. However, it is always important to remember that it is usually helpful to strike a balance between using further tests and investigations appropriately and over-medicalising the disorder. Based on the history and frequency of symptoms it might be useful to check the patient's blood chemistry. In particular, full blood count (FBC), erythrocyte sedimentation rate (ESR), urea and electrolytes (U&E), creatinine (Cr), creatine kinase (CK), glucose (Gluc) and liver function (LFTs) may need to be tested. Tests for any other physical problems should also be carried out, if appropriate. Patients who are taking drugs, for example tricyclic antidepressants, that may affect the QT interval should receive an electrocardiogram (ECG). A useful table for indicators of levels and measures that should cause concern, and for which medical intervention (including guidance on type of intervention, for example, the need and appropriateness of dietary supplements) may be necessary, has been produced by King's College, South London and Maudsley NHS and can be accessed online at their Trust website. It is reproduced at the end of this Appendix with kind permission from Professor Janet Treasure.

Regular monitoring

If the parameters of the measures listed above are in the normal ranges then, at the discretion of the physician, regular review and monitoring of these may be all that is currently required.

Additional testing

It is important that the physician is alert to any changes in the patient's BN that may indicate increased risk (e.g. reports of blood in vomiting, increases in vomiting or purging, addition of new methods of purging) or of any illness or other behaviours that may increase medical risk (e.g. illness that results in dehydration, binge drinking, use of illegal substances, misuse or abuse of over-the-counter medication). Weight, and marked increases in food restriction, must also be monitored regularly. Some patients may move into anorexia nervosa and this can markedly increase medical risk. If such changes occur then it is vital to repeat previous tests as soon as possible.

Medication

Selective serotonin reuptake inhibitors (SSRIs), as well as some other classes of antidepressants, have been shown to reduce binging and vomiting. Fluoxetine hydrochloride (Prozac) is perhaps most often prescribed for BN. The recommended dose is 60mg/day (the patient would typically start on a lower dose and, as side effects are tolerated, the dose would be gradually increased to 60mg). This is rather greater than that often prescribed for other psychiatric disorders. It is important to be aware that antidepressants have a range of side effects, some of which may increase a patient's medical risk. The relatively low risk of side effects with fluoxetine makes it the drug of choice if medication is deemed necessary, and it is the drug endorsed as most helpful in BN by the NICE guidelines for eating disorder (NICE 2004). However, it is also useful to be aware that no consistent predictors of positive response to antidepressants have been identified, and that there is little research investigating impact on features other than bingeing and vomiting. The mechanisms by which they may work are also largely unknown.

Pregnancy

It is advisable to monitor patients with BN who become pregnant particularly carefully and regularly. Their pregnancy should be regarded as high risk, and they need to be referred to an obstetrician for specialist care at an early stage. Any medication they are receiving should be reviewed and stopped if possible, particularly if it is known to be or likely to be problematic during pregnancy. Women with BN who are pregnant may also require advice about safe limits for exercising, especially if this is a key compensatory strategy following binge eating. They are likely to be very concerned about the potential impact of their BN on their unborn child, a concern that may continue postpartum as they worry about feeding their child appropriately. They may value and be helped by a referral to a dietician, both for themselves and later on when beginning to feed their baby.

General medical problems

Many patients with psychiatric illnesses suffer from inadequate general medical care, either because they are reluctant to consult their physician, or because their symptoms are mistakenly attributed to their mental health problems, including by themselves and other professionals. A useful source to consult on this topic is Dean et al. (2001). In general, it is important to ensure that physical symptoms are carefully identified and, if necessary, appropriately investigated. As well as asking about psychological state, physicians have an important role in routinely asking patients with BN about their physical health, including when this may not be the primary focus of the consultation.

Reference

Dean, J., Todd, G., Morrow, H. and Sheldon, K. (2001). Mum I used to be good looking . . . look at me now: The physical health needs of adults with mental health problems: The perspectives of users, carers and front-line staff. *International Journal of Mental Health Promotion, 3*, 16–24.

A rough guide to a summary measure of risk

Written by Professor Janet Treasure

Kings College London, South London and Maudsley NHS Trust, reproduced with kind permission of Professor Janet Treasure.

1. No table scores
   Stable. Regular review and monitoring of above parameters with routine referral to eating disorders unit or secondary services depending on local resources.
   Unstable. If weight is falling ask the person with anorexia nervosa to come up with a plan to ensure that nutritional state does not fall into the risk areas. Regularly review the implementation of this plan.
2. Score/s in the Concern area
   Regular review of parameters (approximately weekly) and assessment of capacity with urgent referral to eating disorders and appropriate medical intervention if needed. As this signifies medical risk this should also be shared with the carer.
3. Score/s in the Alert area
   Immediate contact and referral to eating disorders unit and physicians if outpatient with assessment of capacity. The patient will need urgent specialist and medical assessment. If inpatient – immediate contact with on-call physicians.

Table A.1 gives values of concern for each part of the assessment and is followed by a management protocol based on risk.

Table A.1 A rough guide to a summary measure of risk

System	Test* or Investigation	Concern	Alert
Nutrition	BMI	<14	**<12**
	Weight loss/week	>0.5kg	**>1.0kg**
	Skin breakdown	<0.1cm	**>0.2cm**
	Purpuric rash		**+**
Circulation	Systolic BP	<90	**<80**
	Diastolic BP	<70	**<60**
	Postural drop (sit–stand)	>10	**>20**
	Pulse rate	<50	**<40**
Musculo-skeletal (squat test and sit-up test)	Unable to get up without using arms for balance (yellow)	+	
	Unable to get up without using arms as leverage (red)		**+**
	Unable to sit up without using arms as leverage	+	
	Unable to sit up at all		**+**
Temperature		<35	**<34.5C**
		98.0F	**<97.0F**
Bone marrow	WCC	<4.0	**<2.0**
	Neutrophil count	<1.5	**<1.0**
	Hb	<11	**<9.0**
	Acute Hb drop (MCV and MCH raised – no acute risk)		**+**
	Platelets	<130	**<110**

continues

Table A.1 (continued)

System	Test or Investigation	Concern	Alert
Salt/water balance	1. K+	<3.5	**<3.0**
	2. Na+	<135	**<130**
	3. Mg++	0.5–0.7	**<0.5**
	4. PO4--	0.5–0.8	**<0.5**
	5. Urea	>7	**>10**
Liver	Bilirubin	>20	**>40**
	Alkpase	>110	**>200**
	AsT	>40	**>80**
	ALT	>45	**>90**
	GGT	>45	**>90**
Nutrition	Albumin	<35	**<32**
	Creatinine kinase	>170	**>250**
	Glucose	<3.5	**<2.5**
Differential diagnosis	TFT, ESR		
ECG	Pulse rate	<50	**<40**
	Corrected QT interval (QTC)		**>450msec**
	Arrythmias		**+**

Note: * The baselines for these tests vary between labs. Any abnormal result is an indication for concern and monitoring.

From Treating Bulimia Nervosa and Binge Eating by Myra Cooper, Gillian Todd and Adrian Wells – published by Routledge

APPENDIX 12

MEDICAL ASPECT OF BULIMIA NERVOSA FOR NON-MEDICAL PRACTITIONERS

Physicians must be kept regularly informed about a BN patient's therapy by those who are non-medical practitioners. It is also important to alert the physician if there is any significant change in the patient's physical symptoms, an increase in the frequency, intensity or methods of purging, or significant weight loss, so that appropriate physical tests, and any relevant treatment, can be initiated.

Medical risk can be increased by a range of BN-related behaviours, and it is important that the physician is alerted to these if new behaviours and information emerge that the patient has not previously discussed with the physician. Such behaviours include excessive fluid loading, vomiting blood, misuse of prescribed medications such as insulin or adrenalin (many patients purchase normally prescribed medications over the internet), use of illegal substances, excessive or binge drinking, and misuse or abuse of over-the-counter medications such as anti-decongestants, diet pills, caffeine tablets. Symptoms that may need further investigation by the physician, if not already known and investigated, include cardiovascular and respiratory symptoms such as shortness of breath, palpitations and chest pain. Any neurological symptoms, particularly significant dizziness or marked changes in concentration or memory, should also be reported. Severe reflux should also be discussed by the patient with their physician. Severe abdominal pain on bingeing should be investigated immediately; in a small number of cases this can indicate rupture of the stomach. Patients should also be advised to attend a dental checkup, if this has not been done recently, particularly if they are vomiting regularly, as this can cause significant tooth and gum damage. The patient who is pregnant will need particularly careful medical care; it is important that patients who are or who become pregnant consult with their physician at the earliest possible opportunity. They should be referred on for specialist prenatal care at an early stage, and generally considered to be at high risk of complications.

APPENDIX 13

USEFUL WEBSITE ADDRESSES

www.edr.org.uk Lucy Serpell's eating disorder resources for health professionals

www.rcpsych.ac.uk Royal College of Psychiatrists – mental health information with leaflets downloadable in a pdf format

www.nice.org.uk NICE guidelines

www.babcp.com British Association of Behavioural and Cognitive Psychotherapists – information and downloadable leaflets

www.b-eat.co.uk Beating Eating Disorders – information for patients and carers and professionals

www.aedweb.org Academy of Eating Disorders – international organisation that promotes awareness, research and developments in the treatment of eating disorders

www.iop.kcl.ac.uk Institute of Psychiatry Eating Disorders – information for health professionals

www.bbc.co.uk/health BBC health website – information on eating disorders

www.something-fish.org Pro-recovery website on eating disorders

www.mirror-mirror.org Information for patients with eating disorders

www.mct-institute.com

APPENDIX 14

POSITIVE CORE BELIEFS QUESTIONNAIRE

Name:		Date:	

Instructions

Listed below are different attitudes and beliefs which people sometimes hold. Please read each statement carefully and decide how much you agree or disagree with the statement. Base your answer on what you really feel or believe, and not on what you think you should believe. Choose a rating out of 100 which best describes what you usually believe, rather than how you feel right now. Write the number in the box before the statement.

Rating scale

```
     0    10   20   30   40   50   60   70   80   90   100
```

I do not believe this thought at all

I am completely sure that this thought is true

1. ☐ I am a strong person
2. ☐ I am lovable
3. ☐ I am competent
4. ☐ I am resilient
5. ☐ I am likeable
6. ☐ I have value as a person
7. ☐ I am an achiever
8. ☐ I have a role
9. ☐ I am interesting
10. ☐ I have something to contribute
11. ☐ I am important
12. ☐ I am successful
13. ☐ I am an independent person

14		I am a capable person
15		I fit into a group
16		I am ambitious
17		I am in control of my life
18		I am adventurous
19		I am lucky
20		I am a good person
21		I am a positive thinking person
22		I am confident
23		I am a responsible person
24		I am a friendly person
25		I am trustworthy
26		I am a sociable person
27		I am a fun person

Positive Core Beliefs Questionnaire Scoring

Add up the scores for each item and divide by the total number of items (i.e. 27).

Normative scores (from Noad, Stewart-Brown and Cooper, unpublished).

Positive Core Beliefs Questionnaire	N=224 Mean age =21.6 (SD=5.9) Female=69%	Mean=72.37	Standard deviation =13.23	Range=4–96

Blank worksheets

From Treating Bulimia Nervosa and Binge Eating by Myra Cooper, Gillian Todd and Adrian Wells – published by Routledge

APPENDIX 15

A COST-BENEFIT SHEET

Advantages of change	Disadvantages of change
Conclusion	

THE BINGEING VICIOUS CIRCLE

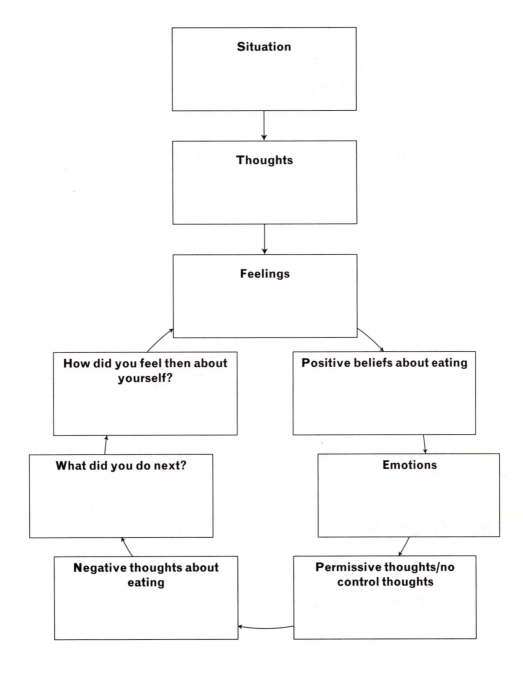

Figure A.1 The bingeing vicious circle

From Treating Bulimia Nervosa and Binge Eating by Myra Cooper, Gillian Todd and Adrian Wells – published by Routledge

WORKSHEET TO ELICIT FORMULATION

What thoughts were running through your mind? What were you thinking to yourself?

What did that mean or say about you?

Did you start eating?

How did you think that would help?

What did you think would happen if you didn't eat?

What thoughts made it easy to keep eating?

How did you feel about your sense of control?

What did you do next?

How did you feel then about yourself?

A MODIFIED DYSFUNCTIONAL THOUGHT RECORD FORM TO RECORD UNCONTROLLABILITY BELIEFS ABOUT EATING

Situation	Feelings (0–100)	Beliefs (0–100)	Behaviour
Where was I? What was I doing? What was I thinking? What was I worrying about?	How did I feel?	What was running through my mind while I was bingeing/ contemplating bingeing? How much did I believe I could control my bingeing?	What evidence do I have against my belief? What evidence do I have that I can control my bingeing?

From Treating Bulimia Nervosa and Binge Eating by Myra Cooper, Gillian Todd and Adrian Wells – published by Routledge

A BEHAVIOURAL EXPERIMENTS WORKSHEET

Thought I want to test (Belief 0–100)	Situation in which I'll test it	Test strategy (what I will do)	Outcome (Belief 0–100)

MODIFIED DYSFUNCTIONAL THOUGHT RECORD FOR IDENTIFYING NEGATIVE BELIEFS ABOUT CONSEQUENCES

Situation	Feelings (0–100)	Beliefs (0–100)	Response to beliefs (0–100)

A DYSFUNCTIONAL THOUGHT RECORD SHEET FOR A POSITIVE BELIEF ABOUT EATING

Situation	Feelings / sensations	Beliefs	Behaviour

AN ADVANTAGES AND DISADVANTAGES ANALYSIS FOR A POSITIVE BELIEF

Positive belief		
Advantages	**Disadvantages**	**Evaluation of advantages**
Conclusion		

From Treating Bulimia Nervosa and Binge Eating by Myra Cooper, Gillian Todd and Adrian Wells – published by Routledge

KEY POSITIVE BELIEF ABOUT EATING, AND THE EVIDENCE FOR IT

Situation	Feelings (0–100)	Beliefs (0–100)	Counter-evidence

Conclusion

From Treating Bulimia Nervosa and Binge Eating by Myra Cooper, Gillian Todd and Adrian Wells – published by Routledge

A BEHAVIOURAL EXPERIMENTS WORKSHEET FOR A POSITIVE BELIEF

Thought I want to test (Belief 0–100)	Situation in which I'll test it	Test strategy (what I will do)	Outcome (Belief 0–100)

From Treating Bulimia Nervosa and Binge Eating by Myra Cooper,
Gillian Todd and Adrian Wells – published by Routledge

A CORE BELIEF WORKSHEET

Old core belief	New core belief
What is the most you've believed this belief this week (intellectually and emotionally 0–100%?)	**What is the most you've believed this belief this week (intellectually and emotionally 0–100%?)**
Intellectually Emotionally	Intellectually Emotionally
What is the least you've believed it this week (intellectually and emotionally 0–100%?)	**What is the least you've believed it this week (intellectually and emotionally 0–100%?)**
Intellectually Emotionally	Intellectually Emotionally
Meaning of the old belief (ask patient to operationalise the belief)	**Meaning of the new belief**
Evidence against old belief (in the last month)	**Evidence to support new belief (in the last month)**

A COGNITIVE CONTINUUM

0%   100%

0%   100%

0%   100%

0%   100%

0%   100%

0%   100%

0%   100%

0%   100%

From Treating Bulimia Nervosa and Binge Eating by Myra Cooper, Gillian Todd and Adrian Wells – published by Routledge

SAMPLE FLASHCARD TEMPLATE

When my core belief (e.g.   ) is triggered I start to think . . . (e.g.

This makes me feel . . . (e.g.

When I'm thinking and feeling like this, my way of coping is to binge eat . . .

However, while binge eating helps in the short term, in the long term I feel . . . (e.g.

List all the evidence against the core belief (e.g.

Right now, what I need to do is (for example):

◉

◉

◉

◉

◉

◉

◉

WORKSHEET FOR THE BLUEPRINT

General questions

What have you learnt in our therapy over the last few months?

What have you found useful or helpful?

What cognitive therapy skills have you developed?

What has been difficult?

What problems are remaining?

How might you work on these? Develop a plan.

Specific questions

The cognitive model: understanding what keeps the problem going

What beliefs and thoughts are important in maintaining binge eating?

How do these beliefs and thoughts play a role in maintaining BN symptoms?

What beliefs make you vulnerable to BN?

Detached mindfulness

What is the aim of detached mindfulness?

What specific DM strategies did you find most helpful?

From Treating Bulimia Nervosa and Binge Eating by Myra Cooper, Gillian Todd and Adrian Wells – published by Routledge

Fears associated with change

What fears did you have about changing?

How did you overcome these?

What was most helpful here?

Challenging negative and positive beliefs about eating

What helped you overcome your negative beliefs about eating?

What was most helpful here?

What helped you overcome your positive beliefs about eating?

What was most helpful here?

Challenging other problem behaviours

What helped you to decrease any other problem eating-related behaviours?

What was most helpful here?

Negative self beliefs

How did you challenge your negative self beliefs?

What strategies were most helpful?

References

Abraham, S.F. and Beumont, P.J.V. (1982). How patients describe bulimia or binge eating. *Psychological Medicine, 12*, 625–635.

Agras, W.S. and Apple, R. (2007). *Overcoming your Eating Disorder: A Cognitive Behavioural Therapy Approach for Bulimia Nervosa and Binge-Eating Disorder, Guided Self Help Workbook*. New York: Oxford University Press.

Agras, W.S., Walsh, T., Fairburn, C.G., Wilson, G.T. and Kraemer, H.C. (2000). A multicentre comparison of cognitive behavioural therapy and interpersonal psychotherapy for bulimia nervosa. *Archives of General Psychiatry, 57*, 459–466.

American Psychiatric Association (APA) (2000). *Diagnostic and Statistical Manual for Mental Disorders*, 4th edition, revised. Washington, DC: APA.

Beck, A.T. and Freeman, A. (1990). *Cognitive Therapy of Personality Disorders*. New York: Guilford.

Beck, A.T. and Steer, R.A. (1990). *Beck Anxiety Inventory Manual*. San Antonio, TX: Psychological Corporation.

Beck, A.T., Rush, A.J., Shaw, B.F. and Emery, G. (1979). *Cognitive Therapy of Depression*. New York: Guilford.

Beck, A.T., Steer, R.A. and Brown, K. (1996). *Beck Depression Inventory. Version 2*. San Antonio, TX: Psychological Corporation, Harcourt Brace.

Beck, J.S. (1995). *Cognitive Therapy: Basics and Beyond*. New York: Guilford.

Beglin, S.J. and Fairburn, C.G. (1992). Evaluation of a new instrument for the detection of eating disorders in community samples. *Psychiatry Research, 44*, 191–201.

Bennett-Levy, J., Butler, G., Fennell, M.J.V., Hackmann, A., Mueller, M. and Westbrook, D. (2004). *The Oxford Handbook of Behavioural Experiments*. Oxford: Oxford University Press.

Blouin, J., Schnarre, K., Carter, J. and Blouin, A. (1995). Factors affecting dropout rate from cognitive-behavioral group treatment for bulimia nervosa. *International Journal of Eating Disorders, 17*, 323–329.

Burns, D.D. (1980). *Feeling Good*. New York: William Morrow.

Butler, G., Fennell, M., Robson, P. and Gelder, M. (1991). Comparison of behaviour therapy and cognitive behaviour therapy in the treatment of generalised anxiety disorder. *Journal of Consulting and Clinical Psychology, 59*, 167–175.

Byrne, S.M. and McLean, N.J. (2002). The cognitive behavioural model of bulimia nervosa: A direct evaluation. *International Journal of Eating Disorders, 31*, 17–31.

Carter, F.A., Bulik, C.M., McIntosh, V.V. and Joyce, P.R. (2000). Changes on the Stroop test following treatment: Relation to word type, treatment condition, and treatment outcome among women with bulimia nervosa. *International Journal of Eating Disorders, 28*, 349–355.

Cooper, J.L., Morrison, T.L., Bigman, O.L., Abramowitz, S.I., Levin, S. and Krener, P. (1988). Mood changes and affective disorder in the bulimic binge-purge cycle. *International Journal of Eating Disorders, 7*, 469–474.

Cooper, M.J. (1997a). Cognitive theory of anorexia nervosa and bulimia nervosa: A review. *Behavioural and Cognitive Psychotherapy, 25*, 113–145.

Cooper, M.J. (1997b). Interpretation of ambiguous scenarios in anorexia nervosa and bulimia nervosa. *Behaviour Research and Therapy, 35*, 619–626.

Cooper, M.J. (2003). *Bulimia Nervosa; A Cognitive Perspective*. Oxford: Oxford University Press.

Cooper, M.J. (2005). Cognitive theory in anorexia nervosa and bulimia nervosa: Progress, development and future directions. *Clinical Psychology Review, 25*, 511–531.

Cooper, M.J. and Fairburn, C.G. (1994). Changes in selective information processing with three psychological treatments for bulimia nervosa. *British Journal of Clinical Psychology, 33*, 353–356.

Cooper, M.J. and Hunt, J. (1998). Core beliefs and underlying assumptions in bulimia nervosa and depression. *Behaviour Research and Therapy, 36*, 895–898.

Cooper, M.J. and Todd, G. (1997). Selective processing of three types of stimuli in eating disorders. *British Journal of Clinical Psychology, 36*, 279–281.

Cooper, M.J., Anastasiades, P. and Fairburn, C.G. (1992). Selective processing of eating, weight and shape related words in bulimia nervosa. *Journal of Abnormal Psychology, 101*, 353–355.

Cooper, M.J., Todd, G. and Cohen-Tovée. E (1996). Core beliefs in eating disorders. *International Cognitive Therapy Newsletter, 10*, Part 2, 2–3.

Cooper, M.J., Cohen-Tovée, E., Todd, G., Wells, A. and Tovee, M. (1997). The eating disorder belief questionnaire: Preliminary development. *Behaviour Research and Therapy, 35*, 381–388.

Cooper, M.J., Todd, G. and Wells, A. (1998). Content, origins and consequences of dysfunctional beliefs in anorexia nervosa and bulimia nervosa. *Journal of Cognitive Psychotherapy, 12*, 213–230.

Cooper, M.J., Todd, G. and Wells, A. (2000). *Bulimia Nervosa: A Cognitive Therapy Programme for Clients*. London: Jessica Kingsley.

Cooper, M.J., Todd, G. and Wells, A. (2002). Content, origins and consequences of dysfunctional beliefs in anorexia nervosa and bulimia nervosa. In R.L. Leahy and E.T. Dowd (eds) *Clinical Advances in Cognitive Psychotherapy*. New York: Springer.

Cooper, M.J., Wells, A. and Todd, G. (2004). A cognitive theory of bulimia nervosa. *British Journal of Clinical Psychology, 43*, 1–16.

Cooper, M.J., Todd, G., Woolrich, R., Somerville, K. and Wells, A. (2006). Assessing eating disorder thoughts and behaviours: The development and preliminary evaluation of two questionnaires. *Cognitive Therapy and Research, 30*, 551–570.

Cooper, M.J., Stockford, K. and Turner, H. (2007a). Stages of change in anorexic and bulimic disorders: The importance of illness representations. *Eating Behaviors, 8*, 474–484.

Cooper, M.J., Todd, G., Turner, H. and Wells, A. (2007b). Cognitive therapy for bulimia nervosa: An A-B replication series. *Clinical Psychology and Psychotherapy, 14*, 402–411.

Cooper, P.J. (1993). *Bulimia Nervosa*. London: Robinson.

Cooper, P.J. (1995). *Bulimia Nervosa and Binge Eating*. London: Robinson.

Cooper, P.J., Taylor, M.J., Cooper, Z. and Fairburn, C.G. (1987). The development and validation of the body shape questionnaire. *International Journal of Eating Disorders, 6*, 485–494.

Currin, L., Schmidt, U., Treasure, J. and Jick, H. (2005). Time trends in eating disorder incidence. *British Journal of Psychiatry, 186*, 132–135.

Dean, J., Todd, G., Morrow, H. and Sheldon, K. (2001). Mum I used to be good looking . . . Look at me now: The physical health needs of adults with mental health problems. The perspectives of users, carers and front-line staff. *International Journal of Mental Health Promotion, 3*, 16–24.

Edwards, D.J.A. (1990). Cognitive therapy and the restructuring of early memories through guided imagery. *Journal of Cognitive Psychotherapy, 4*, 33–50.

Elmore, D.K. and De Castro, J.M. (1990). Self rated moods and hunger in relation to spontaneous eating behaviour in bulimics, recovered bulimics and normals. *International Journal of Eating Disorders, 9*, 179–190.

Engelberg, M.J., Steiger, H., Gauvin, L. and Wonderlich, S.A. (2007). Binge antecedents in bulimic syndromes: An examination of dissociation and negative affect. *International Journal of Eating Disorders, 40*, 531–536.

Fairburn, C.G. (1995). *Overcoming Binge Eating*. New York: Guilford.

Fairburn, C.G. and Beglin, S.J. (1994). Assessment of eating disorders: interview or self-report questionnaire? *International Journal of Eating Disorders, 16*, 363–370.

Fairburn, C.G. and Cooper, Z. (1993). The eating disorder examination. In C.G. Fairburn and G.T. Wilson (eds) *Binge Eating: Nature, Assessment and Treatment*. New York: Guilford.

Fairburn, C.G., Cooper, P.J. and Cooper, Z. (1986). The clinical features and maintenance of bulimia nervosa. In K.D. Brownell and J.P. Foreyt (eds) *Physiology, Psychology and Treatment of the Eating Disorders*. New York: Basic Books.

Fairburn, C.G., Jones, R., Peveler, R.C., Carr, S.J., Solomon, R.A., O'Connor, M.E., Burton, J. and Hope, R.A. (1991). Three psychological treatments for bulimia nervosa: A comparative trial. *Archives of General Psychiatry, 48*, 463–469.

Fairburn, C.G., Marcus, M.D. and Wilson, G.T. (1993). Cognitive behaviour therapy for binge eating and bulimia nervosa: A comprehensive treatment manual. In C.G. Fairburn and G.T. Wilson (eds) *Binge Eating: Nature, Assessment and Treatment*. New York: Guilford.

Fairburn, C.G., Norman, P.A., Welch, S.L., O'Connor, M.E., Doll, H.A. and Peveler, R.C. (1995). A prospective study of outcome in bulimia nervosa and the long term effects of three psychological treatments. *Archives of General Psychiatry, 52*, 304–312.

Fairburn, C.G., Cooper, Z. and Shafran, R. (2003). Cognitive behaviour therapy for eating disorders: A transdiagnostic theory and treatment. *Behaviour Research and Therapy, 41*, 509–528.

Faunce, G.J. (2002). Eating disorders and attentional bias: a review. *Eating Disorders, 10*, 125–139.

First, M.B., Spitzer, R.L., Gibbon, M. and Williams, J.B.W. (1996). *Structured Clinical Interview for DSM-IV Axis 1 Disorders*. New York: Biometrics Research Department, New York State Psychiatric Institute.

Fisher, P. and Wells, A. (2007). Metacognitive therapy for obsessive compulsive disorder: A case series. *Journal of Behaviour Therapy and Experimental Psychiatry, 39*, 117–132.

Flynn, S.V. and McNally, R.J. (1999). Do disorder-relevant biases endure in recovered bulimics? *Behaviour Therapy, 30*, 541–553.

Fombonne, E. (1995). Anorexia nervosa: No evidence of an increase. *British Journal of Psychiatry, 31*, 451–465.

Freeman, A. (2001). Personality disorder. Seminar, World Congress of Cognitive and Behavioural Therapies, Vancouver, Canada, July.

Freeman, A. (2002). Developing treatment conceptualisations in cognitive therapy. In A.

Freeman and F. Dattilio (eds) *Comprehensive Casebook of Cognitive Therapy*. New York: Plenum.

Freeman, A. and Dattilio, F.M. (eds) (1992). *Comprehensive Casebook of Cognitive Therapy*. New York: Springer.

Garner, D.M. (1987). Psychotherapy outcome research with bulimia nervosa. *Psychotherapy and Psychosomatics, 48*, 129–140.

Garner, D.M. (2004). *Eating Disorders Inventory 3*. Lutz, FL: Psychological Assessment Resources Inc.

Garner, D.M. and Bemis, K.M. (1982). A cognitive–behavioural approach to anorexia nervosa. *Cognitive Therapy and Research, 6*, 123–150.

Garner, D.M. and Fairburn, C.G. (1988). Relationship between anorexia nervosa and bulimia nervosa: Diagnostic implications. In D.M. Garner and P.E. Garfinkel (eds) *Diagnostic Issues in Anorexia Nervosa and Bulimia Nervosa*. Monograph Series. New York: Brunner/Mazel.

Garner, D.M., Olmsted, M.P., Bohr, Y. and Garfinkel, P.E. (1982). The eating attitudes test: Psychometric features and clinical correlates. *Psychological Medicine, 12*, 871–878.

Geller, J. (2002). What a motivational approach is and what a motivational approach isn't: Reflections and responses. *European Eating Disorders Review, 10*, 155–160.

Geller, J. and Drab, D.L. (1999). The Readiness and Motivation Interview: A symptom specific measure of readiness for change in the eating disorders. *European Eating Disorders Review, 7*, 259–278.

Geller, J., Johnston, C. and Madson, K. (1997). The role of shape and weight in self-concept: The shape and weight based self esteem inventory. *Cognitive Therapy and Research, 21*, 5–24.

Geller, J., Williams, K. and Srikameswaran, S. (2001). Clinician stance in the treatment of chronic eating disorders. *European Eating Disorders Review, 9*, 1–9.

Giesen-Bloo, J., van Dyck, R., Spinhoven, P., van Tilburg, W., Dirksen, C., van Asselt, T., Kremers, I., Nadort, M. and Arntz, A. (2006). Outpatient psychotherapy for borderline personality disorder: Randomized trial of schema-focused therapy vs transference-focused psychotherapy. *Archives of General Psychiatry, 63*, 649–658.

Grilo, C.M. and Shiffman, S. (1994). Longitudinal investigation of the abstinence violation effect in binge eaters. *Journal of Consulting and Clinical Psychology, 62*, 611–619.

Guertin, T.L. (1999). Eating behaviour of bulimics, self identified binge eaters, and non eating disordered individuals: What differentiates these populations? *Clinical Psychology Review, 19*, 1–23.

Guidano, V.F. and Liotti, G. (1983). *Cognitive Processes and Emotional Disorders: A Structural Approach to Psychotherapy*. New York: Guilford.

Hay, P.J. and Bacaltchuk, J. (2000). *Psychotherapy for Bulimia Nervosa and Bingeing*. The Cochrane Library, 4.

Heatherton, T.F. and Baumeister, R.F. (1991). Binge eating as escape from self-awareness. *Psychological Bulletin, 110*, 86–108.

Hilbert, A. and Tuschen-Caffier, B. (2007). Maintenance of binge eating through negative mood: A naturalistic comparison of binge eating disorder and bulimia nervosa. *International Journal of Eating Disorders, 40*, 521–530.

Hohlstein, L.A., Smith, G.T. and Atlas, J.G. (1998). An application of expectancy theory to eating disorders: Development and validation of measures of eating and dieting expectancies. *Psychological Assessment, 10*, 49–58.

Hostick, T. and Newell, R. (2004). Concordance with community mental health appointments: Service users' reasons for discontinuation. *Journal of Clinical Nursing, 13*, 895–902.

Hsu, L.K.G. (1990). Experiential aspects of bulimia nervosa. *Behaviour Modification, 14*, 50–65.

Hunt, J. and Cooper, M.J. (2001). Selective memory bias in women with bulimia nervosa and depression. *Behavioural and Cognitive Psychotherapy, 29*, 93–102.

Jansen, A. (2001). Towards effective treatment of eating disorders: Nothing is as practical as good theory. *Behaviour Research and Therapy, 39*, 1007–1022.

Joiner, T.E., Schmidt, N.B. and Wonderlich, S.A. (1997). Global self-esteem as contingent on body satisfaction among patients with bulimia nervosa: Lack of diagnostic specificity? *International Journal of Eating Disorders, 21*, 17–22.

Kaye, W.H., Gwirtsman, H.E., George, D.T., Weiss, S.R. and Jimerson, D.C. (1986). Relationship of mood alterations to bingeing behaviour in bulimia. *British Journal of Psychiatry, 149*, 479–485.

Keel, P.K., Fichter, M., Quadflieg, N., Bulik, C.M., Baxter, M.G., Thornton, L., Halmi, K.A., Kaplan, A.S., Strober, M., Woodside, D.B., Crow, S.J., Mitchell, J.E., Rotondo, A., Mauri, M., Cassano, G., Treasure, J., Goldman, D., Berrettini, W.H. and Kaye, W.H. (2004). Application of a latent class analysis to empirically define eating disorder phenotypes. *Archives of General Psychiatry, 61*, 192–200.

Kendler, K., MacLean, C., Neale, M., Kessler, R., Heath, A. and Eaves, L. (1991). The genetic epidemiology of bulimia nervosa. *American Journal of Psychiatry, 148*, 1627–1637.

Leahy, R.L. (2001). *Overcoming Resistance in Cognitive Therapy.* New York: Guilford.

Lee, M. and Shafran, R. (2004). Information processing biases in eating disorders. *Clinical Psychology Review, 24*, 215–238.

Leung, N., Waller, G. and Thomas, G. (1999). Core beliefs in anorexic and bulimic women. *Journal of Nervous and Mental Disease, 187*, 736–741.

Leung, N., Thomas, G. and Waller, G. (2000). The relationship between parental bonding and core beliefs in anorexic and bulimic women. *British Journal of Clinical Psychology, 39*, 205–213.

Linehan, M.M. (1993). *Cognitive Behavioural Treatment of Borderline Personality Disorder.* New York: Guilford.

Luck, A., Waller, G., Meyer, C., Ussher, M. and Lacey, H. (2005). The role of schema processes in the eating disorders. *Cognitive Therapy and Research, 29*, 717–732.

Meyer, C., Leung, N., Feary, R. and Mann, B. (2001). Core beliefs and bulimic symptomatology in non-eating-disordered women: The mediating role of borderline characteristics. *International Journal of Eating Disorders, 30*, 434–440.

Meyer, D.F. (2001). Help-seeking for eating disorders in female adolescents. *Journal of College Student Psychotherapy, 15*, 23–36.

Miller, W.R. and Rollnick, S. (2002). *Motivational Interviewing: Preparing People for Change.* New York: Guilford.

Mumford, D.B. and Whitehouse, A.M. (1988). Increased prevalence of bulimia nervosa among Asian schoolgirls. *British Medical Journal, 297*, 718.

National Institute for Clinical Excellence (NICE) (2004). *Core Interventions in the Treatment and Management of Anorexia Nervosa, Bulimia Nervosa and Related Eating Disorders.* London: NICE.

Noad, R., Stewart-Brown, S. and Cooper, M.J. (2006). The role of positive cognitive processes in psychological well-being. Unpublished manuscript.

Padesky, C.A. (1990). Schema as self prejudice. *International Cognitive Therapy Newsletter, 6*, 6–7.

Padesky, C.A. (1993). *Socratic Questioning: Changing Minds or Guided Discovery?* London: European Congress of Behavioural and Cognitive Therapies.

Padesky, C.A. (1994). Schema change processes in cognitive therapy. *Clinical Psychology and Psychotherapy, 1*, 267–278.

Padesky, C.A. and Greenberger, D. (1995). *Clinician's Guide to Mind over Mood*. New York: Guilford.

Peake, K.J., Limbert, C. and Whitehead, L. (2005). Evaluation of the Oxford Adult Eating Disorders Service between 1994 and 2002. *European Eating Disorders Review, 13*, 427–435.

Pinel, J.F.J. (2000). *Biopsychology*. Needham Heights, MA: Allyn & Bacon.

Pritchard, B.J., Bergin, J.L. and Wade, T.D. (2004). A case series evaluation of guided self-help for bulimia nervosa using a cognitive manual. *International Journal of Eating Disorders, 36*, 144–156.

Prochaska, J.O. and DiClemente, C.C. (1982). Transtheoretical therapy: towards an integrative model of change. *Psychotherapy Theory and Research Practice, 19*, 276–288.

Reas, D.L., Williamson, D.A., Martin, C.K. and Zucker, N.L. (2000). Duration of illness predicts outcome for bulimia nervosa: A long-term follow-up study. *International Journal of Eating Disorders, 27*, 428–434.

Rieger, E., Schotte, D.E., Touyz, S.W., Beumont, P.J., Griffiths, R. and Russell, J. (1998). Attentional biases in eating disorders: A visual probe detection procedure. *International Journal of Eating Disorders, 23*, 199–205.

Rogers, C.R. (1951). *Client-Centered Therapy: Its Current Practice, Implications and Theory*. Boston, MA: Houghton Mifflin.

Root, M.P.P., Fallon, P. and Friedrich, W.N. (1986). *Bulimia: A Systems Approach to Treatment*. New York: Norton.

Rorty, M., Yager, J. and Rossotto, E. (1994). Childhood sexual, physical, and psychological abuse in bulimia nervosa. *American Journal of Psychiatry, 151*, 1122–1126.

Rose, K.S., Cooper, M.J. and Turner, H. (2006). The Eating Disorders Belief Questionnaire: Psychometric properties in an adolescent sample. *Eating Behaviours, 7*, 410–418.

Rosenberg, M. (1967). *Society and the Adolescent Self Image*. Princeton, NJ: Princeton University Press.

Rouf, K., Fennell, M.J.V., Westbrook, D., Cooper, M.J. and Bennett-Levy, J. (2004). Devising effective behavioural experiments. In J. Bennett-Levy, G. Butler, M.J.V. Fennell, A. Hackmann, M. Mueller and D. Westbrook (eds) *The Oxford Handbook of Behavioural Experiments*. Oxford: Oxford University Press.

Safer, D.L., Telch, C.F. and Agras, W.S. (2001). Dialectical behavior therapy for bulimia nervosa. *American Journal of Psychiatry, 158*, 632–634.

Safran, J.D. and Muran, J.C. (2000). *Negotiating the Therapeutic Alliance: A Relational Treatment Guide*. New York: Guilford.

Schmidt, U. and Treasure, J. (1993). *Getting Better Bit(e) by Bit(e)*. Hove, UK: Psychology Press.

Schmidt, U. and Treasure, J. (1997). *Getting Better Bit(e) by Bit(e)*. Hove, UK: Psychology Press.

Segal, Z.V., Williams, J.M.G. and Teasdale, J. (2002). *Mindfulness-Based Cognitive Therapy for Depression: A New Approach to Preventing Relapse*. New York: Guilford.

Sherwood, N.E., Crowther, J.H., Wills, L. and Ben-Porath, Y.S. (2000). The perceived function of eating for bulimic, subclinical bulimic, and non-eating disordered women. *Behavior Therapy, 31,* 777–793.

Somerville, K. and Cooper, M.J. (2007). The presence and characteristics of core beliefs in women with bulimia nervosa, dieting and non-dieting women accessed using imagery. *Eating Behaviors, 8,* 450–456.

Somerville, K., Cooper, M.J. and Hackmann, A. (2007). Spontaneous imagery in women with bulimia nervosa: An investigation into content, characteristics and links to childhood memories. *Journal of Behaviour Therapy and Experimental Psychiatry, 38,* 435–446.

Steel, Z., Jones, J., Adcock, S., Clancy, R., Bridgford-West, L. and Austin, J. (2000). Why the high rate of dropout from individualized cognitive-behavior therapy for bulimia nervosa? *International Journal of Eating Disorders, 28,* 209–214.

Steiger, H., Gauvin, L., Jabalpurwala, S., Séguin, J.R. and Stotland, S. (1999a). Hypersensitivity to social interactions in bulimic syndromes: Relationship to binge eating. *Journal of Consulting and Clinical Psychology, 67,* 765–775.

Steiger, H., Lehoux, P.M. and Gauvin, L. (1999b). Impulsivity, dietary control and the urge to binge in bulimic syndromes. *International Journal of Eating Disorders, 26,* 261–274.

Stein, R.I., Kenardy, J., Wiseman, C.V., Dounchis, J.Z., Arnow, B.A. and Wilfley, D.E. (2007). What's driving the binge in binge eating disorder? A prospective examination of precursors and consequences. *International Journal of Eating Disorders, 40,* 195–203.

Stice, E. (2005). Using risk factor findings to design eating disorder prevention programmes: Tales of success and failure. Paper presented to Academy of Eating Disorders Conference, Montreal, Quebec, Canada, April.

Stice, E., Nemeroff, C. and Shaw, H.E. (1996). A test of the dual pathway model of bulimia nervosa: Evidence for restrained eating and affect regulation mechanisms. *Journal of Social and Clinical Psychology, 15,* 340–363.

Stockford, K., Turner, H. and Cooper, M.J. (2007). Illness perception and its relationship to readiness to change in the eating disorders: A preliminary investigation. *British Journal of Clinical Psychology, 46,* 139–154.

Thompson-Brenner, H., Glass, S. and Western, D., (2003). A multidimensional meta-analysis of psychotherapy for bulimia nervosa. *Clinical Psychology: Science and Practice, 10,* 269–287.

Todd, G. (2006). Cognitive factors in bulimia nervosa. Doctoral dissertation, Darwin College, University of Cambridge.

Tozzi, F., Thornton, L.M., Klump, K.L., Fichter, M.M, Halmi, K.A., Kaplan, A.S., Strober, M., Woodside, D.B., Crow, S., Mitchell, J., Rotondo, A, Mauri, M., Cassano, G., Keel, P., Plotnicov, K.H., Pollice, C., Lilenfeld, L.R., Berrettini, W.H., Bulik, C.M. and Kaye, W.H. (2005). Symptom fluctuation in eating disorders: Correlates of diagnostic crossover. *American Journal of Psychiatry, 162,* 732–740.

Treasure, J. (2004). Motivational interviewing. *Advances in Psychiatric Treatment, 10,* 331–337

van Son, G.E., van Hoeken, D., Bartelds, A.I.M., van Furth, E.F. and Hoek, H.W. (2006). Time trends in the incidence of eating disorders: A primary care study in the Netherlands. *International Journal of Eating Disorders, 39,* 565–569.

Waller, G., Ohanian, V., Meyer, C. and Osman, S. (2000). Cognitive content among bulimic women: The role of core beliefs. *International Journal of Eating Disorders, 28,* 235–241.

Waller, G., Kennerley, H. and Ohanian, V. (2007). Schema focussed cognitive behavioural therapy for eating disorders. In L.P. Riso, P. du Toit, D.J. Stein and J.E. Young (eds) *Cognitive Schemas and Core Beliefs in Psychological Problems: A Scientist Practitioner Guide*. Washington, DC: American Psychological Association.

Waters, A., Hill, A. and Waller, G. (2001). Bulimics' responses to food cravings: Is binge eating a product of hunger of emotional state? *Behaviour Research and Therapy*, *39*, 877–886.

Welch, S.L. and Fairburn, C.G. (1994). Sexual abuse and bulimia nervosa: Three integrated case control comparisons. *American Journal of Psychiatry*, *151*, 402–407.

Wells, A. (1995). Worry, metacognition, and GAD: Nature, consequences, and treatment. *Journal of Cognitive Psychotherapy*, 16, 179–192.

Wells, A. (1997). *Cognitive Therapy of Anxiety Disorders*. Chichester: Wiley.

Wells, A. (2000). *Emotional Disorders and Metacognition*. Chichester: Wiley.

Wells, A. (2006). Detached mindfulness in cognitive therapy: A metacognitive analysis and ten techniques. *Journal of Rational-Emotive and Cognitive-Behavior Therapy*, *23*, 337–355.

Wells, A. (2008). *Metacognitive Therapy: A Practical Guide*. New York: Guilford.

Wells, A. and Cartwright-Hatton, S. (2004). A short form of the metacognitions questionnaire: Properties of the MCQ-30. *Behaviour Research and Therapy*, *42*, 385–396.

Wells, A. and Hackmann, A. (1993). Imagery and core beliefs in health anxiety: Content and origins. *Behavioural and Cognitive Psychotherapy*, *21*, 265–273.

Wells, A. and Matthews, G. (1994). *Attention and Emotion*. Hove, UK: Laurence Erlbaum Associates.

Wells, A. and Matthews, G. (1996). Modeling cognition in emotional disorder: The S-REF model. *Behaviour Research and Therapy*, *34*, 881–888.

Wells, A. and Sembi, S. (2004). Metacognitive therapy for PTSD: A core treatment manual. *Cognitive and Behavioral Practice*, *11*, 365–377.

Williamson, D.A., Muller, S.L., Reas, D.L. and Thaw, J.M. (1999). Cognitive bias in eating disorders: Implications for theory and treatment. *Behavior Modification*, *23*, 556–577.

Wilson, G.T. and Schlam, T.R. (2004). The transtheoretical model and motivational interviewing in the treatment of eating and weight disorders. *Clinical Psychology Review*, *24*, 361–378.

Wonderlich, S., Klein, M.H. and Council, J.R. (1996). Relationship of social perceptions and self-concept in bulimia nervosa. *Journal of Consulting and Clinical Psychology*, *64*, 1231–1237.

Woolrich, R., Cooper, M.J. and Turner, H. (2006). A preliminary study of negative self beliefs in anorexia nervosa: Exploring their content, origins and functional links to 'not eating enough' and other characteristic behaviors. *Cognitive Therapy and Research*, *30*, 735–748.

World Health Organization (WHO) (1992). *The ICD-10 Classification of Mental and Behavioural Disorders*. Geneva: WHO.

Young, J.E. (1990). *Cognitive Therapy for Personality Disorders: A Schema Focussed Approach*. Sarasota, FL: Professional Resource Exchange.

Young, J.E. (1998). Young schema questionnaire (available at http://www.schematherapy.com).

Young, J.E. and Klosko, J.S. (1994). *Reinventing your Life*. New York: Plume.

Young, J.E., Klosko, J.S. and Weishaar, M.E. (2003). *Schema Therapy*. New York: Guilford.

Index